PRAISE FOR E. PATRICK JOHNSON

More praise for *Honeypot*

"In this critically singular work E. Patrick Johnson excavates heretofore unexplored stories of contemporary southern black women whose narratives of loving other women subvert their erasure in queer histories of LGBTQ communities. Gesturing toward black storytelling traditions within which both myth and fact shape the story, Johnson values and gives value to black women's understandings of themselves and the transformative power of self-initiated freedoms. I've never read an oral history as powerful as *Honeypot*."
—Alexis De Veaux, author of *Yabo*

"E. Patrick Johnson's *Honeypot* simmers with delight and insight as black lesbian women share their stories of triumph and horror. Never before have I encountered space ruled by these voices, and never before have they been invited to bare it all unashamedly. It's about time!"
—Daniel Black, author of *Perfect Peace*

Praise for *Black. Queer. Southern. Women.*

"A courageous and eminently readable book that will be celebrated and cherished by a generation of readers inside and outside the academy."
—Nan Alamilla Boyd, San Francisco State University

"An amazing work that reflects Johnson's passion, care for his subjects, sharp analytical skills, and standing in the field."
—Beverly Guy-Sheftall, Spelman College

Praise for *Sweet Tea*

"It's pretty rare to pick up a book, turn randomly to any page, and find such a powerful personal story that you have to close the book for a moment to take it in. But the oral histories featured in *Sweet Tea* . . . cast just that kind of spell."—*The Advocate*

"*Sweet Tea* is an amazing book. Engaging from the very start, it is well written and thought provoking throughout. There were times I simply could not put it down"

D1570064

"This fascinating . . . oral history subverts countless preconceptions in its illustration of black gay subcultures thriving in just about every imaginable rural and religious milieu in the South. . . . The courage and honesty of Johnson's interviewees humble, and readers will find much to treasure in the stories."
—*Publishers Weekly*

Performances

"[Johnson] has a poised delivery and can plunge himself into moments of lively theatricality—during the show he sings gospel, executes an infectious ring shout and, in a particularly enjoyable scene, channels the tambourine-waving exuberance of an eccentric pastor. . . . The show trains its eye far beyond any specific veranda. In one of the play's particularly moving lines, Gerome, the tambourine-shaking pastor, explains that he has turned his back on narrow perspectives and learned to see creation 'as a whole picture.' *Sweet Tea* invites us to gaze at that picture, too."—*The Washington Post*

"Perhaps the most wonderful thing about *Sweet Tea* is that the artist has achieved the near impossible: [Johnson's] stories of self do not scream 'me me me,' but rather sing of an us that is rarely seen or lauded. As he said after the show, 'the best autobiographical work is work that opens out.'"—*Indy Week* (Durham, NC)

HONEYPOT

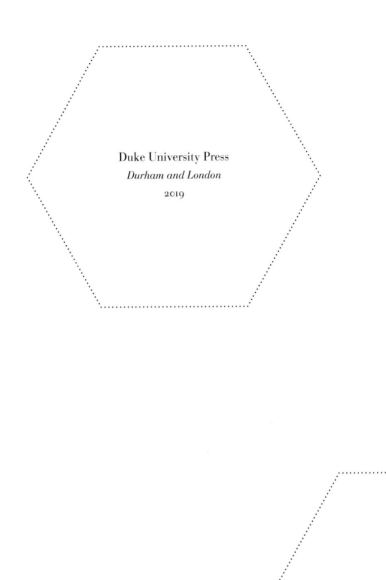

Duke University Press
Durham and London
2019

Honeypot

BLACK

SOUTHERN WOMEN WHO

LOVE WOMEN

E. PATRICK JOHNSON

With a foreword by
ALEXIS PAULINE GUMBS

Cover design by Courtney Leigh Baker
Text design by Aimee C. Harrison
Typeset in Bauer Bodoni, Trade Gothic,
and Whitman by Copperline Books

Library of Congress Cataloging-in-Publication Data
Names: Johnson, E. Patrick, [date] author.
Title: Honeypot : black Southern women who love women /
E. Patrick Johnson.
Description: Durham : Duke University Press, 2019. |
Includes bibliographical references and index.
Identifiers: LCCN 2019010883 (print)
LCCN 2019980052 (ebook)
ISBN 9781478005902 (hardcover : alk. paper)
ISBN 9781478006534 (pbk. : alk. paper)
ISBN 9781478007241 (ebook)
Subjects: LCSH: African American lesbians—Southern States
—Biography. | African American lesbians—Southern States—
History—20th century. | African American lesbians—
Southern States—History—21st century.
Classification: LCC HQ75.6.U52 S684 2019 (print)
LCC HQ75.6. U52 (ebook) | DDC 306.76/630923896073—dc23
LC record available at https://lccn.loc.gov/2019010883
LC ebook record available at https://lccn.loc.gov/2019980052

Cover art: Jamea Richmond-Edwards,
Wings Not Meant to Fly, 2012. Ink, acrylic, and mixed
media collage on canvas, 36 in. × 36 in.
© Jamea Richmond-Edwards. Courtesy of the artist.

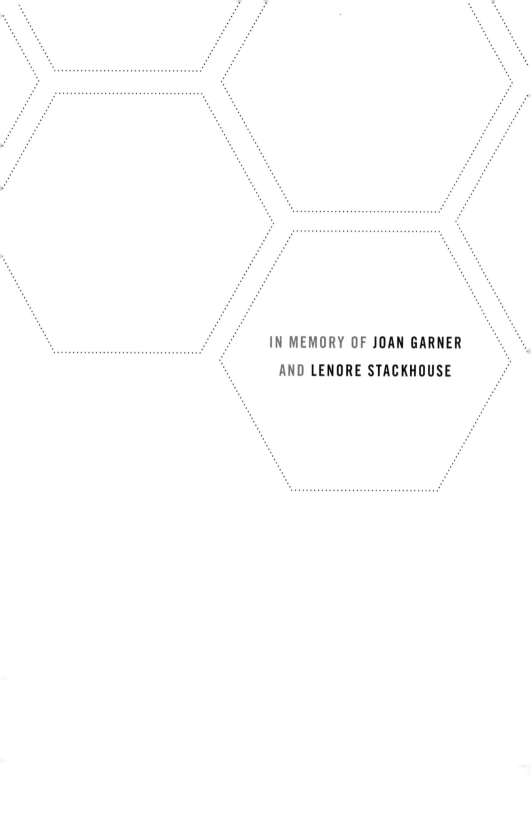

IN MEMORY OF **JOAN GARNER**
AND **LENORE STACKHOUSE**

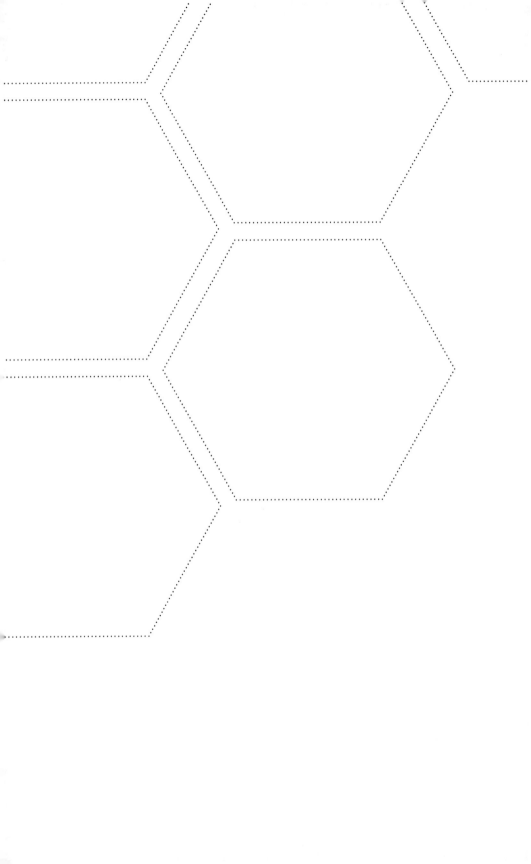

Contents

Foreword

ALEXIS PAULINE GUMBS

For a year, my partner and I lived in an apartment with a brick floor. At least three times that year, I dropped glass jars of honey on that floor and they cracked open. Precious local honey oozed out over my shiny brick floors. Like a message or a meditation. Have you ever seen the way honey works? So thick that it slows down time. So sweet that it convinces you your skin can and should touch broken glass. So golden and brown that it calls the light from all directions.

What E. Patrick Johnson offers here is a work of honey. A time travel testament, a beautiful hexagonal prism, a strategic sweetness that allows us to drink in the painful edges of life in a world that is violent to Black women and even more so to Black lesbians in the South.

In this book, E. Patrick Johnson creates an afro-surreal world for the real-life stories of Black lesbians from and in the South. A world populated by fly (and sometimes actually flying) girls, grown women, grandmas, butch daddies, and dapper self-identified dykes. As we journey with him and the archetypal Miss B., through this world we encounter a queer ecology of witness.

Johnson centers himself as a sometimes uplifted, sometimes conflicted, sometimes reluctant, and sometimes even confused listener. He therefore gives us permission to feel however we feel when we are confronted with the realities of sexual violence enacted on Black girls by the men in their communities and families; the inspiration of the contributions Black southern lesbians have made to their communities through their art and activism; and the drama, excitement, and sweetness of their evolving love lives over time.

Through this work, and through his brave honesty about how the stories affect him, refract his own story, and challenge him on his journey, Johnson models how the life experiences of Black lesbians in the South are relevant to everyone in the world. While as a Black queer woman who grew up mostly in the southern United States I appreciated the reflection I found in stories that resonated with my own life experiences and even learned a new context about the lives of people in my own communities, or whom my partner Sangodare (Julia Roxanne Wallace—who was interviewed for this book) and I met on our cross-country Mobile Homecoming tour of listening to and honoring Black LGBTQ feminist elders, the most revolutionary approach to this book is as a practice of what Audre Lorde called "the creative power of difference." As you travel on this journey, you will be experiencing a different form of oral history. You will be led to learn from the very different lives of each of the women interviewed. And, most importantly, you will be called on to know yourself differently through the transformative truths of these heartbreaks, adventures, spiritual insights, and resilient examples.

When I think of the impact of this book on the world and our communities, I think not only of the sweetness of honey but also of its medicinal properties. Allow this work to clean you out, awaken your body's aliveness to the air around you, inspire you to listen deeper, love bravely, and be a part of the buzz that transforms the world.

Preface

YOU CATCH MORE BEES WITH HONEY THAN WITH VINEGAR

> Sitting next to a hive, watching
> bees flying in and out, my mind clears
> of conscious thought as I enter a deep state of
> "bee meditation." . . . The bees draw us into this
> opening heart and welcome us there. It is a
> heart filled with great love and great activity.
> —Jacqueline Freeman, *The Song of Increase*

If you've ever tried to pour honey from a jar or even squeeze it from a bottle, you know that it moves on its own time. Never mind the hot buttered biscuit cracked open, just waiting to be smothered in tawny, gooey deliciousness. Or freshly brewed tea sitting in the sun standing at the ready to get sweetened. Or granddaddy's whiskey that needs to be cut with something to make the cold remedy go down just a little bit easier. No. Honey will make you wait while it traverses that long and slow trail to the rim of the jar, the tip of the bear bottle, or the edge of the teaspoon before descending into a snail's free fall, spindling its way over mounds of billowy biscuit innards, dissolving bitterness to sweetness in tea, or joining hands with Jack Daniels and lemon for a sweet hour of prayer. The payoff is worth the wait.

And so it is with this book. I have waited over a decade to write it, finally nudged by my queer sisters who were fans of my previous book, *Sweet Tea: Black Gay Men of the South—An Oral History*. After reading the stories of black gay men of the South, many black women who attended my book signings or my performances were eager to have their stories collected in a similar fashion. I believed that someone would collect these stories, but after a decade, no one had seemed to step forward. Then in 2012, I decided that I would travel back to the South of my childhood—again—and bear witness to my sisters telling their tales. This book is the culmination, then, of two years of oral histories I collected from African American women, all of whom express same-sex desire and who were born, reared, and continue to reside in the US South. I found the majority of these women by putting out a call on a few listservs, where the word about this book spread fairly quickly. In fact, while it took me two years to collect seventy-seven narratives for *Sweet Tea*, in fourteen months I conducted the same number of interviews for *Honeypot*. The women range in age from eighteen to seventy-four and hail from states below the Mason-Dixon Line including, Texas, Louisiana, Arkansas, Alabama, Mississippi, Tennessee, Georgia, South Carolina, Florida, North Carolina, Virginia, Kentucky, Washington, DC, and Maryland. They range in social class from factory workers, local government administrators, entrepreneurs, counselors, professors, librarians, schoolteachers, musicians, writers, community organizers, disc jockeys, truck drivers, and housewives to those who are unemployed. Educational backgrounds also differed, but the majority of the women had completed high school, many had had some college education, and a few had postgraduate and professional degrees. The criteria for being interviewed were that the woman be born in a southern state, meaning a state below the Mason-Dixon Line or a state that had previously been slave-holding, such as Missouri and Oklahoma; be primarily reared in the South for a significant portion of her life; and, be currently living in the South. I made a few exceptions to these criteria if a woman had not been born in the South as I have defined it but had been reared there as an infant or toddler. I also made one exception by including a woman born in the global South, in Puerto Rico, and who identifies as a black Puerto Rican. The women were given the option of remaining anonymous, but most agreed to use their real names. In those instances where the narrator wanted to remain anonymous, I gave them a pseudonym, which is indicated in the appendix by their name. One of the people I interviewed identified as female at the time but now identifies as male and wanted to be included in the book as "Bluhe."

As anyone who has read any of my other work comes to realize, I am very much invested in playful titles. The title of this book is no different. Like the title for *Sweet Tea*, the title for this book stems from its associations with the South, as well as pejorative, celebratory, and vernacular uses of the word "honey."

In southern black vernacular among women, "honey" is a term of endearment or expression of sisterhood, as in "Honey, let me tell you what this fool did!"; or, when combined with the word "child" to form "honeychild" or "honeychile," as in "Honeychild, don't worry about what people say about you."[1] One of the more provocative riffs on the word was revealed to me through Michelle, one of the women I interviewed, who spent many of her college years around black gay men who also have a penchant for camping up language, as any episode of *RuPaul's Drag Race* will attest. In her narrative Michelle playfully draws on black camp culture in her pronunciation of the word as "hunty" (i.e., "honey" plus "cunty"),[2] fully aware of the sexually explicit connotations of her usage. Moving from the profane to the sacred (depending on one's perspective), biblical references to honey are widely thought of as positive, as in God promising the Israelites "a land of milk and honey" (Leviticus 20:24). At the same time there are biblical associations of honey with loose and/or untrustworthy women, as in Proverbs 5:3: "For the Lips of the adulterous woman drip honey, and her speech is smoother than oil." Moreover, the folk saying, "You catch more bees with honey than with vinegar" equates the "sweetness" of honey with one's temperament and manners. Finally, the honeycomb's shape—a hexagon—is the symbol of the heart and represents sweetness of the heart and the symbol of the sun and its energies.

The women of *Honeypot* have remixed all of these definitions of "honey" by reimagining the negative connotations and highlighting the positive symbols and appropriating them for sexual and nonsexual references. As I spoke with women who shared their stories, I learned that in black lesbian vernacular, "honeypot" refers to a woman's vagina. But the reference is not just a receptacle— the women I interviewed designate the honeypot as a space where sexual expression, desire, and power reside. It is no coincidence, then, that honey is also one of the proprieties of the Yoruba deity of love and beauty, Osun. More than a few of the women I interviewed, such as Julia from Gastonia, North Carolina, who was in the midst of her initiation at the time, engage in Yoruba-based practices, and one of the most venerated deities among these women is Osun. Osun is the patron deity of the Osun River in Nigeria, which bears her namesake, and is why she is associated with fresh water. She also symbolizes sensuality, divine beauty, fertility, luxury, and abundance of all kinds. Through these literal and figurative associations of honey with spirituality, sexuality, and desire, it is apropos, then, that I use the term in the title to capture its symbolism for these women.

As I began to realize the importance of these metaphors to these women, it struck a deep personal chord, and I reflected on my own childhood and my fascination with bees. As a child, my friends and I used to "borrow" my mother's mason jars and, as a game, see how many bees we could catch. It was often a dangerous adventure (which made it even more thrilling) as we stalked, lionlike, our beautiful prey as they danced on summer dandelions. Honeybees were fine, but if we caught a larger bumblebee, which we called "blackjacks," we got extra points—and if we got stung by a bumblebee it was that much more painful than a honeybee. The snuff that Mama Kate, my godmother and sometimes babysitter, mixed with her spit to make a salve for the sting was sometimes enough of a deterrent for me not to catch bees for at least a few days, since I hated the smell and look of snuff. And yet, there was something beautiful about the bees all collected together with broken dandelions we had dropped into the jar. We were beekeepers in the making since we also somehow knew to "smoke" the bees by lighting matches, blowing them out and dropping them into the jar to calm them. Back then I had no idea that we could not survive without bees, for they pollinate flowers, plants, and trees that produce our fruit and vegetables. They are the only insects that produce food—honey—that humans eat. Now, as I consider the importance of bees—to the South of my childhood and to humanity in general—I want to draw parallels between what Sue Monk Kid calls the "secret life of bees" and the not-so-secret lives of black southern women who love women.[3]

One of the most interesting things about the life of bees is that their colonies are essentially female-dominated communities of "worker bees," so called because they maintain the colony by flying off to collect pollen and nectar for the hive, keeping the hive clean, building the honeycombs, storing the food, nursing and feeding the larvae, and making honey. Given the history of slave labor in the South in particular, where women worked both in the fields and in the plantation home, bore and nursed her master's children and her own, and did so with dignity and pride, it is not a stretch to make an analogy to the work of female bees. Indeed, metaphors about the industriousness of bees or sayings such as "busy as a bee" apply to the lives of black women who, as fiction writer and folklorist Zora Neale Hurston suggests through the wisdom of her character Nanny, are the "mules of the world."[4] And, according to one group of scientists, it is likely that honeybees all had one common ancestor in Africa.[5] Thus, the connection between the history of black women—of any sexual orientation—and bees abounds. Even the designation "bee charmer" is a southern slang term for lesbians who are particularly adept at seducing other lesbians!

Male bees, called "drones," are fewer in number. They are larger and wider than female worker bees and do not contribute to the maintenance of the hive—that is, cleaning, foraging for food, production of honey, and so on—

beyond reproduction. They hang together in a group called a "scarp," where they detect queen bees in flight. A drone competes for copulation rights, and if he wins those rights, he injects his sperm into the queen's abdomen while mounted to her and flying in midair, his penis and other abdominal tissue ripped from his body after copulation. He then dies, while the queen continues on in search of more drones to mate with. If a drone does survive copulation and returns to the hive, or if he never mates with a queen and never leaves the hive, the worker bees eventually push him out—typically in autumn before the hive goes dormant for the winter—because he is of no further use to the hive. The connections between drones and men in general, and black men specifically, are not as obvious, and those comparisons that might be made run the risk of reinforcing stereotypes of black men as lazy and promiscuous. For example, over 80 percent of the women I interviewed recount stories of sexual assault at the hands of male relatives.[6] But it would be unfair to make an analogy between black men and drones in this regard because the sex between drones and queen bees is necessary and solicited by the queen bee in order to populate the hive, and is not the same as sexual assault. In *Honeypot*, then, the drones represent not so much a direct analogy to the role that they play in a real hive but represent more a composite of the male behavior described by the women I interviewed, some of which includes sexual assault, misogyny, and sexism, as well as protectors, confidants, and lovers.

All of these parallels between the life of bees and the life of the women I interviewed inspired me to think more creatively about how to represent their stories in addition to a traditional "academic" text. In the process, I was challenged to think differently about false distinctions we make about myth and truth, since many of us—and especially those who are marginalized—are constantly compelled to prove the validity of our experiences or the stories we tell about them. And, in any event, myth, lore, and story create the foundation of what maintains a culture's past, present, and future, and African American culture is no exception—and in this instance, black southern women who love women aren't either.

What I offer here, then, is the vision that came to me as these stories flowed—like honey—over me. What emerged was a character named "Miss B.," who functions as a liaison between the world of black southern women who love women—a hive—and me. Perhaps it was pure serendipity that this bee first appeared in the epilogue of a draft of my book *Black. Queer. Southern. Women.—An Oral History*,[7] which is drawn from the same oral histories as this book but presented in a traditional academic format. But as I made the decision to write two separate books based on the same source material—one academic, and one creative—the bee decided that she wanted her own story. In the tradition of many African oral traditions, Miss B. is a trickster figure that is both of this world and outside it. She blurs the line between the sacred and the profane; she exists in the past, present, and future, transcending time and space. She is a composite of many black southern women I know, who, much like my grandmother, cursed like sailors out of the same mouth that they praised Jesus—women for whom this contradiction spoke to their humanity rather than to what some might deem hypocrisy. She is also a composite of the women I interviewed for this book, some of whom were open to sharing their stories while at the same time understandably cautious about relaying some of the most intimate details of their lives to a male listener. Miss B. is often crass but never cruel; confident but also vulnerable; a chain smoker despite knowing it's bad for her.[8] She's that family member who gets on everyone's last nerve with her antics but whom no one could imagine the world without. What she is ultimately—bee, human, ancestor figure—is left to the reader, but for me, Miss B. serves both as my guide and my conscience about what it meant for me to bear witness to these stories. She is also what Jacqueline Freeman refers to as an "Overlighting Being," a bee who is "the representative of the hive and at the same time has the responsibility to the bee kingdom . . . the repository of the hive's history and the emissary who speaks on their behalf."[9]

Bees are a part of the insect order Hymenoptera. I find it productive, then, to allegorize the root name of the order—"hymen"—as the name of the hive over which Miss B. presides. In *Honeypot*, Hymen is located in the nether regions of the South under which a massive river flows. Miss B. is both the keeper of the word and protector of Hymen. No one may enter without her blessing. Along our journey in this otherworldly place, Miss B. and I engage in conversations about life, love, politics, and her sisters. Though it is she who chooses me to collect these stories, she reminds me of the stakes and responsibilities of bearing witness to another's humanity. As we reveal ourselves to one another—and to ourselves—so do the women whose stories buzz in the sacred space of the hive.[10]

Acknowledgments

This book willed itself into existence. It all started with a pesky bee(ing) who decided that she warranted her own book. So, my first "thank you" is to Miss B. who knew that these stories deserved more than one way to exist in the world. To my husband and mate for life, Stephen J. Lewis, you are always my biggest fan. Thank you for being the first reader of this manuscript and for helping me strengthen the book in important ways. To D. Soyini Madison, to whom I'll forever be indebted for introducing me to oral history, ethnography, and poetic writing, thank you for reading a very early draft of this manuscript—twice!—and encouraging me to trust my instincts. Thanks to other colleagues who gave me valuable feedback on drafts of the manuscript: Marlon M. Bailey, Stephanie Batiste, Lauren Berlant, Martha Biondi, Joanne Braxton, Sharon Bridgforth, Jennifer Brier, Cedric Brown, Chris Cunningham, Nicole Fleetwood, Kai M. Green, Trudier Harris, Dwight A. McBride, Daniel Alexander Jones, Omi Osun Joni L. Jones, Ramon Rivera-Servera, and Deborah Thomas.

I would be remiss if I did not acknowledge all of my colleagues around the country who have supported this work through encouragement or inviting me to give talks at their institutions. They include Tami Albin, Renee Alexander-Craft, Juan Battle, Katie Batza, Karen Baxter, Lauren Berlant, Robin Bernstein, Joanne Braxton, Daphne Brooks, Ashley Coleman, Tommy DeFrantz, Jill Dolan, Alexis De Veaux, Lisa Duggan, Jackie Goldsby, Gayatri Gopinath, Kai M. Green, Beverly Guy-Sheftall, Michael Hanchard, Trudier Harris, Jaime Harker, Holly Hughes, John L. Jackson, Jr., Jajuan Johnson, Kareem Khubchandani, Susan Lanser, Bill Leap, A. J. Lewis, Jeffrey McCune, Leisa Meyer, Gregory Mitchell, Kathy Peiss, Della Pollock, Joseph Roach, Patricia Rose, Barbara Savage, Elmo Terry-Morgan, Deborah Thomas, Emilie Townes, Valerie Traub, Red Tremmel, Sherrie Tucker, Mary Helen Washington, Heather Williams, Eldie Wong, Michelle M. Wright, Vershawn Young, and Barbie Zelizer.

Thanks to my graduate research assistants who did dramaturgical research on bees, Yoruba spiritual practices, and who copyedited versions of the book: Julian Glover, S. Tay Glover, Jonathan Magat, Gervais Marsh, Shoniqua Roach, and Cinnamon Williams.

I received financial support from the Sexualities Project at Northwestern (SPAN) for two grants without which this research could have never taken place.

Miss B. first came to life in Oakland at the dining room table of Cedric Brown and Ray Pifferrer. I thank them for providing that space to write and imagine otherwise. Miss B. was further developed at the dining room table of Nicky Solomon and Glen McGillivray, in Sydney, Australia. They have welcomed me into their home for over sixteen years. Thank you for allowing me to escape to the other side of the world and for always providing me inspiration, great food, and an opportunity to cook!

To my editor, Courtney Berger, thank you for not only taking a chance on this manuscript but also for believing in my ability to make it work. You will never know how much I appreciate your candor, support, and friendship. And, as always, the folks at Duke University Press know how to make beautiful books. This time was no exception.

And, finally, to all of the women who invited me inside the hive to listen and bear witness, I say keep on buzzing about. Keep on telling your tales. Know that the beekeeper is always on duty.

Introduction

THE ADVENTURES
OF MISS B. AND ME

Some dreams you want to remember—and don't want interrupted. Flying dreams. Food dreams. Fuck dreams. Dreams that propel you into suspenseful delight to see what's going to happen next—from up above, in your mouth, to the body beneath you—or on top of you. And then there are those other dreams. You. Alone. In the dark. And whatever that something is, is chasing you. No one hears your scream, and your feet seem to be stuck in quicksand as the whatever your unconscious has unleashed on you devours every last bit of hope you had of escaping. You awaken. Heart racing and brow beaded with sweat. You realize it was just a dream. Comforted, you adjust your pillow and your body position (Mama always told you it was bad luck to sleep on your back!) and drift back off to sleep—only for the dream to pick up where it left off. The whatever it is, is on your heels. Damn.

And then there are the in-between dreams. Neither hopeful nor nightmarish, but nonetheless curious. You want to see and hear more, but you have a reticence. Will it turn nightmarish? Will it just be boring? Is it worth staying asleep for? You won't be too disappointed if you are awakened by your alarm clock music of Jill Scott singing, "Is it the way you love me baby?" or by finally noticing that your lover's side of the bed is cold—and empty. But you also wouldn't mind staying in this dreamscape to prolong the inevitable—the drudgery of the day's dilemmas: What am I going to wear today? What are we having for dinner? How many emails do I need to return? When is that essay due? How many more letters of recommendation do I have to write? The in-between dream sounds like a much better choice, so you stay asleep. Suspended. Waiting. Until you're awakened from the in-between dream by a knock at the door.

My dog, Bailey, is barking and scratching at the bedroom door. He is ready for his morning walk, pee, and poop. "Is the doorbell broken?" I mumble to myself as I stumble out of bed, grabbing my jeans and shirt from the floor. Whoever is at the door is going to be knocked out by my bad morning breath, but it serves them right for waking me up just when my dream was about to get good. I push Bailey back from the bedroom door and close it behind me, as I run down the stairs, trying to zip up my jeans and button up my shirt. It's Monday morning, so I know it's not Jehovah's Witnesses. The knocking turns to pounding, and I become worried that something has happened to Stephen. I notice I'm barefoot as I reach to turn the lock. Before I can get the door fully open, she blasts past me talking a mile a minute.

"Whew! I thought you were never gonna open that damn door! Don't you know it's cold out there? This is Chicago and I really ain't got no business being here this time of year anyway. I hibernate in the winter."

Adjusting what looks like a scarf draped around her neck, she pauses, briefly, realizing that I'm standing with my mouth agape and wondering who this person is who has just barged into my house. "Oh, baby, I'm sorry. Where are my manners? I just buzzed in here without greeting you properly. I'm Miss B."

She extends her hand. I do not return the courtesy, confused by what is happening. Seeing my confusion but still annoyed that I don't extend my hand to shake, she drops her hand to her side, only to place it on one of her hips.

"Hmmph. And you supposed to be a southerner. Could've fooled me." She begins to dig into what seems to be a purse, but looks more like a gold basket. The word "PANNIER" is embossed in all caps on the lower right corner in black letters. She starts a long string of almost inaudible non sequiturs: "I thought I had my card down in here somewhere . . . I bet you one of those drones been digging around in my . . . Lord, who done took my last c—."

We both feel the whip of cold air from the front door being left ajar. She finally looks up from her . . . purse. "Well, ain't you going to close the door? You letting all the heat out. And it sounds like that dog is about to lose its mind with all of that barking." I move to close the door while she removes her hat, scarf, and gloves and parks herself on one of our living room chairs. I want to run upstairs to calm Bailey, and take him out for his walk, but he'll have to wait. I need to attend to the business at hand.

"Ma'am, I think you're lost. Who are you looking for?" I say in my most respectful voice, but notably tinged with impatience.

She laughs. "Oh, I'm in the right place alright. And if you had a semblance of anything that looked like manners, you would have offered me some tea with a little honey."

I stare at her with even more disbelief.

"I'll take organic dandelion if you have it. And put the honey on the side. And that should be organic, too. So many pesticides and chemicals are used these days. It's scan'less." She fumbles some more with her purse.

"I don't have organic dandelion tea. The only organic tea I have is green tea. Would you like some of that?" I say, pinching myself to awaken from what must be a dream.

"From the looks of this house, I thought you were a bourgie Negro, but you can't be bourgie and ain't got no organic dandelion tea! Green tea is so last year. But if that's all you got." Her side eye is stunningly arrogant.

I make my way to the kitchen and open the cabinet where we keep the tea. I scan the two shelves of tea and there, on the bottom shelf, is a collection of teas in silver tins that I purchased in Portland, OR while visiting some friends. Well, I'll be damned. Organic dandelion.

I hear a low buzzing sound and then quiet. Buzzing. Quiet. Buzzing. Quiet. Surely, a fly has not survived the winter. I'm almost afraid to peek around the corner to see what she's doing in the living room. Instead, I focus on the task of preparing this dandelion tea that I didn't even know I had and trying to find my "bourgie" honey from Whole Foods. Luckily, there is still a little left in the jar in the refrigerator, but it has coagulated from the cold. I scoop a little out and put it in a ramekin and place it in the microwave for a few seconds. The tea has steeped long enough, so I pour it into a proper china teacup and place both on a tray and head back to the living room.

"Here's your *organic* tea and honey," I say, sitting the tray down on the coffee table.

She picks up the ramekin of honey, studies it for a minute before sticking the tip of her tongue into it very lightly. "Not bad. And by the way, you need to invest in a good fly swatter. You got bluebottles flying everywhere. You know they say that cleanliness is next to godliness, so I'd say you have a ways to go to get . . . godly," she says, not looking at me and taking another sip of tea. I say nothing but stare at her with all of the incredulity I can muster. Paying me no mind, she continues, "Okay, so now that we have the pleasantries out of the way, why don't you run on up and put on some shoes while I enjoy my tea so that we can go?"

"I'm not going anywhere with you."

"Okay. Sit down and let me explain to you how this is going to go."

"Uh, no. *You* are going to stand up and get out of my house."

The house goes quiet.

Without saying a word, Miss B. stands up and begins to gather her things. She slips on her gloves and then slowly, methodically, wraps her scarf around her neck, winding it round as if she's stuck in slow motion. It is at this moment that I get a closer look at her face. It is heart shaped. Her eyes are as dark as night, but rather than absorb the light, their glossiness seems to reflect it. Their blackness is a beautiful contrast to her tawny skin tone. On each of her cheeks is a small cluster of moles, similar to the ones on my mother's face, that resemble constellations on a clear night. Her hair looks as if she stuck her finger into an electrical socket—a blowout kit gone wrong. And to be cute, she has twisted two small bunches of the electrified hair on either side of her forehead such that they drape down toward her eyes to resemble tendrils. Tragic and fly all at the same time. She puts on her coat just as methodically as she did her scarf before bending over to slip on her shoes. I clutch my pearls when I notice that she doesn't shave her legs. Black mossy patches of hair extend up to her knees. It is then that I catch sight of her ass, which seems to blossom from her body, extended out far beyond any ass I have ever seen—including my own. She squishes her ill-fitting hat on top of her head, adjusting it on either side while pretending to look into an imaginary mirror. After she adorns herself in her outerwear, she takes one last slurp from the tea and moves silently toward the door. My dog's barking has reached a fever pitch, as if he senses that something is off.

"I hope that you find the person you are looking for, Miss B.," I say, wrapped in a bouquet of condescension.

She turns and extends her hand—again. This time I oblige. As our hands meet, she says, "I already have." And with that we are off.

One

THE HIVE

smooth soft flow

       quiet

           float

               float flow float

                still

river smooth

       river soft

         river flow

            river speaks   tongues

               shhhh

who/dat/man/she/done/brought/to/the/hive   he/must/be

   special   if/she/brought/him/to/the/nether/region/of/hymen

   blasphemy   sacrilege   waspy

           how/she/know/he/the/one

                  he/the/one

       how/she/know

            oh/she/know

she/missb.

                she/know

and/he/will/know/too

river quiet

river thinks

river still

river sing

wonderment of the senses   heterophony of solo and chorus

peak

dip

simmer

s-t-e-a-d-y s-t-r-e-a-m

hummmmmmmmmmmiiiiiiiiiiiiiinnnnnnnnnnggggggggggg

lower register sink

d

e

e

p

Heart (flutter) breath (stilted) eyes (wet)

soloist disrupts with flourish

melisma queen! high e flat! high f sharp! low b natural!

somebody tell her to cool it she raising the temperature of the hive

with/all/those/vocal/theatrics

paradox of harmony is   unison vibration rhythm

touch

swoon/sway/jiggle/swoon/sway/jiggle

too dizzying to keep up with it all

perfumes preside

patchouli thinks musk is too strong

lilac ducks beneath lavender

rose and honeysuckle stay quiet

jasmine rains

reigns

I awaken. My eyes are wet with dreams. We are by a river, my hands and knees covered in silt. Miss B. helps me to my feet and keeps her arms around me until I am calm enough to speak.

"Where are we?"

She continues to hold me, but does not respond. She puts her finger under my chin and tilts my head up until I see it: suspended in midair and hovering like a UFO is a gourd-shaped mountain. Its massive girth makes it impossible to see around.

"That, my dear, is Hymen. And we are at the river of Osun."

"I don't know what kind of drugs you gave me, but please, can you take me back to Chicago? My husband doesn't know where I am. My poor dog is still in his crate and needs to go out and I have not prepared for my class that I'm supposed to teach today."

She moves to the river and dips her hands into the water. She walks back to me and places her wet hands over my eyes, closing my lids as she does. When I open my eyes, we have been transported to yet another place.

"Dr. EPJ, you have been chosen by my people to share our stories. I am charged with making sure that our history is collected and passed down to the next generation. Why you were chosen will be revealed in time, but for now, you need to open your heart and mind so that you can receive the gift of story from my sisters. I have some brothers, too, but their days are numbered. Besides, you already know their stories. This is about the sisterhood. Don't worry. I will be with you every step of the way and introduce you to the sisters whose stories need telling. There might be some sisters whose stories you don't want to hear, but that is not your decision to make. You must receive and record those, too. It's most important that you bear witness.

"We—for good or bad—all work toward one purpose and that is maintaining our hive. The river of Osun that flows beneath us is our spiritual foundation. She, too, will be helpful to you when you need her. When you stumble, or feel stuck, go to the river. Wade in the water and listen. Now, are you ready to get your tour of the hive?"

"No. I want to go home. And I don't want to talk to your 'sisters.' I have things to do and places to be," I snap.

"I see you're going to have to learn that you can't always be in control," she says nonchalantly, walking by me but not looking in my direction. A strong, unrecognizable scent fills the air. Its intoxicating redolence draws me so strongly that I'm walking behind Miss B. against my will. I realize that I have no choice in the matter and follow her through the entrance of the hive.

Every street is filled with crowds of folks on their way somewhere, hovered in a circle, or carrying something. Streets seem to wind around at angles—almost circular but not really. Intersections are confusing because there is traffic from six directions rather than four. Miss B., of course, is unbothered by all of this and barrels her way through the crowds up a steep spiraling path until we get to what appears to be a clearing, much like an open market square.

"We'll stop here for now while some folks are away grabbing lunch. This way I can give you an aerial view."

"But why isn't anyone speaking?"

"Oh, they're talking. You just have to tune in to their frequency in order to hear what they're saying. Don't worry. You will. So close your mouth and open your ears—and your heart."

"Umm hmm," I say, pursing my lips as I scan the scene. There are rays of sun shining through the otherwise cloudy day. The temperature is just right, not too hot and a very nice breeze.

"I'll get you something to drink in a minute," Miss B. says. "I'm not rude like *some* people. I offer them something to drink right away when they enter *my* house." She grabs me by the hand and pulls me a few feet further down the road. There are a group of children doing chores: taking out garbage, beating rugs, and filling up water pails. Interestingly, they don't look bothered by the chores like the children I know, or the child I was. Instead, they seem to have a fierce look of dedication to the task at hand, trance-like, moving from one thing to the next and staying out of each other's way.

"We come out of the womb working," Miss B. says. "You have to fight your way into this world to take your first breath and you have to fight your way to stay here."

We stop in front of what looks like a warehouse. Hundreds of old women stand in line carrying gourds on their heads. We walk around the line to see the opening of the warehouse where there are younger women greeting the older women with a kiss on either cheek and then taking the gourds from them and carrying them off—to where, I don't know.

"What is this?" I ask.

"This is our honey factory. Those old women have traveled near and far gathering food to feed the whole hive. The young folk take the food from them and sort it out in the warehouse. It's stored there for the winter. If you're lucky, you'll get to see the old women do the waggle."[1]

We continue to walk a little further and pass a small group of elderly men playing checkers on an old tree stump. They look up momentarily to acknowledge our presence and then turn back to their game. We then reach an old convenience store. It looks more like a junkyard than a store: cigarette butts, old car parts, chicken bones, and empty Wild Irish Rose and Jim Bean bottles are scattered about. On the side of the store is a huge sweetbay magnolia tree and several tree stumps, where a few men are gathered, shooting craps and drinking. Miss B.'s posture changes and her eyes narrow.

"Hey, B.! What you know good?" one of the men yells at her. She ignores him, her walking picking up pace. "I see you ain't speaking today. Alright, then. You know I'm still going to hit that one of these days!" The other men laugh before fixing their eyes on me. "Your friend's ass is as big as yours. Maybe I'll ask *him* for a piece if you won't give me none!" More laughter.

Miss B. stops walking and turns to face the cat caller.

"Beau Willie Drone, don't let your *mouth* start something your *ass* can't finish. You *wish* you were man enough to handle all of this, but last I heard, your buzz saw working more like a *hand* saw. You bettah take you a dose of saltpeter. And you keep your mouth off of my friend. He's more man than you'll ever be and more woman than you'll ever get!"

The men buckle over in laughter at their friend's humiliation, while Beau Willie gives Miss B. the middle finger. Miss B. takes off down the road, marching as if off to war. "I see you give as good as you get. Who are those men?" I ask, once we are out of earshot.

"A necessary evil," she hisses back.

"What does that mean?"

After a pause, her tone changes.

"They mostly harmless. They just have to be put in their place from time to time, especially Beau Willie. Once he gets deep in that bottle, he loses his mind. He gets on my nerves so bad it makes my ass want to cut stove wood."

"I don't know what that means, but I assume you don't like him."

"Anyhoo, those are the drones and they hang out by that tree every day until around midday and then fly off somewhere in search of trouble."

I believe her, but I also know there is more to their story. But I don't intend to be in this "hive" long enough to find out.

"So, that's pretty much everybody who lives in Hymen. But I want you to get the lay of the land." She picks up a stick and begins to draw a circle in the dirt. She then draws sections within the dirt circle and inscribes two initials in each of the different shapes she's sketched out: "NC," "VA," "MS," "LA," and so on.

"We are here," she says, pointing to a section with "MS" in it. But I'm going to take you to all of these areas of the hive where my sisters live. Now, what you need to know is that not all of us are alike, depending on where we live in the hive. And we got different ways of doing things, as well. Some places got different tasting honey. I don't eat everybody's honey. I have to see how it's made, because you know everybody's kitchen ain't clean. You know what I mean?"

I'm only half listening to what she's saying, but I shake my head in agreement.

"We'll start down here in MS and work our way 'round the hive so you can get different perspectives based on where folks live. And don't you worry, I'll introduce you to everybody. They're expecting us." She walks ahead of me and then stops. "The other thing I forgot to tell you is that even though we are into unity and so on, we do have our little cliques. We have some saddity folks who live in the more populated areas; we got some masons, carpenters, and miners who live in more rural areas and tend to be a little country;[2] we even have some miners who came here from Europe who mostly keep to themselves. They always look ashy to me; I keep telling my good girlfriend, Nancy, who I'll introduce you to, that those folks need to discover the butters, starting with cocoa! And Lord, don't let 'em get wet.

"You talkin' 'bout smellin' like the funk of ten thousand years, I'm here to tell you. Anyway, in addition to being stank and ashy, they are not to be trusted. They will lie, steal, and cheat and claim that it's your fault that you've been lied on, cheated, talked about, and mistreated. We have tried for years to get along with them—and sometimes we do—but you can't trust them as far as you can throw 'em. So our strategy is to keep a close eye on them. Some of us do that by hitching up with them, but I guess you know all about that, huh?"

"I have no idea what you're talking about. You don't know nothing about me." I roll my eyes at her. She's living up to her name so far—Miss B.

She continues, paying me no mind. "The point is that they have, and still do, make our lives very difficult. It's been really, really hard dealing with the 'ashies.'[3] That's what I call 'em."

She pulls out a pad and flips through it, skimming over each of the pages. "Ooooookay. I think that's it. I think I've covered everything—at least for now. Any questions?"

"I don't have any questions because I'm not going to be asking any. I don't know how many times I have to tell you that I need to get back home. The only questions I need to be thinking about are the ones for the exam I need to write for my class. You do know that kidnapping is illegal, don't you, or don't you have laws here in Hymen?" I can barely repress the smirk stretching across my face.

Miss B. ignores me and digs inside her purse, producing a pad, pencil, and recorder. "Here," she says, extending the items to me.

"What part of 'I'm not interviewing anybody' don't you understand?" I say, feeling a bit uneasy about pushing back too hard at this point given that I don't know where the hell I am.

"I knew you were hardheaded, but damn. Don't you know a hard head makes a soft behind? You done felt yo'se'f too strong,/An' you sholy got me wrong.[4]

"Now you're quoting Paul Laurence Dunbar as if those are your words?" I laugh out loud. This woman is crazy and a fake.

"I was just testing your academic credentials," she lies.

I take the pad, pencil, and recorder from her hand. "Well, can't I have a few more days just to prepare? I haven't even thought about what questions to ask," I say, recoiling and trying to stall.

I can see her patience is wearing very thin. "No, you cannot have a few more days," she snaps. "You better pull it together before I get you together."

I take a deep breath, purse my lips and say, plaintively, "Okay. Let's go."

It's odd that I can never remember the journey to our destination—only the arrival. Miss B. has changed clothes. She's wearing a bright yellow blouse, black pants, and black patent leather stilettos.

"Aren't you going to be uncomfortable in those shoes?" I ask, not really concerned about *her* comfort at this point.

"Aren't you going to be uncomfortable in *those* shoes?" she retorts without missing a beat. I look down at my feet and realize I'm barefoot. I don't have a comeback. She laughs, looks down at my feet, and suddenly I'm wearing my loafers.

"Okay. We need to get down to business. I'll start you off with one of my younger sisters. She might be young but she has had some firsthand experiences with the ashies. She even knows a big-time movie star, but I'll let her tell you all about it."

"Can you first start by telling me where we are?"

"Hold up. Let me light my cigarette." She digs inside her yellow basket. "Whew, that's much better," she says dragging on her smoke. "We are in the deepest part of the hive in a place called Jackson, MS. There's a lot of history here. The good thing, though, is that there are a lot more of us than of them—them being the ashies." Her cigarette dangling from her mouth, she balances her basket on the middle of her left arm while she burrows down inside it again with her right hand in search of something. "I know my cell phone is down in here somewhere," she says to herself, her fag dangerously on the edge of her lips. "Ah, here we are." She produces the cell phone. "I can't remember exactly where Laura lives, so I'm going to look it up on my GPS." She punches in some coordinates, studies the phone for a bit, and then begins walking. Used to being left behind, I follow her.

We walk for about ten minutes through what feels like downtown. There are small knickknack shops and lots of beauty supply places. Just about everyone speaks to us as they walk by.

"Okay, we almost there. We're meeting her at Sugar's Place. They have some of the best catfish in MS!"

"Oh! We're meeting her at a restaurant? Isn't it going to be noisy in there? It might be hard for the recorder to pick up her voice if it's really busy."

She ignores me and picks up her pace. We come to the corner of Lamar and Griffith Streets and she stops.

"The restaurant is just down there on Griffith," she says pointing. "Go on down there, she's waiting for you. She'll be wearing a black pantsuit."

"Aren't you coming with me?"

"I'll meet up with y'all in a minute. I have an errand to run."

I walk down Griffith to Sugar's Place. I glance back up the street and Miss B. is still standing in the same spot looking at her phone, puffing on her cigarette. I enter the restaurant looking for a young woman in a black pantsuit and don't immediately see anyone fitting that description. The restaurant is more of a diner than anything else. The tables are covered with red-and-white checkered plastic tablecloths and there's a long counter to place orders. The food on people's plates looks tasty. I tell the server that I'm meeting someone and she says to take any empty table. I take a seat at a table next to the window so that I can easily spot Laura when she arrives. I was hoping that it would be too noisy to do the interview and this Laura person and I could just have a nice unhealthy lunch. Much to my chagrin, it was a slow day and not very loud at all and quite conducive to doing an interview. I let out a long sigh of resignation as I slump down in the chair.

Fifteen minutes pass and Laura still has not shown up—neither has Miss B. Perhaps they ran into each other on the street and are on their way. Half an hour passes, and now I'm concerned. The waiter comes over and fills my water glass up for a third time. I can tell she's annoyed because I've been sitting for a half hour, taking up a table, and haven't ordered any food. Hungry and a bit panicked, I place an order: fried catfish, black-eyed peas, collard greens, and sweet tea, for good measure. I might as well go all in or not at all with my heart-attack-on-a-plate meal. While waiting for my food, I begin to wonder if Miss B. is some crazy person after all and I've been duped into going on some wild goose chase with her. No one would ever believe this. And after I collect these stories, what am I going to do with them? This onslaught of questions gurgling in my head makes me dizzy. It's either that or I'm just hungry. Fortunately, the food comes out quickly. I inhale it. Just as I am washing down my last bit of cornbread with sweet tea, I realize that I do not have my wallet on me. Where is Miss B.?

I am about to explain to the waitress that I can't pay for my meal when in walks Miss B. Everyone turns to look.

"BAM!" she shouts, holding out her hands to reveal her new nail job. "Baby, Nail Envy on Medgar Evers Boulevard was having a special on nail service today and I could NOT pass that up. How do you like them?"

They are hideous. Half-black and half-neon yellow to match her blouse, and tiny bumblebee decals glued on the tips.

"If you like it, I love it."

"That's the line I use when I don't want to hurt somebody's feelings. That's just like saying, 'Girl, you were on that stage!' to one of your friends when you don't know what the hell to say when they were in a god-awful play. You can't out passive-aggressive me, Professor! I know the shit ugly, but I thought I would try something different. Do you really think they look that bad?"

I frown and nod my head.

"Well, you just going to have to live with it." She begins to chuckle from the inside out. She's searching for a cigarette. "Damn, I need to run to the store on our way out."

"Uh, Laura never showed up," I explain before she asks me how the interview went.

She looks up at me, her eyes studying my face. "I know."

"What do you mean, 'you know'? Did she call you and tell you she wasn't coming? Why didn't you come back and let me know instead of making me sit here for over an hour when I could be back at *my* home, working on *my* questions for *my* students? This is some bullshit."

She is not happy, beads of sweat dripping from her brow, her mole clusters moist with anger. "This was lesson number one. It ain't about you and what *you* want. You so full of, oh let me think of a big professor word, 'hubris,' that you think your shit don't stink. Well, it's awfully smelly up in here. This was a test of humility and you failed miserably. Did you even think about *why* Laura might have cancelled? No! You just went in on me. Well, Dr., you better pull your shit tight or this is going to be a very long journey for you."

I'm mad and embarrassed. The other customers are trying—unsuccessfully—not to stare at us. The only thing I can say is, "I don't have any money to pay for my food."

"Really? Lord Jesus, help me to hold out. Oooooh, I'm seeing red right now and I can't even see red! How much do you owe for this food?"

"The food was $7.95 and the sweet tea was a dollar. So, $9 plus tip."

"Tip? It's hot outside. How about that for a tip? Boy, this ain't Chicago."

Now I am doubly embarrassed and just want to disappear the same way I appeared—out of thin air. The waitress is standing right next to my table and hears the entire exchange. Miss B. picks up the check and carries it to the counter to pay. I try to avoid eye contact with the waitress. The waitress, on the other hand, appears unbothered. She comes back to my table and refills my glass with tea and whispers, "You might need something a little stronger than tea if you going to be dealing with her much longer." I wordlessly praise her shade.

Miss B. gets her change and tosses it into her yellow basket. She turns and scans the restaurant, as if daring anyone to judge her. She starts walking my way, sashaying like she's on a runway, except her heels are entirely too high for her to walk gracefully. She arrives at the table, plops down her pocketbook, and begins to rummage, I think, for a cigarette. Instead, she pulls out two crisp dollar bills, pulling on them to make sure that no others are stuck to them. Assured that they are indeed singles, she lays them on the table and puts the greasy salt and pepper shakers on top of them and looks back over her shoulder at the waitress and then at me. "You ready?" she says, more as a command than a question. I take another sip of my tea, gather my pad, pencil, and recorder, and stand to leave. She self-consciously closes her yellow basket and drapes it over her left arm. "Evah mo'nin' on dis place, seem lak I mus' lose my grace,"[5] she says, heading to the door. I open the door for her and we leave Sugar's Place. Miss B. saunters ahead of me, sparks flying from her stilettos scraping the sidewalk and from the tension in the air between us. She looks back and motions for me to catch up.

We walk for about fifteen minutes back down Griffith. My shirt is soaked and I need to pee. Miss B. seems preoccupied and has barely said two words to me since we left Sugar's.

"Where are we going? It's hot and I need to use the bathroom."

She keeps walking.

I finally concede. "I'm sorry, Miss B."

"Umm humm. You sure are. Give me your hand."

As soon as I touch her, the scene changes from urban to rural. We're stand-ing on the side of a two-lane road; on both sides is open field with high brush.

"Uh, what just happened? Where are we now?"

"You really do ask too many questions. If you must know, I took a little short-cut to get us here. I don't have my new set of wheels yet, but I will after this visit. Miss B. is going to take you on a road trip by the by." She abruptly changes the subject. "You said you needed to go, so go on over there and do your business."

"I'm not going to pee outside! That is so country."

"Don't get all new on me just because you live in a nice house now. You grew up without a pot to piss in, and now you don't want to piss outside? Fine. Hold it then. Nature will always take its course."

I really am about to wet myself, which makes me hold even more contempt for her. I turn and march into the brush and relieve myself. When I return she is the one smirking.

"Feel bettah, don't you?" she says as she hands me some hand sanitizer from her purse.

"I thought you wanted to stop to get some cigarettes on the way," I say to diffuse the tension.

"Chile, I always have a fag or two hanging out in my purse. I have enough to get by. How do you feel about dead people?"

"Dead people! I thought you were going to introduce me to the living?"

"I am going to introduce you to the living, but it ain't that much difference between the two. One is just above ground and the other ain't. Same shit, dif-ferent realms. I asked you because the next person I'm going to introduce you to runs a funeral home."

"Oh. I don't do funeral homes. You can ask all of my friends. I don't do hos-pitals and I don't do funerals."

"Well, you're going to do one today," she snaps. "I can tell this is going to be a long journey." She walks off mumbling under her breath: "Lord, give me strength today. These young people are something else, talking 'bout 'I'm not going to pee outside,' 'I don't do hospitals and funerals.' Where the hell do he think we enter and exit this world?" As she bumbles off into the distance, I look down again at my feet and discover that somehow I'm wearing sandals now. I am headed to a funeral home and now my shoes have changed without me changing them. This ain't right. This ain't right at all.

After a good little walk, we turn down a street named Fred Street. Off on the right is a small building with a white portico that extends the width of the building. I look up at the sign on the front of the building and it reads "Johnson Funeral Home."

FIGURE 1.1: JOHNSON FUNERAL HOME. PHOTO BY THE AUTHOR.

"Is this a joke, Miss B.? This is not funny. Johnson Funeral Home? Really? Seriously?"

Miss B. doesn't respond, only darts me a look—the look that my mama or grandmamma used to give when I was *thinking* about acting out in church. She keeps her eyes locked on me as I walk up next to her.

"You going to act like you got some sense one of these days. I done told you that everything ain't about you. Now, take out that pad I gave you and write down these notes before I knock on the door."

I take out my pad and pencil and she begins to tell me a little about the woman we're going to meet.

"You're going to love Miss Dedra. She's a soft-spoken woman with a spirit of fire. Like I told you, she runs her family funeral home, the only black funeral home in Prentiss, MS. She and her wife, Laurinda, who I'm also going to introduce you to, were married in NY before it was legal everywhere and live openly as spouses in Prentiss. Dedra is quiet but no-nonsense. That's how she runs her business and her life. You got all of that?"

"Yes, I think so. But wouldn't it just be easier if you just recorded all of this like I'm going to record the interviews?"

"You know, I've really been tryin' to cut down on my cussin' but you are really making that difficult, you little . . ." she stops short, glares at me, and then knocks on the door. Dedra opens the door and invites us in. I turn around and Miss B. is nowhere to be found. I have no idea where she has gone. Dedra senses that I am nervous and offers me some water. When she walks away to what I presume is a kitchen in the back of the funeral home, I notice how much the place doesn't feel like a funeral home—at least ones that I've been to. The front door doesn't open into a sanctuary with pews on either side of an aisle. Instead, it opens into what feels like a living room. There's a couch, two chairs, and a coffee table sitting off to the right of the door, and a bookshelf full of what looks like catalogues—probably of caskets. Just as I begin to have a flashback of walking through a room full of caskets in my hometown funeral home when my family was picking out one for my uncle, Dedra returns with a glass of water and leads me down a hallway to where we'll do the interview. I am praying that we don't go too close to where services happen. I'm already freaking out that I'm actually in a funeral home about to interview a stranger, in a strange town that I was brought to by a strange woman who has just disappeared. God, help me.

We enter what looks like an office, and I'm immediately relieved. There are framed pictures on the walls and on a small bookcase behind the desk—most likely of family members. The fluorescent light is harsh in the space and gives everything a bluish hue. We sit on either side of a small side table, and I begin fiddling with the recorder. Dedra sits patiently, watching me nervously prepare. She is a short, plump, caramel-colored woman with a round happy face, her short, curly hair adding a nice frame. Her slight smile immediately puts me at ease as I ask the first question.

Dedra

My father died when I was eight, and of course they had the business.

And what was the business?

Johnson Funeral Home. And after he died my mother took over the business and I had six brothers and one sister. My sister was the oldest and she was a nurse and she had moved away to Jackson and had a family up there. My oldest brother kind of stepped in as the backbone. He was in medical school when my father died. After my father died he had a nervous breakdown, came out of medical school, and came back to work in the funeral home, went to mortuary science school to run the funeral home for my mother. My mother must've been in her forties. My daddy was like forty-four when he died. She had all of us, so seven children, one in college, and the rest in high school, and I was in third grade.

It's a small town. The competition took an opportunity to hit her below her knees as far as business. They put on a lot of rumors that she was gonna close down; she was a woman; she couldn't run the business; she couldn't do it; and, she's from Alabama, scared of the white man. And she fought relentlessly [with] the white people. And when I say white people, [I mean] bill collectors, not white people coming to take the business, but bill collectors. She fought relentlessly [with] black people talking about her. Just, you name it, they did it. I watched her from eight years old just struggle with the business but . . . once my oldest brother got his mortuary science license he came and he stayed probably about four years and helped her get the business kind of leveled out . . . after the impact of my father dying. And once he did that then he went back to Ole Miss to pharmacy school and he finished and he was a pharmacist. So he was her backbone. So things kind of leveled out.

Where did you fall in the family?

I was [the] baby. I was right behind her every day watching her struggle. I used to hear her say, "Lord, have mercy," and [as] an eight-year-old, it frightened me because my father had just died and not knowing what she meant by "Lord, have mercy." I thought she was going to die, so that stayed with me years and years and years and years, and just to watch her just have to deal with this. So, I didn't have a childhood, basically. I didn't have a childhood because my brothers . . . went out into the world and experienced drugs and alcohol, and they come back and they want her to give them money, and they want to use the vehicles that she used for the funeral services, and just kind of took advantage of her. And I watched that but she still stayed strong. That was in '75. So her son, in '93, died. He was gay. He was HIV-positive so we took another hit, but at this point I knew that the responsibility was going to be on me because I was her right hand and kind of expected that. Two years before he passed away, she actually retired to take care of him, and in '93, he passed away and I took over the business and that's my job.

What are your best memories of growing up?

Going with my father before he died out to the pasture to feed the cows, when he would get out the truck and he would say, "Woo," and they would all come to him, and riding in the truck with him. I think that's why I have a love for trucks. But the little time that I remembered of him, if he had lived, wouldn't be in Prentiss. I wouldn't be here. So, that and just being out, being able to go outside and just kind of be free. After he died, then, of course I had an aunt that stayed next door, and her husband had a farm that's probably about four or five miles down, and in the evening times I would go down with him and we['d] get on the tractor and go feed the cows and ride out in the countryside.

What are your worst memories?

My brothers being on drugs and alcoholics. It wasn't segregation or anything like that because I wasn't really exposed to that. Them being on drugs. All of them went through a period of being that way, but they survived. They went to recovery and one had to go twice but they finally got it together. But to watch that, and I think even though I was gay that helped to turn me further against men. It did.

You associated being on drugs with being a man?

Alcoholic: I associated that with men. I associated the way they took advantage of my mother. I associated that with a man because she couldn't drive and it was either she give them the keys to what they want, or they were raising a fuss or threatening to do things all because it was something they want to go to do. And all the same time she's trying to run a business so she could feed them.

I've still got to go back to my mamma. Watching her . . . struggle helped me to be humble, helped me to appreciate [things] because even though she had a business, there were times where—now our lights were never turned off, water was never turned off—but there were times that she didn't have money to do other things, and it made me humble, [taught me how] to appreciate, and not look down on people that don't have. And try to at least give everybody a fair shot and try to kind of understand what the next person is going through because even though [they knew] my grandfather, [people thought] the Johnsons . . . had everything. The Johnsons were so high up on this pole that when I would go out in different places when I was young they'd say, "Oh you're a Johnson, you're one of them Johnsons, y'all got this, y'all got that." When I got grown, I was looking for what the Johnsons had and guess what? The Johnsons didn't have nothing. They didn't have nothing. And to live under that Johnson façade: "The Johnsons, oh you one of them Johnsons. You one of them Johnsons with that good hair. Y'all got [everything], your granddaddy had this, your granddaddy had that, y'all got that." You know when you go in the store, "Let me have five dollars. You a Johnson, you got money. You got this. You got that." No, we didn't have that. So, probably watching my mother helped me to be humble.

As I'm leaving the funeral home, I spot Miss B. outside smoking a cigarette. She has changed clothes yet again. It's dusk, so I can't tell exactly what color her dress is, but it's shimmering in the last bits of sunset. Her silhouetted figure is even more voluptuous—and she knows it.

"Where did you go? I turned around and you were nowhere to be found."

"Stay out of grown folks' business," she quips, blowing smoke out the side of her mouth and smacking her arm to kill a mosquito. "We need to get on the road. I don't like being in this part of the hive late at night. The ashies down here are super crazy."

"I heard. Dedra said that when we get back on the road that we should be very careful when we get to Mendenhall because there is a speed trap right when you enter the city limits. Although I'm sure you'll be able to talk your way out of any ticket wearing that dress."

Her face goes blank. She takes a long drag of the cigarette and blows a long stream of smoke before dropping it to the ground and crushing it into the graveled driveway. The sun winks past the horizon and darkness descends. The cicadas lift their voices in song.

"Is that why you think I'm wearing this dress? To get out of a speeding ticket? Boy, don't you know that these cracker heads would just as soon see you and me swinging from a tree for far less than a damn speeding ticket—and that would be *after* they had their way with me? If you ever say something like that to me again, I'll jerk a knot in your head. Get in the car."

She lights up another cigarette. I don't move. She knows that I was trying to joke with her the way she has with me and I'm not sure why my comment has crossed the line. I was in this situation before with a female friend in graduate school with whom I had joked about her "coochie cutter" shorts. She told me that my comment was sexist because she had the right to wear anything she wanted without a reference to her gender. Her chastising stung because I was embarrassed but also because I thought that as a gay friend I had more leeway than straight male friends. Back then I was a graduate student. I had a lot to learn about male privilege. What was my excuse now as a professor who taught gender and sexuality studies? Still, I could not let Miss B. see my culpability.

"You got something to say?"

"Did you hear me say something?" I sass, startled out of memory.

"I can tell you now that this is going to be a long trip if you don't get an attitude adjustment. I'm a woman—a *black* woman—and you don't know nothing about it. Trust me." She finishes the second cigarette and tosses it out into the street. It looks like a smoldering firework as it torpedoes down to the asphalt. "But, like I said, you'll learn."

I'm seething. I feel powerless because at every turn Miss B. has the upper hand—she won't take me home; she's making me do these interviews; and now she's mocking me. I begin walking back toward the door of the funeral home to ask Dedra if I can use her phone to call my husband so that he can come and get me. Then, I remember, I'm in a hive. A fucking *hive!* Deflated, I stop dead in my tracks and turn back toward Miss B.

She laughs. "The way you were making a beeline toward that funeral home you'd never know that you were afraid of the dead. So what's it's going to be? You going in there or are you coming with me? It's up to you." She opens the car door. I don't move.

"You a trip, but I like you. Come on and get in the car. We need to get on the road for real. We have a long drive ahead of us. We're going up the East Coast to NC. We're going to talk to one of my little sisters from Winston-Salem. It might seem a little familiar to you."

"Where did you get this car?" It's a black Lexus sedan with all of the bells and whistles.

"Stupid questions deserve stupid answers. I bought it. Duh." Her laughter pierces the thick night air.

"Umm hmm," I say, still pissed and giving her the hardest side eye I can as I sink down into my seat, praying to any god that will listen to get me back home.

Sunrise is less tense than sunset. Thank goodness. I roll down the window to enjoy the fresh air before it turns stagnant as the heat of the day ramps up. Miss B. drives the whole way. I imagine that I drifted off to sleep at some point, but given my tour guide, who knows how we got from point A to point B.

"Good morning, Sunshine! Did you sleep well?"

"Was I asleep long?"

"How about the entire thirteen-hour drive!"

"Really? I couldn't have been asleep for thirteen hours," I say, not believing my own words. "I must have been really tired."

"I don't know why. You ain't done nothing."

I know better than to take the bait. "You're right. It must be the jet lag. I have traveled quite a long way from home, after all." She knows I'm dodging.

"You're cute, Dr. EPJ, but not that cute. Look inside my purse and hand me another cigarette. I think it's on the floor on your side."

I reach down and pull her yellow basket to my lap. I open it to find the cigarettes and get a glimpse of all kinds of odd things: broken flowers, half-empty perfume bottles, packets of honey, and a switchblade.

She turns to me. "You don't see them?"

"Yes, I see them, but I was going to try to take it out of the pack and light it for you." The lie rolls off my tongue like snake oil. "How long have you been a smoker?" I ask to quickly move past my being caught snooping through her purse.

"I don't even remember. Ever since my nerves got bad. The smoke calms me, keeps me focused. You got it lit yet?" She extends her right arm with her index and middle fingers spread apart to retrieve the cancer stick. I light it and give it to her. She puts it to her lips quickly and takes a long drag—like it's her last—and exhales, the smoke thankfully trailing out the driver's side window. I don't dare tell her how much I hate cigarette smoke. How I can't stand the smell of it. How I think she's going to die from cancer. How it's a disgusting habit not befitting a woman who says she takes pride in how she looks. Instead, I stare out the window watching the pops of color from the fields of flowers planted on the side of the highway.

"We're about to pass downtown Winston-Salem. If you're lucky, you'll be able to smell the fresh Krispy Kreme donuts. That 'hot' light is a curse. You know they even have a Krispy Kreme app that tells you when the donuts are coming out of the fryer? That is all kinds of wrong." She takes another drag and speeds past a highway trooper.

"You better slow down, Miss B. If the state troopers here are anything like the ones in Chicago, they'll pull you over in a heartbeat," I warn, making sure this time not to mention anything about her low-cut dress.

"Yes, I know. I was only going five miles over the limit. I think they allow you nine. Besides, I can always show my titties and get out of it. Ain't that right?" I can tell she's looking at me, but I continue to stare out the window.

I finally break the silence. "I thought we were going to see someone in Winston-Salem."

"We're going to have to work on your listening skills. Remind me to take you back to Osun to meditate. I didn't say we were going to Winston-Salem, I said we were going to meet one of my sisters who is *from* Winston-Salem. She lives in Durham."

I continue to ignore her baiting. "Tell me a little bit about her. For starters, what is her name?"

"Ah, okay. I see how you're going to be, Mr. EPJ. Excuse me, *Dr.* EPJ." She tosses the cigarette butt out of the window and extends her hand for another. I dive into her purse again, get a fag, light it, and hand it to her. She moves out of the fast lane and turns the radio on. Surfing over various stations, she lands on a country and western channel. The female voice sings, *Turn the radio on to drown out the sound of goodbye.* "That is my song! Chely Wright's 'Shut up and Drive.'"

"I think it captures the moment quite nicely," I signify. "Can we stop somewhere to get something to eat before we arrive at this woman's house? I'm pretty hungry."

"Sure. There's a Waffle House a few exits up the road, or we can just stop at Hardee's and get a biscuit. I love their biscuits. They even serve them with honey now," she says, her cigarette now dangling from her mouth.

"Hardee's is fine," I say, as Chely Wright croons, *Shut up and drive. Shut up and drive. Shut up and drive.*

We go through the drive-thru and get our biscuits and get back on the highway. Between the whizzing of cars and the faint sound of yet another country song are the sounds of us smacking on the biscuits. I see the sign that says the exit for Durham is only two miles away. I'm relieved that we'll finally be out of the car. I also hope that she decides to "disappear" during the interview like last time. I really need a break from this woman.

"I'm going to stay for the interview this time. I'll be in the room the whole time."

I roll my eyes.

"But let me hurry up and tell you about my little sister. Her name is Kate. And like I said before, she was born in Winston-Salem, NC, in 1981." She stops abruptly and looks at me. "You're not writing this down, Dr. EPJ. Write it down." I let out a deep sigh and begin to write. "Good. She has her own bowtie company called Distinguished Cravat. She describes herself as a 'Southern Belle,' but Kate's gender and sartorial presentation—see, I know some big words, too!—'sartorial presentation.' Anyway, her sartorial presentation puts a twist on that southern belle image as she appears more as what one might think of as a dandy—we used to call 'em 'man ladies'—anyway she's been through quite a bit, but she's a survivor."

We arrive at Kate's neighborhood. It's a set of low-rise apartment buildings. We drive around in what seems like circles before we get to her building. The buildings look like they have been painted several times and have a 1970s feel.

We walk up two sets of iron staircases until we reach Kate's apartment. Miss B. knocks on the door. A young, thin woman with closely cropped hair opens the door, greets us, and invites us in. It's a small apartment but very neat. There's a couch positioned perpendicular to the wall. Both the couch and the wall are worn and look like they, too, have stories. Miss B. sits next to me on the couch while Kate sits in an adjacent armchair. She is wearing one of her bowties. It's made of wood and is quite a piece of art. Before I can ask anything, Miss B. says, "Now, Kate, sweetie, I want you to start by telling Dr. EPJ about your neighborhood where you grew up."

Kate
....

My neighborhood. Oh, it was absolutely [an] all-black neighborhood. And it was so black that I remember there was a time that if you looked slightly mixed you were like the cutest thing in the neighborhood. I think that it just came from the fact that we never saw anything other than us. [. . .] Even though we were a close-knit community you still had people killing one another. And I think as a child I saw so many people killed, which is why in my older days I deal with death different than a lot of my friends. A lot of my friends today other than their grandparents or something, great grandparents, they've never really had an experience. But I mean you look out your window as a kid and there's a guy laying on the ground and he's been shot and he was one of your uncle's friends. And now he's dead. And I would just cry. [. . .] But the community as a whole, it was one of those communities where if you needed some ketchup you could knock on your neighbor's door and ask for some ketchup. The one thing I will say is like my house was clean. We always had food. My mom always washed our clothes. Some of my other friends, they weren't that fortunate. I would go to their house and there would only be an ice tray in the freezer. I remember this. And so, like I said, those were the kids with the ice trays in there, those were the houses where we could chill at. Because either their parents were on drugs and they were gone all the time, or either they would just party or they would drink and it was like we weren't even there, if you will. But like I said there were a lot of people who killed each other because of drugs. That was one thing that really made me question just how much did they love one another. I remember my next-door neighbor; he walks up the street and shoots the guy in the head who was like his best friend. And I see the police going up the street and I ask, "What happened?" And my friend tells me, "You know Jonathan killed [man's name]." He just walked up the street and blew his brains out. Just a lot of death. [. . .]

There was a lot of drugs in that community. A lot of the older guys who used to sell drugs, I go back to my hometown now, and they're either alcoholics or drug addicts themselves. And interestingly enough a lot of them who "caught time" as they call it, when my mom got her time, a lot of them are now coming home. Because they had like heavy sentences. I mean they were giving these guys like fifty years. And some of them were like twenty [years old]. But they didn't do the whole fifty. They did like maybe twenty-five years or some are home at forty-five, and they left when they were like teenagers, if you will. And so it's going to be interesting to see them come home, especially when they're coming home to nothing. Winston-Salem is growing, but I would never move back home. You couldn't pay me to. I think that the mentality is just different. I'll give you an example. I flew home one time and I stayed in Burlington. And I remember sitting in the car with my godsister and I just started crying as I looked at the people because I felt like they had no hope. I felt like they were at the point in their lives where they were settling. I felt like there was no sense of hope. And I felt like . . . they were just happy with where they were. And they were just fine with that. And I'm not saying that happiness necessarily has to do with material things. But I think hope and happiness definitely go hand in hand.

I am struck by how Kate's story is filled with so much despair, yet she has the tenacity to move away, start her own business, and be open about being a gender nonconforming lesbian. Although she's fifteen years my junior, we have similar backgrounds relative to growing up in public housing, with the major difference being my community was not as plagued by drugs—perhaps because I came of age in the seventies and she the eighties, when black communities were being ravaged. So much for Nancy Reagan's "Just Say No" campaign. Did Miss B. know that Kate and I had growing up in the projects in common?

As we're leaving Kate's place I can sense that Miss B. is tired. How could she not be? I can't imagine how much energy it takes to keep all of that talking and shade throwing going.

"I can drive to the next interview, Miss B. That way, you can get some rest. Just put the address in the GPS."

"You think I'm a sucker, don't you? You think you can find your way back to Chicago while I'm asleep if I let you drive. Good luck with that. But I sure will take you up on your offer. My feet are killing me and I could use a good old-fashioned nap. We're only about three hours away from Nancy's place. I'll punch in the address." She hops in the passenger side of the car and begins to put the address into the GPS. I open the driver's side door, but can't sit because the seat is pulled almost to the steering wheel. "What are you waiting on? Get in the car. I'll pull the seat back."

"I got it," I say, beating her to the button on the side of the seat to move it back. I take a seat and put my hands on the steering wheel, which feels sticky.

"So, let me tell you a little bit about Nancy. She and I go way back."

I put the car in reverse as she begins to tell me about her sister.

"Nancy was born in Maxton, NC, in 1950. That side of NC is full of ashies, and during the fifties, you can best be sure it was not a cute time to be black or a honeypot licker. We called that side of the NC "Helms Country," because there was a very powerful ashy minor named Jesse Helms. You talk about hateful! He was meaner than a rabid pit bull. And I always thought his mouth looked like a chicken's ass, which made sense 'cause nothing came out of his mouth but chicken shit! Thankfully, his reign of terror is over, but he was the worst of the worst ashies!" She frowns at the memory. "Back to Nancy. She's an anthropology professor, so you two 'academics' should have something in common, except Nancy ain't bourgie. And she pulls no punches when it comes to speaking her mind, so don't try get cute with your questions. While she is not closed about her sexuality, she's more about being a race woman, if you get my drift."

I keep my eyes straight ahead but silently acknowledge her comment. I'm hoping that, like its effect on babies, the car ride will put her to sleep so that I can have some peace and quiet. The Lord grants my wish, and before long, she's knocked out and sleeps the entire three-hour drive to Nancy's. Miss B. reminds me so much of my grandmother that it's scary. My grandmother was one of the most generous people I have ever known and would do anything to help someone out. At the same time, she was set in her ways, and there was no way of getting around her fussing and complaining about something. Even when we grandchildren became adults and often joked about grandmama's aggravating ways, we dare not step out of line. Miss B. was my grandmother reincarnated—just a bit more . . . urban.

We pull into Nancy's driveway. The house is a modest white frame home with a front porch. Miss B. is still asleep, and I don't disturb her. I get out and walk up the stairs to the porch, where Nancy is sitting having a glass of ice tea. I introduce myself and have a seat in the chair next to her.

I understand why she and Miss B. are friends. She has a self-confidence about her that lets you know not to cross her—and she smokes, which I'm really surprised by since she's a professor. On the other hand, I have plenty of colleagues who smoke, so why I'm surprised about Nancy smoking is not completely rational. At least we're outside, so the smoke won't bother me. It's hot and sticky, which explains Nancy's attire of a thin blouse, shorts, and flip-flops. She offers me a glass of tea, which I gladly accept. I take a few gulps of my tea and begin the interview with questions about her childhood.

Nancy

Well I grew up in the segregated South, so white people were not a part of my daily experience. So you knew racism existed but you created another world. Your parents had more racist encounters than you did, than you would have as a child, because you know I lived in a black community and went to all-black schools. The racial experiences that I had would be like a white boy exposing his penis, thinking that's cute. Or a group of white girls trying to figure out who's going to move off the sidewalk. None of us want to move, so we would bump shoulders, whatever, to try to push each other off the sidewalk.

Is this in transit to school?

My home or wherever I was going. Their communities had sidewalks. Of course, ours didn't. So, you're walking to town and go to town for your parents or get something, whatever, and you're walking down the street and you're walking through their neighborhood. Or you're riding on your bicycle through their neighborhood and one of their dogs comes walking after you. That's why I don't like dogs. People tell me, "My dog is friendly." Please, uh-uh. I don't believe that.

Was your town segregated physically by a railroad track or river or road or some physical thing?

There was a railroad track. It's true. In the western part of the town is where I lived, and it's separated by a railroad track that ran north and south. Then you have the white sections of town and then another black section of town. So I just happened to live closer to the railroad track. People who lived in the most eastern part of the town, they were white, I mean black. In the middle, you had a lot of white folks.

And when you went to the white side of town, was it usually with your parents?

I don't recall myself going there. What I did was go through there so I could go downtown to get whatever my mom was sending me for or whatever. I had to go through their neighborhood to get to school sometimes. Different activities that you might get involved in. But to say, "I'm going into the white community to see someone," no, that never happened.

One time I had to go see my aunt. She was at work and my mom had to tell me, "You must go to the back door. You cannot go to the front door. Your aunt will lose her job." So I went to the back door. I remember that. The only time I went to a white person's house in my hometown.

Your aunt was a maid?

Yes. But my mom was a stay-home mom. My father worked two jobs because he said his wife was not going to take care of white children at the neglect of her own children. So, we had land, so we grew almost everything. We had pigs. We had a cow. We had chickens, working-class people with a little land and a small house, but I don't ever recall wanting for anything.

How would you describe your family's beliefs and attitudes about people who were different from you?

My father was very forthcoming, even truthful about white people. My father said something to his friends and I was serving him coffee and I'll never forget it. He said there isn't a Negro alive that can steal as much as a white man. He said they stole us from Africa, they stole Native American land, and they still stealing our labor. My father was very political. I remember that. I wasn't even twelve or thirteen at that time. I remember that. So, my father told me the truth about white people. My mother did not work outside the family, so my mom basically showed you how to be diplomatic and to work within the black community. My father gave you what you needed to do when you had to work around white people. You could not say the word "nigger." You could not call each other that. That was a sinful word in my family. Probably could get away with cursing better than you could calling someone "nigger." When it came to class, because we grew up in a small town, you know you don't say "middle class," "working class." I use the term "working class" now because I understand it, that concept. But then you were either better off or worse off. So, everything is relative. My good friend who came from a family where both parents were teaching, they had far more material goods than we had. So, they were better off than us. But I had somebody live down the street who were worse off than us and they have to borrow my shoes when they go to like a school program. Okay. So, class wasn't a big issue. What was a better issue is probably respectability. Being a respectful, dutiful person who's working trying to take care of the family. If you weren't doing that then people would talk about you, so class wasn't a big issue, but you knew that some people were better off and some had less. Whites were a big issue. I grew up in a town with three ethnic groups. Native Americans belonged to my county, so they came to town. They're called the Lumbee. My father grew up around Lumbees, so some of his Lumbee friends used to come to the house and sometimes we would work on a Lumbee person's farm. They had a big farm and needed extra work hands or something like that. Sometimes we did that. What I didn't know, my mom had a Lumbee friend. They tended to live in the county, but when they lived in town they lived in the black community when I was a child.

I had lots of chores. First of all, you would have to clean, help clean the house on the weekends. When you were going to school, one of us had to get up early to help my mom make breakfast because we had [a] freshly prepared meal for breakfast and dinner, so somebody was always in the kitchen helping her on duty. Those who weren't in the kitchen helping her fed the pig, cow, or made sure the chickens were in or fetched firewood. We had a woodstove to heat the bedroom. So, we worked. In summertime, you worked, they used to give us like a row while we worked in our parent's garden. But they would give you a row and you would have your little corn and tomatoes, little things you would grow. And you would be like so proud of them and stuff like that. We worked. And I don't regret that.

Did you think it gave you a sense of the value of things, having to work for something?

Yeah. Oh yeah. I can remember looking out over the field sometime and seeing heat waves and thinking, "Shit, I am not going to be caught in this little town. I'm getting out of here. I don't know how I'm going to do it, but

I'm getting out of here." But work was good because you learned things. I never felt overworked or anything like that, but we worked. From the time I was thirteen I would work tobacco in the summer and save up money for my schoolbooks. God bless the child that's got his own. If you made money, your parents bragged about you. I didn't know any lazy kids. You got a chance to work and make your own money, you did it, 'cause then everybody would be praising you.

My father and some of his friends would go down to the beach and get all kinds of shellfish and shrimp and stuff and have like a craw boil in the fall. Everybody would be out, talking, eating, and having fun. Kids running, teenagers trying to kiss each other, whatever. Adults winking and nodding at each other. Those were fun times. Going to school. I loved going to school. I loved learning. When I was little I used to look at *National Geographic*. It doesn't surprise me that I turned out to be an anthropologist because I always wanted to go see the world. I wanted to see the world beyond my hometown. But going dancing; I love dancing. To this day every Saturday night we go dancing. I loved those parties where we danced. I didn't grow up in a town where people were fighting and killing each other, young people when they go to events. Sometimes a bunch of boys from another town would ride up and start fighting our boys. Serious violence. I never was taught to fear black people, always feared violence from white people. I will never forget it. One day I was walking down a street in Harlem. It was evening, early evening. It was fall. I was walking going to the bus stop. So, these guys said, "Hey baby. How you doing?" I said, "I'm not too bad. How you all doing?" They said, "You're not from New York, right?" I asked, "Why is that important?" You got a certain ease about yourself. I went to Harlem [and] I wasn't scared of black people. I still am not scared of black people. The people I'm scared of are the people I can't fucking predict. White people. I can predict black people. I can't fucking predict white people. This fear of a people has never been of my own people. It's what those people could do to us.

I remember something from my childhood that hurt me. Sometimes husbands and wives would fight, and I saw this man fighting his wife. I saw him dragging her. Two days later I see her with a bandage on her arm and sitting all up under him and everything. I said to my mama, "That will never happen to me." Somebody whip my butt and I'm going to be hugged up on them the next day. My mom said, "Honey, life isn't that simple." Life is simple to me. My mom knew my dad was a ladies' man. Sometimes it hurt her and she would be crying. I said, "I'm sorry but I would not cry for that."

How would you describe the importance of your southern upbringing on your character?

Well, I try to be helpful. If I can't be helpful, I won't be around. My mom would say, "If you ain't got nothing good to say, shut the hell up." Don't add to the craziness. Then there's an expression which is "Honey attracts more flies than shit." That is a southern expression. A lot of people call southerners phony, but I know what they doing. They being sweet so they get what they want. It doesn't have to be something conniving or mean. "Honey," "baby," "sweetheart": all those terms of affection. I like that stuff. I like southern culture. I know that we can talk about folks, and then they enter the room, and it's "Honey, how you doing?" The person comes in the room and I would tell my mother, "I know they been talking about me." I mean some people say the South is very two-faced, but I don't. Everybody know who's talking about who. I like the civility. I like the hospitality of the South. People in the North would say to me, "You are so southern." I would give something to someone and not think anything about it, no big deal. I would hear, "You so kind." I don't know any other way to do this. There are mean people in the South, but the South encourages you to be a kind person. You know scholars now say there's a great difference between the North and the South. Always has been. Northern cultures have been greatly influenced by Northwestern European cultures: English, French, Irish, and Norwegian. The South was influenced equally by African cultures. So, this civility that we have in the South, whether white or black people, that shit comes straight out of Africa. You go over there and it tells you right away why we do the shit that's good and why we do the shit we do that's bad. 'Cause Africans be talking about your ass, you come in the room, they change the whole conversation. So, I like trying to build consensus, but at some point let's get on with it. Southerners take too long. You can't always build consensus. White people will do everything to build a consensus. We are not going to agree. Let's be respectful of each other and move on. Please. I can do that with black people more than white people.

It's almost sundown, and the air is still heavy, but honeysuckle sweet. Nancy's story gets me to thinking about how dramatically different someone's outlook on life is affected just by where they live. I also begin to think about how different my own life might have been had I grown up in Chicago as opposed to a small town in North Carolina, despite Chicago being considered "up south." I don't know that I think black people are more predictable than white people, especially if I take my immediate family as an example. Still, the observation gives me something to chew on. Nancy goes into the house to take the tea glasses while I go to the car to check on Miss B., who's still asleep.

"Miss B.! Wake up! Wake up!" I shout to annoy her the way she has annoyed me.

"Why are you yelling? I'm right here. Damn. I was into my third dream about a land of milk and honey. And I was just about to get my honey milkshake before you come yelling at me. Hand me my purse."

I anticipated that she would want a cigarette when she woke up, so I bummed one from Nancy to have ready for her. She looks at me and then at the cigarette.

"You think you are so smart. How did you know I was going to look in my purse for a cigarette? I could have needed my purse to get to my phone or get a piece of gum." She snatches the fag out of my hand and smiles slightly. "Well, you going to light me up?" I fetch the lighter from her purse, cup my hand around hers with the cigarette, and light it.

"Did you have a good nap?"

"More important, did you have a good interview? Nancy is my ace. We are like two peas in a pod. No nonsense. I'm surprised she didn't come out here to the car and wake my ass up. But she knows we older queens need our rest." She blows smoke in my face.

"She's had a colorful life. It was also interesting interviewing another academic. She gave me lots to think about. I see why the two of you are such good friends." She knows I'm signifying but doesn't take the bait, so I try to cover and add, "I didn't realize she has a daughter, who is also a lesbian, a mother—and a chaplain."

"Yep. Her daughter's name is Malu. I'll tell Nancy to call her over for you to talk to her. In fact, why don't I introduce you to some daughters and mothers?"

"You mean there's more than just Nancy and Malu who are mother/daughter lesbians?" That doesn't quite come out right, and I see Miss B. frowning.

"Err uhh, I don't know what a 'mother/daughter lesbian' is, but I'm assuming you're asking me if there are other mothers who have daughters who also love women. And the answer is yes.

"Regardless of that, though, in general, we in the hive have special bonds with our mothers, which sometimes makes the fallouts that much harder. My mother been dead for years now, but couldn't nobody sting me like her. She loved me hard and she hurt me hard. Most do, especially if you *that way*.

"Here in Hymen, our mothers take a long time to prepare to bring us into the world. I think that's why they are so hard on us. They want to protect us. But they also want to make sure we understand that we must all pull our own weight if we are to survive. Hell, I was working in a food storage factory at the age of twelve. As I got older, mama let me go out of the hive with her to go shopping. Those trips were so much fun because she would always buy me some honey lollipops if I was able to find a good sale in the store. Although these trips to the store would take all day because we had to go to sometimes three or four different stores to look for different things—Winn Dixie for canned goods, Harris Teeter for meat, Kroger for housewares, Bi-Lo for vegetables, and sometimes the Piggly Wiggly for chitlins—I didn't care because I knew that I would get my honey lollipop when we got back to the hive. And I earned that candy 'cause Mama would make me carry the bags. I believe to this day that that is why my hips are so big—it's from carrying all them damn bags every week.

"Anyway, I don't have any children, but I have been mother to many. That is our way here: 'I am because we are.' That's what Mama used to say all the time. 'I am because we are.' I never forgot that." Melancholy overcomes her face, dissolving into indifference then jubilance, and finally resignation. It is like watching the seasons change over the course of a nanosecond. "Let me run in here and say hey to Nancy. I can't believe that heifer didn't come to the car and speak. Me being asleep has never stopped her from running her mouth before! By the way, Malu was born up north in 1980 but was raised down here from the time she was a little thing, so we claim her as part of the hive. She's as cute as a button—and tough as nails. She's her mother's child."

Miss B. goes up the steps of the porch, gives a few rapid knocks on the door before entering the house. The door is barely closed before I hear her booming voice cutting through the air. I sit down on the porch and watch the last bit of the sun wink past the horizon. The pink, purple, and orange-lit clouds resemble bags of cotton candy at the county fair. A car pulls up into the driveway behind our car and a young woman emerges. She is the spitting image of Nancy, so I know that it's Malu. She walks up and introduces herself and tells me that her mother called and asked if she would agree to be interviewed. Before I can introduce myself, Miss B. comes to the door.

"Malu? Is that you? Girl, if you ain't grown I don't know who is. Come and give your godmother a hug." Malu walks to the door and hugs Miss B. "I assume you've met my friend, Dr. EPJ. He's recording our stories and I thought it would be good for him to talk to some young people whose mamas are also in the life. You go on and sit down here on the porch and I'm going to go on back in here and finish catching up with your mama. Chile, she is bringing me up to speed about her neighbors. What a soap opera! Holla if you need me, Dr. EPJ." She turns and retreats back inside, her voice still rattling the windows. Malu smiles while shaking her head and sits down in the same rocking chair where her mother had just sat.

Miss B. described Malu as "cute," but I disagree—she's too much of a woman for such a description. Perhaps she described her as cute because her beauty has an innocence that her body betrays. As the old folks say, she *favors* her mother, but they could pass for sisters rather than mother and daughter. She is much more femme than her mother, her high cheek bones perched perfectly on her deep caramel face surrounded by henna-colored spirals of tight curls. Her smile is a lullaby.

Malu

What was your coming-out experience like?

Oh, so dramatic. And I don't know why. [*Laughter.*] I was so dramatic. I was crying and all. It wasn't so much of who I was with; it was the fact that I had had a sexual experience, that I was horrified to say that to my mom. Like, I was horrified, because we'd always talked about waiting until I got older, and the responsibility of it, and what that looks like. Now, most of it was coming out of a more heteronormative context in terms of pregnancy and disease, but I didn't think about that. What I thought was, "My momma told me I should wait until I get older," and here I am, like, I think fifteen, being like, "Momma." I mean, I was so drama[tic]—oh, I cried so hard. Now we talked about it. . . . She kept a straight face, and then she went to call my aunt. It was like, "Girl, Malu finally done come out." And they had a good laugh about it. [*Laughter.*]—"Girl, please. Didn't she know she was gay?" We talked about it years later. But at the time, I just remember I was so emotional, because I was so concerned that she would have feelings about that. The actual act of sex. Or yeah, that was where I was like, "Oh, God, what is she gonna think?"

So, it wasn't about the fact that it was with the same sex, it was about you having sex at all.

Um-hmm.

So, what compelled you to tell her?

I have no idea. I really don't. I do not remember anymore. Whatever it was, I felt like I needed to be . . . in intimate relationships . . . there's a certain amount of transparency and integrity that I need to have with them. And that's just who I am. I lied to my mom one time in third grade, and I came back and told her I lied and put myself on punishment, and she told me that my punishment was harsher than what she was gonna do. But she was like, "Yeah, sure, go with that. No *Cosby*, no *Different World* for like two weeks." That's serious punishment when you're eight years old. I wanted to be honest about who I was. This is a big difference: whereas once I had no idea what an orgasm is, I now know what that is; I have shared it with somebody else. That's a big deal. So, "Mom, you need to know that about me. But I'm also freaking out that I'm gonna tell you this." And I don't think I said all those words; I'm confident I didn't. But it's more so just about transparency and showing up in that relationship. How can I be in a real relationship and not show up?

And at that point, she hadn't come out to you, or she had?

Oh, yeah. My mom told me she was, yeah, she told me that a long time ago. And my response was, "I like boys. You can be gay if you want to, but I like boys."

Really?

I was real young . . . don't remember how young I was, but I was young. And she just kinda gave me the side-eye, like, "Okay," and I was like, "Alright." That was really my only question. "Does that mean I have to like girls, too?" That was kinda my thing. "No." Okay, well, whatever.

And then when you came out to her, what was her reaction?

[*Pursing her lips*] "Um-hmm." [*Laughter.*] It was kinda like, "Right." [*Laughter.*] I mean, I think it was kinda like, "You don't think I know that's your girlfriend? I ain't stupid." Like, "Yeah, I know." I mean, she didn't say that, but kinda, you know. She was like, "Okay."

My son was born in 2005, so that shifted everything. I understood parents; I didn't understand, like, coparent family unit. When it came to him [their son] and us [her and her ex] having that discussion about what it means to coparent a child together and, whether we could break up tomorrow, but once we say this, under the commitment to him, I understood. I've known her [her ex] since I was a teenager. She's from this area, so we've known each other off and on since I was like sixteen or seventeen. But we linked up again for dating purposes. I was twenty-four.

When you and Linda got together, you made a conscious decision that one of you would have a child?

No.

No.

[*Laughter*.] Oh, my son, the little surprise. So, Linda was raised Pentecostal; her mom's a Pentecostal missionary. Now, I mean, at this point her mom was like a whole new level. But she was raised working class, Pentecostal, missionary, with her family having some roots that are like Trinidadian, some roots that are Geechee, [and] her father happens to be Liberian. But her family context was very, very conservative, very, very holy. I mean, her mom doesn't wear pants, doesn't wear earrings. She grew up going to church all the time. So, her journey of being able to say that she was a lesbian was far more painful, I would say, than my own, especially in reaction with her family, I mean, her nuclear family. So, anyway, she had been engaged to a man there for a while; and I don't doubt that she loved him, but I think a large part of it was "I am not going to be gay." Anyway, she was engaged to him and they broke up and, as people do sometimes, you dip back into old experiences. And he [her son] was a surprise out of that. So, yeah, I was there when she learned she was pregnant. She didn't know that. We didn't know she was pregnant when we first started dating—had no idea. So, that was a funny moment. She wasn't feeling well, so I took her to the ER trying to figure out [what was wrong]. 'Cause she has bad asthma. And so, I was like, "Well, you're about to have an asthma attack?" "I don't know." I'm like, "We're going to the doctor. I don't know what's about to happen."

And this little white lady, she's so funny, she said, "Well, I need to tell you something. Do you want your friend to stay?" And Linda was like, "Yeah." And she was like, "Are you sure you want your friend to stay?" And she looks at me real sweet with this look in her eyes, and I'm like, "What?" By the way she said "friend," I knew she knew. So, we're just like, "Yeah," and so the doctor says, "Well, honey, you're pregnant." And I remember they both just turned and looked at me. And I was like [*laughter*], "For what? Hey, like are y'all really both staring at me?" And they did. Both just complete silence, just looking at me. And I was like, "Dang." So, I think we all kinda recovered. And then there was a lot of conversation after that, like, "What does that mean?" And "Okay, you're pregnant and are we going to stay together? Are we going to break up? Are you trying to give it one more try with this dude? You were engaged to him. What does this look like?" It was a lot of conversation, a lot of heavy intense conversations for people so young. And I know some people don't think that's all that young, 'cause people have babies earlier than that, but when you put in the dynamic of being same-gender-loving and having a surprise kid . . . I haven't heard a lot of stories that are similar—put it that way. So, a lot of conversations, and I prayed a lot. And the way I talk about it is that was my first calling, like my first calling from God was to motherhood. I was like, "This is my kid. Okay. Huh, okay." So, I need to get on that and adjust my life accordingly, and figure out what it means to be a mother. "Wow. Alright." Which I didn't think I would do until in my thirties somewhere. But we figured it out—not well initially, in terms of our relationship—but [our son is] always well-loved, has what [he] needs and he's kinda spoiled, but . . .

Well, with three mommies now.

Right. Three mommies, two grandmas in his life on a consistent basis. But then Mika, that's his stepmom; she has a mom, so he has her. [. . .] [*Laughter.*]

And what does he call all of y'all?

Mika, he calls by her name, he calls her Mika. Initially, I was like, "No, that's not your mama." I didn't tell him that, but I made it very clear when they first dated, I was like, "Yes, this is great. Y'all can date, that's not a problem, but that's my child." Now, six years later, very different experience. So, if he's with one of us, it's just "Mommy." But if he's with [one of them], then "Mommy Lu" or "Mommy Lin." He just distinguishes like that. When he talks about his other mom, he's gonna talk about her wherever he is. If he's in the street, if he's in the store, he talks openly about his family. He has even told strangers before, "I have three moms." And I'm looking at them, trying to hold my energy, 'cause I'm like, "You'd better not. I don't care what you think, you better . . ." And sometimes people are like, "Oh." "Well, isn't that beautiful?" Or "Aren't you special?" Or "Isn't that unique?" People have not said anything rude to him, [for] which I'm grateful. Because who knows what they're really thinking. But my thing is, whatever you think, I don't care. Just don't say it to him.

Malu and I talk for a little over an hour, interrupted sporadically by cackles coming from inside the house, when she looks at her watch and realizes that she's late to pick up her son. She tells me to tell her mom that she'll call her later and to tell Miss B. goodbye. She runs to the car and drives off, just when Miss B. comes to the door.

"Where is Malu running off to? She didn't even say goodbye. That girl is always rippin' and runnin.'" She puts her hands on her hips in exasperation.

"She had to go pick up her son. She said to tell you goodbye."

"Well, I'm glad she was able to come over and talk to you. Unless you didn't notice, Nancy and I had a good time catching up. She's talking about retiring, leaving the hive and moving to Africa. I told her to take me with her, 'cause Lord knows I'm good and tired." She plops down in the rocking chair across from me. We sit for a while listening to the cicadas and watching the lightning bugs' night show. After a while, she breaks the silence. "I know you're tired, so I asked Nancy if we can stay here tonight. We'll start fresh in the morning."

"Oh." I say, disappointed that we're not going back to Chicago.

"Pouting doesn't become you," she says. "You'll feel better in the morning after a good night's rest. And Nancy is a good cook, so she'll put her baby toe in something special for us tomorrow morning for breakfast." She rises, walks over to me, and rubs my face with the back of her hand. It's almost a tender moment, except I feel the condescension through her touch. Unbothered, I rise, too, and follow her into the house.

I awake the next morning to the smell of biscuits. I hear Miss B. and Nancy talking from the kitchen. I look at the alarm clock and it's already eight o'clock. I slept in my clothes and am feeling funky fresh, so I stumble to the bathroom and wash my face, hit the highs and lows, and then head to the kitchen, where the two are sitting at the kitchen table having a cup of coffee.

"Well, if it isn't Mr. Sleepy Head himself. I was just about to come back there and get you. You can't sleep your life away, we gots bills to pay." She does an internal chuckle.

"Perhaps if I weren't snatched from my house I could be at work making money to pay my bills," I retort with the sass of a teenage girl from the 'hood. Nancy purses her lips and gives Miss B. the side eye as if to say "You walked right into that one."

Miss B. is impressed with my quick comeback but is too prideful to admit it. "Boy, you better sit down somewhere. I ain't got time to be playing with you this morning, we need to get to our next stop." I take a seat at the table and Nancy gets up and retrieves a plate of food from the stove and places it before me: grits, eggs, liver mush, and homemade biscuits. I almost begin to cry at how good it looks. As I begin to eat, the two go to the front porch, leaving me to eat alone. I have eaten in this place many times before. It reminds me of my Aunt Bertha's kitchen, where everything is in its place, despite the whirlwind of activity it took to prepare the meal that I'm now consuming; flour tossed and smoothed out on the counter, eggs cracked, butter churned, grits poured, grease splashed. The canary yellow walls glisten with decades of stories spilling out of every corner. I'm then transported to my mother's kitchen, where she pressed hair; my grandmother's kitchen, where she made chow chow and fried bologna sandwiches with weeks-old grease from the Crisco can; my Aunt Mary Lee's kitchen, where she pierced ears with a needle, thread, and straw from a broom. So much love and care—and labor—happens in this space called the kitchen. Maybe that's why the back of the nape is also so named because it takes so much work to straighten out the naps. I wash down my last bit of biscuit with a swig of orange juice and place my plate in the sink, over which are three shelves of canning jars, neatly labeled "Apple Butter," "Crab Apple Jam," and "Blackberry Jam." I think about asking Nancy if I can have a jar of the apple butter but remember that I have no idea where I'm off to next and have no way of keeping it. I walk outside to the porch, where Miss B. and Nancy are sitting, both having a cigarette.

"I told you Nancy was going to send you off with a full belly. This woman know she can burn in the kitchen." She winks at Nancy.

"It was delicious. Thank you so much for all of your hospitality." Nancy nods and takes a long drag on her cigarette.

Miss B. stands up, stretching her hands up to the sky. "Well, kiddo. You ready to roll? I'm leaving the car here. I'll get it later. Nancy said she'll watch it for me. I don't feel like driving that far today, so we'll do it the old-fashioned way. Grab my hand."

This time the transportation seemed to take longer, though I still remember nothing of the trip. We are standing outside a building where lots of children are running in and out. There is a middle-aged woman standing in the doorway.

Miss B. has changed outfits again, and this time she's wearing something more modest—a white blouse and long black skirt and flat shoes. She lights up and looks over at the entrance to the building. "That's Miss Alpha, who you're going to interview. We're in a place called Dallas in north TX. Alpha was born here in 1957. Like many of us, she has a lot of siblings. She's a mother to a queer daughter, but she also had some issues with her own mother. She'll tell you about it. Go on over there and introduce yourself."

"Where are you going?" I ask, but not really interested in the answer.

"I'm going to tend to my business while you tend to yours, Sweetie. Now go on over there and talk to Alpha. I won't be far."

I respond with a deep sigh and turn toward the building and begin to approach the woman standing in the doorway. She's busy chastising the children who are darting in and out of the door. I realize that the building is a community center. When I make it to the door, she greets me with a serious smile, the kind of smile that is welcoming but cautious. Though she is short, her presence is commanding. Her oak-colored face is quite a setting for the mane of rope-sized salt-and-pepper locks sprouting from her head and trailing down her back. I know she has an interesting story to tell.

We walk down a long hallway to a big room that looks like a romper room. She pulls up two chairs and places them in the middle of the room, where we sit for the interview.

Alpha

You are a mother. Talk about your decision to become a mother and a little bit about your relationship with your daughter, being a black same-gender-loving woman.

Yes, I was in a relationship with a woman who—well, we both decided that we wanted another child. She had a child from a previous marriage. But we both wanted a daughter. And so we decided that I would go through Child Protective Services as a single parent and adopt a child. So I did. And so that's how I became a mother. My daughter came into my life when she was eight months old. I requested a toddler. I wanted a child between the ages of two and four, because I wanted to bypass all the diapers and a lot of that. Because I used to have issues about getting urine and fecal material on my hands. But when God blessed me with this eight-month-old child, I overcame all of that finicky stuff, okay? I started telling my daughter about me being a same-gender-loving person when she was able to talk. Because . . . my partner and I made up our minds that we were going to be very open and honest with our children, because I adopted her. As an out lesbian, I was open with the state. But my partner and I, at that time we decided that we didn't want to have any secrets in our family. And we wanted both of our children to grow up in a healthy, wholesome home. So, as I said, the minute my daughter was able to talk, I started telling her, "You have two mommies." And we had books, like *Heather Has Two Mommies*. And we used to read that book to our daughter. And we also wanted to be open with her about being adopted. So we had a book from *Sesame Street* that dealt with being adopted. But we've always been open and honest with our children about being same-gender-loving.

And then when my daughter was two, the relationship ended. My partner decided that she wanted a husband, so our relationship ended. So I raised my daughter alone. Well, with the help of the community, the school, and the community. And so, my daughter, when she was a teenager, that's when we really talked about what it means to be same-gender-loving and to have a mama who is same-gender-loving. Now, I'm a revolutionary, and I put that spirit in my daughter. So I told my daughter over the years that nobody defines us, we define ourselves. We define family, not the church, not the community, not the school, not even our immediate family. You will have people who will say, "Oh, your mommy is blah, blah, blah. She's a bulldagger. She's gay. She's a freak. She a lesbian." I always taught my daughter, "Don't let that get to you. When people come at you with the poison, you're not gonna be a part of that. And I want you to remember, I want you to hear my voice when the negative people come at you with this, because they're gonna come." And then I taught her what my mentor taught me about just because the wolves come for you doesn't mean they have to eat you. So my daughter really was never teased about having a same-gender-loving mama.

I locked my daughter's hair when she was two years old. And when she started school, the children teased her about her hair. But she never really was teased about having a same-gender-loving mama. Now, when my daughter was in high school, she attended a single-gender school here in the Dallas community. And she started writing papers on gay adoptions and what it means to grow up in a same-gender-loving or a gay home, a gay household. And even when she went to college, she wrote papers on gay adoptions and growing up in a gay household. Actually, she did a presentation in one of her classes in college on growing up in a same-gender-loving home and having a same-gender-loving mama. So, as I said, she's a little revolutionary, like me.

And she kind of went through this phase in college, because she attended a single-gender college in Oakland, California, Mills College. And, well, you know California is very liberated . . . and blah, blah, blah. So, she kind of had crushes on a few female students there. But I reminded her, I said, "Girl, let me tell you. This is nothing to play around with." Because she likes what she calls "studs." She said, "Ooh, they're so cute; they're like cute little boys." I said, "I want to remind you that they may be cute, dress nice, and all that, maybe look like a guy. But trust me, when she takes off her clothes, she's gonna have breasts and a pussy." I was just honest with her. And I said, "She's not gonna have a penis or a dick dangling between her legs. Now, she may have sex with you maybe with a dildo. But remember, she's still a woman. She's not a man. And I'm not teaching you to have this little fantasy in your mind about studs, thinking that, "Oh, is she gonna be just like a guy?" No. I said, "This is a very dangerous playground to play on, if you're not same-gender-loving or you calling yourself bicurious. No." I said, "You can't play on the playground like that, big girl. Somebody will hurt you possibly, because they may fall in love with you. And here you are, you just want to play house. But this person has become emotionally connected with you and maybe even loves you. And I'm telling you, it can be a very dangerous, winding road. So you need to really know what you're doing if you're going to play on that playground, because that's nothing to play with, big girl." So she got over her little stud fascination. So I'm a grandmother now. My daughter has an eight-month-old child. And I stay at home and I'm helping my daughter raise her, because my daughter is a Bill Gates scholarship recipient. And I don't want her to lose that scholarship just because she's a mother. So she's studying nursing. And so I know that's not an easy major, so I didn't want her to have any excuses for not being able to study and to graduate, just because she's a mom.

How old is she now?

She's twenty-one now. When there's certain things in the media about the LGBT community, she'll call me and say, "Mama, turn on channel blah, blah, blah. And blah, blah, blah is on. They're talking about gay rights or bisexuality or whatever." So that makes me feel good, because she is open-minded. And what I wanted for her, the open-mindedness, the love, the care, the compassion, and all of that, for humanity is in her. Because I told her that in our home, we have no place for discrimination, prejudice, and what have you. Because we've had other issues that we've had to deal with, like immigration. And I told her we don't have negative attitudes or behavior towards people who don't have their legal status. So, I'm proud of my daughter, because the things that I put into her in terms of that foundation, they're there. And they're surfacing through her behavior and even things that she says, conversations that we have. So, I'm proud of myself as a parent. I feel that I've done a great job with my daughter. And she can speak out on what it means to have a same-gender-loving mama, knowing that she was raised in a healthy, wholesome, loving environment. Her mama made her a Gates Scholar, and she graduated sixth in her class of twenty-one students, with a GPA of 3.6 on a 4.0 scale. So I'm proud of myself, you know. And when she was a student at Mills College, she was involved in the LGBT community there at the college. So kudos to her, I feel really good, about the job I did with her.

My [own] mother was mentally ill and she was also a religious fanatic. And we experienced a lot of emotional, psychological, spiritual, and physical abuse. So I did not have a happy childhood.

Were you an only child?

No, I come from a family of fifteen children. I'm number eleven. I'm Alpha and I have a sister named Omega. My mother was very religious. She named all of her children from the Bible.

Really?

Yes. But, you know, my childhood was very traumatic for me.

So, did you know your father?

Yes, I come from a two-parent household. Actually, I was raised by my sister and her husband. But I did frequently visit my birth family.

So, you said you're number eleven of fifteen children?

Yes, mmm-hmm.

And what are the age ranges?

Well, my oldest brother, he's deceased, but he would probably be close to eighty. And my youngest brother is like in his early forties.

And you said that your sister and her husband raised you?

Yes, I have a sister who's seventy-seven. And she and her husband—they raised me.

How did that come about?

That came about as a result of me not wanting to live in the same household with my parents because things were so dysfunctional. During that time, I was seven years old. And because of the dysfunctionalism that existed at home, at age seven, I made just a serious decision that I didn't want to live in that type of environment. And it was at a time when they were integrating schools. So I used the excuse of not wanting to attend an integrated school, as opposed to telling my parents, "Y'all fight too much, and that's really why I don't want to live with you." So, with my sister and her husband, now I did not know this, but they fought, too. So I just really jumped out of one bad situation and entered another one. But my sister and her husband economically were in a better shape than my parents because they only had one child. And so I had my own room that I shared with a nephew. But we had plenty of food. I mean, you know, coming from a family where there are fifteen children, if we were not home at a certain time, we didn't eat. So living with my sister and her husband, I didn't have to experience those hardships.

What did your father do for work?

He was a construction worker. And my mother, she was a domestic worker, when she worked. But most of the time, she was a stay-at-home mom.

And did you consider your sister your mother, in a way, because you moved in with her so early?

I never really considered her my mom. But my sister forced me to call her mom.

She did?

She did. Because I was telling people that she was my sister. And for whatever reason, she did not like that, so she threatened me, and told me that I better tell people that she's my mom and not my sister. So, I was terrified, and I was like, "Oh, okay."

Well, how did your mother feel about that?

Well, she wasn't really crazy about it. My mom and my sister, they really didn't get along well. Because this sister came from a previous marriage from my father. So there was a lot of friction between my mom and my sister. We never said we were half-sisters or anything like that. Our parents just taught us that we were all sisters and brothers. But this particular sister and my mom, they had a lot of problems with each other. So my mother wasn't happy about it, but she was a very passive woman. And she just let it be.

Growing up, what role did church or religion play in your life?

Oh, church and religion played a major role in my life. As a matter of fact, my mother was Pentecostal, and we went to church every Sunday. We also went to tarrying.

What's that?

It's like in the Pentecostal church, when you spend the entire night praying. You stay up all night just praying. And so, we did that. I hated church because our mother, she used religion to really shame and embarrass us. [. . .] She would always tell us that the devil was in us. I know now that my mother was mentally ill. But growing up as a child, I didn't know that she was sick. But she used to always tell us that the devil was in us, and the devil made us do this, the devil made us do that. Mom referred so much to the devil that I always said, "If I ever meet that motherfucker in person, I'm going to kick his ass." [*Laughter.*] That's how much I hated the devil, you know.

Did you even have a concept of who the devil was?

Not really, you know. She just always talked about the devil, and I just grew up hating him. And I always said if I ever meet him in person, I'm going to do him a good ass whipping. And so, my mother was a fanatic. And as I said, I know now that she was mentally ill. And religion—it divided my parents. They used to have these religious debates a lot of times. And my mother was very committed and dedicated to the church. I mean, she put more in church than she did at home. So, yes, religion played a very big role in my life. And when I came out to my family, my mother exorcised me. And that was extremely traumatic.

How old were you?

Seventeen.

Wow. And what did she do exactly?

Well, first she told me that God made woman for man and not for another woman. And that homosexuality was of the devil and evil. And then she laid hands on me. She took her hand and put it on my head and began to speak in tongues and do this little ritual to remove the devil from me. And I grew up in a household where we were taught that everything your parents tell you is right. You never question them because they love you and they know what's best for you. So we went through the ritual.

Who was there?

Just the two of us. We were outside in our garden. We had been picking fruit because we had fruit trees. I had just recently come out to my family. And so she just told me, she says, "You know, you're really not a homosexual. That's a demon in you that's making you think that. And I'm going to drive that demon out of you." And so that's when the ritual started of her placing her hand on my head and praying and speaking in tongues. And she was saying, "Come out, in the name of Jesus! Hallelujah! [Speaking in tongues]." And I'm thinking, "Oh, my God." I had this demon in me, because this is my mother, who had me and who loves me, telling me this. "Oh, God, please." I was praying silently that the devil would come out of me. And so we finished with the ritual. I went inside of our house and I laid down. And I was doing this self-talk. I said, "Oh, my God. I'm possessed by the devil because I'm a homosexual. Well, let me go to sleep, and when I wake up, the devil is going to be out of me." And remember, I was seventeen years old, just a kid, with nobody really to talk to and to explain to me that I was really okay. So, I laid down and went to sleep. And when I woke up, I expected to be heterosexual. But it didn't happen, you know, it didn't work. So, I was like, "Well, you're still gay. Well, you just better accept it." But I internalized a lot of shame and fear. And that was a battle for me, you know. I just began this struggle to feel good about myself and to love myself. But I made it through, you know. I stopped going to church on and off. And I just became so very defensive about being gay that anytime I would hear people say negative things about being gay, I was ready to whoop ass. And it got so bad that after I graduated from college, I had difficulty functioning in the professional world because when I would hear people say negative things about gays and lesbians, I would immediately just click back in my mind to being exorcised by my mom—and also experiencing the negativity from some of my siblings because they shamed me, too. They told me they were embarrassed of me and that we didn't have homosexuals in our family. And that I was basically a disgrace.

Both of my parents are deceased now—but I really do believe that my mother was a lesbian, too.

Really?

I do believe that. Because there was this certain look that my mom gave me. And it was like, it was a look like, "I wish I could do the things that you're doing. I wish that I could be as brave as you are." And, I mean, I just felt that connection with her. So, I believe that lesbianism is in my genes. And I don't mean my 501's. [*Laughter.*] I believe that I inherited it from my mom. And I'm okay with myself now. It has taken me many years to learn how to feel good about myself and to be okay with who I am. And it's a great feeling. It's a really great feeling.

So, how did your relationship with your mother evolve after the exorcism? Between then and, say twenty-one or twenty-two? What happened in those years? Because obviously, the exorcism didn't work.

Right. Well, I come from a family where we just pretended like everything was okay. So she never mentioned anything to me about being a lesbian after that again. All she always talked about was the devil and going to hell. But there was a time over the years when I wrote my mom a letter, too. Actually, I wrote a letter to my entire family. And I did mention being lesbian in those letters. And [Mom] wrote me letters back. But every sentence was a biblical quote. That's when I really realized the sickness of my mom. Because she never really addressed any of the issues that I addressed in the letters. Everything was just scriptural quotes. And I'm like, "Oh, my God, my mom is out of touch. She's really ill." And so, we just went on from there. I just never really talked about it anymore.

And in her later years, when she was a lot older, did you and she ever sort of reconcile or come to some kind of understanding or be at peace with each other?

That never happened until my mother was dying. When she was dying, it was important to me to go to her, to make peace with her. Because I do not like shame, guilt, and fear, but especially guilt. And I did not want to live with any guilt regarding my mom. So I took it upon myself to go to her on her deathbed and make peace with her. I told her that I love her and that I was sorry for the things that had transpired between us. And the fact that we had our differences and we never were able to get past those differences. And that I did not want her to pass away without us talking as mother-daughter. Nor did I want her to face Jesus and God with us not being able to make resolution between us. So I asked her for forgiveness, for whatever I had done to maybe hate or to hurt her, or what have you. I just said, "Mama, please forgive me for whatever hurt or pain I've caused you. And I also want to let you know, Mom, that I forgive you for the hurt and the pain that I have experienced with you. And I just want us to have a clean slate. And I want you to have peace with me. And I want you to have serenity." And she really was unable to speak. But then she, some kind of way, I believe through the power of God, was able to say the word, "serenity." And so that's how things transpired with us. And so today, I do have a peace of mind in reference to my mom because I was the only sibling that went to her to make amends. And so it was a very good feeling. But before doing that, I spent probably like an hour, an hour and a half, communicating with God, and just wailing to God, asking him to give me what I needed, to be able to go to my mom's bedside and say the things that I needed to say to her. And I feel that God did empower me with what I needed to do that because I was able to do it, and it gave me such a peace of mind.

Alpha's story has me overcome with sadness. I can't imagine being estranged from my own mother for most of my life, reconciling with her only on her deathbed. I think of the final scene in the 1959 remake of *Imitation of Life* starring Lana Turner, in which the character Sarah Jane, who shuns her dark-skinned mother for years because she doesn't want people to know that she's black, melodramatically clings to her mother's casket asking for forgiveness while Mahalia Jackson sings "Trouble of the World." Alpha's relationship with her mother is not as melancholy, but no less melodramatic; and yet, for her, finding "peace of mind" with her own mother is probably what makes her such a great mother to her own daughter. I still can't shake the sadness.

I think about the journey I had with my own mother around my being gay. She, too, is a religious woman, but she never tried to exorcise the gayness out of me or even pray it away. She chose instead to act as if I never told her and for years ignored the fact that I was in a relationship with another man—and specifically a white man. But unlike Alpha's mother, my mother eventually came around. Not only did she attend our commitment ceremony, but she eventually began to call my husband her "other" son. I think my sadness about Alpha, then, is because although she and her mother found peace, it was too late. Unlike me, she'll never get to share her experiences with her partner with her mother. I should count my blessings.

As I'm walking outside the building, I see Miss B. from afar, lying on the ground on her back. I walk over to her and she looks so peaceful lying there, her back slightly arched, buttocks balanced gracefully over the earth, and her hands clasped over her abdomen, sinking and rising with each unlabored breath. Her body is drenched in sunshine.

"What you looking at?" she asks, disturbing the peaceful scene.

"Nothing." I pause. "Nothing at all." She knows I have gotten her.

"Okay. I opened the door for you for that one. But the score is still like ninety-nine to one! Help me up." I help her to her feet. "Where is my purse? I have gone a whole two hours without a cigarette!" I spot her yellow basket on the ground, retrieve it, and hand it to her. I have no idea where she's getting cigarettes from because we haven't stopped to buy any and there were only two in her purse the last time I pilfered through it.

"I think I'm going to take you back east again to TN. There is someone that you MUST talk to. Her name is Emilie. We call her the 'high priestess' because she runs a divinity school, the first from our hive to get such a position. Her mother was a very cool woman, who I knew very well. Emilie was born in Durham, NC in 1955." She finishes her smoke and walks about ten feet to a trash can to throw the butt away. "I try never to litter."

"But you did throw your butt out the car window when we were in Winston-Salem."

"Baby, if I threw *my* butt out the car window, you would have read about it in the *Georgia Voice* or the *Washington Blade*. And, in any case, I said I *try* not to litter if I can help it. Don't judge me." She enjoys the ribbing. "Okay. You know the drill, take my hand."

We are standing inside a building with a very long hallway. It looks very serious and is eerily quiet. We walk to the end of the very long hallway and then turn down another long hallway until we arrive at a beautiful wooden door, beside which there is a sign on the wall that reads, "Vanderbilt Divinity School. Dean's Office." Miss B. opens the door and walks up to the receptionist.

"Hello. I believe the dean is expecting Dr. EPJ and me, Miss B. We have an appointment."

"Yes, yes," the woman says. "The dean will be with you in just a moment. She's finishing up a call. Can I get you some refreshments while you wait? We have some dandelion tea."

Miss B. cuts her eyes over at me. "Why, yes, thank you. Some dandelion tea would be extraordinary. That is *so* nice of you. It's one of my favorite teas."

I can tell by the look on the woman's face that she thinks Miss B. is a little off. If only she knew! She shows us to some chairs on the other side of her desk and goes off to get the tea. Miss B. sits with her legs crossed at the knee, bouncing the right leg up and down over the left leg like an impatient child. She hasn't had a cigarette. The receptionist comes back with the tea and places it on the table between our chairs.

"The dean will be with you shortly," she says, and goes back to her desk.

Miss B. takes a sip of her tea and frowns. "Needs some honey." She stands up.

"You go ahead and do the interview by yourself. Tell Emilie I'll catch up with her later."

"Where are you going? You're already here. Isn't that rude?" I say, trying to whisper.

She doesn't respond and heads toward the door. "I'll be back in a couple of hours." She vanishes.

I sit patiently, shaking my head, wondering why Miss B. always conveniently "disappears" when I'm about to conduct an interview. I'm beginning to wonder if she really knows these women or if she's just some trickster. Before I get too far lost in my paranoid thoughts about Miss B., Emilie opens her door.

This must be salt-and-pepper locks day, but unlike Alpha, Emilie's locks are smaller and intertwined into a bun on the back of her head. She is a formidable presence, the kind one would expect of a dean of a divinity school: someone who tempers justice with mercy. She invites me into her office, which is also formidable, with lots of wooden panels and bookshelves. I can tell that white men once occupied this office now sanctified by a womanist holy ghost. I'm loving this black desecration of space. We sink into her comfortable leather chairs as I prepare my recorder.

Emilie
....

My mother was a molecular biologist. My father taught exercise. Mom was the first black woman to get a PhD in cell physiology at the University of Michigan. So it's not something she talked about a lot. The most she would say to me was it was lonely. And she said, "And I don't care to relive that by retelling it." I knew enough to leave that one alone.

Were both of them from the South?

No. Mom was from Southern Pines, North Carolina. Dad was from Mechanicsville, Pennsylvania.

How did they meet?

At North Carolina Central University.

Oh, so they went to school there.

No. They were both teaching at that point and [had] friends who knew them individually. The wife knew my mother; the husband knew my father. [And their friends] decided it might work if they got them together. And it sort of did.

What were the thoughts or beliefs about people that were different from you in your household, whether that be religion, race . . . ?

What I was taught was that we're all equal. I could see differences in behavior from both my parents. Mom was a little more consistent than Dad because Dad was a homophobe. Mom was not. And I often wondered what both of them saw in the world. Because Mom was a light-skinned black woman, so much so that when I was a little kid, I thought she was white. I didn't get a spanking. The worst whipping I got in my life was when I said, "Oh, mama's white," not knowing what I was saying. My dad lit into me like white on rice—so much so that mom stood by to make sure he didn't kill me. And I wasn't a child that got a lot of whippings. I didn't know what I was saying. After he finished and stormed off, that's when mom sat me down and said, "Here's what you need to know." It was my first lesson in colorism. Because dad was a dark-skinned black man. I had no idea what I had stumbled into because I was just commenting on what I saw—not having any idea of what I had opened up.

And so, you have a very light-skinned mother. When she was younger, could she have passed?

Almost, not quite. But she could have come close. There's no way Dad could pass for anything other than boot-black. And the two different worlds they inhabited because of that—not only because of gender but also because of color—has often left me wondering. Because Dad was a staunch Methodist layman. He knew what he should believe, and that's mostly what he taught me. And Mom had had more church from her mother growing up; she said she was working on her backlog. [*Laughter.*] She had gotten enough growing up that she didn't need to go to church. She tithed every month, but she preferred to stay home and listen to the Duke Chapel Services on the radio.

My parents were sneaky. They would leave stuff in our family library for me to find, so there was the *Playboy* joke book down there as well as Raddyffe Hall's *The Well of Loneliness*. And other books. But I realized as I got older they left that down there for me to find and read. And, of course, I never told them I was reading any of it, especially that *Playboy*. I didn't know what I was getting into with *The Well of Loneliness*, but I figured it out. Because my mother was very technical. She was a scientist, so when I asked her where babies come from she gave me the technical explanation. "There's a penis and a vagina and the male inserts the penis into the vagina. If the woman has eggs, the male's penis has semen and, boom, baby happens." So I had no idea why everybody was so hopped up about sex because it's like, "That's pretty perfunctory." Until I started reading some of those books down there and I'm like, "Oh, the difference is this feels good." But that's how they taught, expanding on sex ed. Because nobody said it directly: "This stuff feels good, which is why people do it." But I know. I'm [like], "Okay, now I know what the thing is about sex. It's pleasurable." So, I never got the message it was dirty or nasty, interestingly enough. I got the message it was pleasurable, but you keep it to yourself. As I'm reading these books downstairs, where hardly anybody would have, except me in the library in the basement, reading.

The last night I was home [after graduating from college] it just so happened that Mom and Trisha [her sister] and I were all sitting in the kitchen, and Dad was watching TV in the living room. In retrospect I realize what I did. I pulled Trisha to sit in my lap so there was somebody. I was Dad's favorite, Trisha was mom's favorite, so I had her favorite in front of me. [*Laughter.*] And

I said, "Mom, I got something to tell you." And she said, "Yes?" I said, "Mom, I'm gay." Mom said, "Uh huh." I said, "Mom, did you hear me? I just told you I'm gay." She said, "I heard you. I've known for a long time." I'm like, "Really?" She said, "Mmm hmm. You brought all these women. Yes, I knew this." I'm like, "Really, Mom?" She said, "I am so sorry but we are not gonna have drama here tonight. I've known. Do not tell your father." I said, "Mom, I kind of had thought that wouldn't be a good idea." She said, "He would not be able to handle it. You've heard what he's had to say about gay men in this house and you two have already had words about it. Just don't do it." I said, "Okay, I can live with that." And I looked at Mom and said, "I think he knows." She said, "He probably does, but until you tell him, he doesn't. And he's happy with that." Never told him. Next month I'm doing laundry, getting ready to get on the road. Mom was in the family room in the basement reading. Her favorite thing was reading. She's the most avid reader I have ever seen in my life. And I was going back and forth, down the stairs and from the couch at one point and I heard, "м&м?" I knew something was important because she only used that name, it was a term of endearment, it wasn't said often, and when it was she wanted my attention. So, I stopped, and I was like, "Yes, ma'am." She said, "I am afraid for you." And I said, "Oh?" She said, "The lifestyle you've chosen to lead will be dangerous, and you will have a difficult time in life. And I'm afraid for you because people get killed." And I said, "I know, Mom, but you and Dad taught me to live my life with integrity, which is why I told you." And she said, "I know. I know why you told me. And I know what you're going through, because if I had had courage, I would have made the same choice as you." Which I knew! I knew because my girlfriend and I had talked about "How queer is your mama, Emilie?" "Thank you, Mama. I will be careful. I will take care of myself. I want to be old when I die." And she said, "Thank you. But I just had to tell you my fears." I said, "I understand." [*Whispers.*] I was cool. I just went up the steps, got in the room, and closed the door and, "Girl! You would not *believe* what Mama just told me!"

I laughed far more than I thought I was going to during my interview with Emilie. For some reason, I thought she was going to be serious the whole time because of her position, but that was not the case. It may sound blasphemous to say such about a person of the cloth, but I found her a little devilish—which was so refreshing. It was so much fun to watch her turn into that young woman filled with unbridled glee at the confirmation that her mother is also queer—that she can't wait to run upstairs and call her girlfriend. After Alpha's story, I needed this.

I exit the office still chuckling. Miss B. is sitting in the reception area sipping some tea and flipping through a copy of *Essence*.

"I can't believe you didn't stay for this interview. Emilie asked me what happened to you."

Miss B. puts the magazine down and looks over her shoulder at the receptionist and then leans into me, whispering, "That tea tasted like fly pee. It wasn't organic. I went down to the Whole Foods and bought the real stuff. I snuck back there and threw that old stuff out and replaced it with the good stuff." She leans back in her chair and takes a sip of the tea. I can do nothing but shake my head in disbelief. Miss B. continues, "While you were in there talking to Emilie, it made me realize that you need to talk to some of my sisters about spirituality. We are *very* spiritual—more than what some of those heathens who call themselves spiritual think we ought to lay claim to. I've called a meeting at the river with some women. You must go there by yourself and meditate in order to hear their stories."

Two

BLESSED BEE

I am back at the river of Osun. There is a stillness here. Anticipatory. Unsettling, then calm. Miss B. says that I must take the river an offering of honey, yam, and oranges. She has wrapped all of these in a cotton cloth coated with beeswax. She tells me to remove my shoes and wade into the water up to my waist and then feed the river the offering. I remove my sandals and feel my toes slide into the silt. I slowly move into the water, carrying the satchel of offering. The current covers first my feet, then ankles and shins, the warmth of the water radiating rhythmically up my spine. Once it reaches my waist, I slowly open the cloth and release the honey, yam, and oranges. As they are caught in the downward stream, I feel the pressure of the river on my back. I tie the cloth around my neck and, as Miss B. has instructed, I close my eyes and focus on the rhythm of the river. I am standing still, yet I am moving with her.

First, seduction. Slow, steady djembe drumming a Yankadi. Arms flailing toward the sky. Feet pound the river basin in time.

dip. drop. kick. gasp. dip. drop. kick. gasp.

stop

shift

clave

salsa/songo/son salsa/songo/son salsa/songo/son salsa/songo/son

stop

shift

deep house

bounce bounce bounce bounce

bounce bounce bounce bounce

bounce bounce bounce bounce

bounce bounce bounce bounce

stop

shift

holyghostpentecostalwon'tturnmeloose

The rhythms continue to shift until I feel an exhaustion. Miss B. said this would happen, at which point, I must offer a song. The song must come from the heart and must be from my spiritual tradition. I spread my arms out by my sides and throw my head back:

Why should I feel discouraged and why should the shadows come?
Why should my heart be lonely and long for Heaven and home?
When Jesus is my portion, a constant friend is He
His eye is on the sparrow and I know He watches me.

My feet sink deeper into the basin of the river and begin to burn. The wind has picked up and whistles around my ears. The chorus bubbles up.

I sing (I sing) because (because) I'm happy;
There are voices echoing mine!
I sing (I siiiiinnnnng) because (beCAUSE) I'm free (I. AM. FREEE!)
His eye is on the spaaaaaarroooooooow, yes it is, and . . . I . . . know
       (and I know)
Three voices are singing with me.

And . . . I . . . know (and I know that I know that I know that I know)
And I know (Oh, I know, I know, I know)
Six voices all together in varying harmonies
He watches me!

I open my eyes and I am surrounded by five women, two on one side of the river and three on the other side. They are dressed in all white from head to toe. Their beauty is unspeakable, their voices unknowable. They begin a soft chant and the river becomes still. They wade into the water and take each other's hands to form a circle around me. One by one they share their testimony.

Spirit

I go to the Mississippi River at least three or four times a week. I love her. I sit by her to just be at peace, to just feel like that water and hear it and like what is being said, like what are the messages. So within that work I definitely have been calling on a higher power, my creator, my ancestors. I've been asking for divine guidance, surrendering to divine . . . real and divine time. So, less church these days and more working with spirit and being obedient to spirit and listening. And when I get a feeling about someone or when I . . . it's like just acting. "Don't do that. You don't need to go there." "Okay, I won't go there." "I'll do this instead." "Okay." And just being very obedient and wise and seeing what happens. It opens up a whole lot, makes life a lot easier. So, I haven't really been doing much that is religious in terms of traditional but there are a lot of cultures represented in this city [New Orleans], so in terms of Ifá and Candomblé, I've been getting readings from time to time with priests of Candomblé . . . and just having my ears wide open for the message in however it will get to me and whomever brings it. And going back to roots, that very rooted, very practical application, earth wisdom, wind wisdom. And New Orleans . . . is prime, fertile ground for that kind of work and it really encourages it. The spirits talk. They carry on here. [*Laughter.*] They just been carrying on, which is very healing and wonderful. And also, can be very heavy and present sometimes as well.

The circle shifts counterclockwise. The air turns sweet. Seagulls dip and graze the river for fish.

Shannon S.

I went to church every Sunday, when she [her mother] was with me, when I didn't skip with my godbrother. I'm Catholic. I learned a lot being Catholic, catechism and stuff like that. No religion likes homosexuals. I don't care what religion it is. At nineteen I decided to be converted to Baptist just to try it, because I wanted to please my grandmother, because she was still in denial about me being gay. And I went there one Sunday, and he gave this fire-in-hell brimstone speech sermon about being gay, and I was like I can't believe a God that's so full of love would have this much hate towards things that he created. I couldn't believe it, and it broke my heart, because it's like, "Is this what my grandmother thinks of me?" I didn't want to be that. Stopped going to church. Well, religion, it played a big role because of the values that I have. I'm not Jesus. I ain't going to turn the other cheek, but I can love you from a distance, but it's not all bad.

Did you enjoy going to church?

I did. I did. I did. Not the Baptist Church, because I don't like all that screaming and hollering. The Catholic Church, they get right to the lesson and you're out in forty-five minutes, which was perfect for me. The saints, I admire stuff like that. I enjoy stuff like that. I still light white candles to this day and pray and worship and give homage to the saints. I still do that. Every once in a while, I still cross myself when I pass by a Catholic church I respect, because it wasn't all bad. I can only recall one time that I actually heard them mention homosexuality. One time. So, I mean, they alright. The Catholics all right by me.

I'm scared that when I walk in the church it's going to catch on fire. [*Laughter.*] I still pass by. I just don't think I belong. I went to a gay church one time here, and I just don't feel like I belong really. Strange as that may sound. I listen to a lot of Joyce Meyer. I listen to a lot of Creflo Dollar. I read a lot. I read the Koran. I'm studying feng shui right now. I still read my Bible. I still read the Catholic Bible. I study different religions, Buddhism. I studied Judaism. I even studied Scientology. They all say the same thing about homosexuality. So it's like I never belong. So I try to keep God in my heart and be a good person. That's what I try to do. I don't do it all the time because I am human. I still pray to my saints. I still like my white lights. I just don't feel like I belong in the church, because I went to a church and I joined a church, and it always happens. I enjoy the church. I had went there and visited a couple of times. I went with my sister. Baptist Church, Greater Beulah Baptist as a matter of fact. Ironically enough, the man went to college with my mother and my aunts, and he invited them to church. And after they told him who I was and one Sunday, the deacon, who's a closeted queen, gave "the homosexuality going to hell" [sermon]. I just can't go somewhere where when you see me that's what you think. I got the incentive because a friend of mine killed herself when she came out, and you don't know my story. Everybody got one. Everybody's story not in Barnes and Noble, and I just don't feel like I belong, honestly. Do I want to go to church? Yes. I do. I get invited to church a lot. A friend of mine from school invited me to her church, and my fear is always when I walk in and then scan the crowd what the sermon's going to be, and I just—it hurts, because I was raised in the church, and I think sometimes that's why I have it harder than I should, because I feel like that's God tugging at my heart telling me, "You're still mine. I'm still yours, but you won't give me a place to go." That's how I feel. You know it's not fair, because we love God, too. We really do, because in the end that's all we have. It's not that I don't want to. I just can't find where I belong.

Shannon steps back in the circle of women and they all begin to sink down into the river. I am unsure of what is happening. When the water has submerged all but their heads, they slowly rise up again and gather on either side of me, their wet bodies sticking to each other and to me. One woman to my far right breaks from the huddle and slowly wades in the water to the river bank, ascends to shore, and climbs on top of a rock.

Darlene

As long as I have been a Hudson, I have been in church. That's all my life. I can remember Easter speeches, Christmas plays. I can remember baptism.

I come up Baptist. We did Sunday school, we did church, and we did BTU [Baptist Training Union]. That's right. We got three doses of it. *Three* in one day. You got plenty of Jesus that day, and that became my pattern and I lived for that. That was my life. I loved church. I still love church. I never was begrudging or didn't want to go. I *loved* church.

I loved the singing; I loved the hymns. I love hymns now, but back then I just loved singing and it kind of was a training ground. And I didn't know it at the time because [as] you do your speeches you're learning to speak publicly. You going to learn your speech and you're going to get up there and [*in a child's voice*] "Happy Easter Day," but my sister was the biggest crybaby about that stuff. Anthony, my cousin, was the biggest crybaby in the family about saying the Easter speech, and believe it or not, as a child I was really kind of awkward and very shy. But I love church. I did.

Were you in the choir?

I most certainly was in the children's choir. As a matter of fact, when we lived in Pine Bluff, that's when the whole church world really took off. We was singing in the choir and then I had friends at other schools that was singing in choir. They would come over to *my* church when we were having rehearsal. I said, "Let's all sing together then," and honey, I formed me the citywide mass choir. I was in the seventh or eighth grade. Sure did. And the other little junior piano players came. Everybody came. After a while, that thing got pretty hot because we was steady growing up and sure did form me the citywide youth mass choir, sure did. I had people from Dolloway, Watson Chapel, had a little bit of everybody coming together. Next thing I know honey [*snaps finger*], we was jamming and I went on to college and became the university choir director for the gospel choir, what they called the Ebony Singers. We were ambassadors. We traveled everywhere. And then I became a part of the Church of God in Christ. I put my membership with the New Calvary Temple Church of God in Christ in Little Rock because I went to school in Conway, Arkansas, for college.

Was that Central?

University of Central Arkansas, UCA, sure did. And I graduated from there in '84, '85. Then I went and I became, I was a choir director. I mean, my bishop took me straight up to the choir and said, "Listen, she's a choir director, put her to work." Those musicians looked at me like, really? But they had to do what he said. And so, next thing I know, I was directing the choir for the bishop at this church. I didn't even understand all the pieces of it, but then I became a jurisdictional kind of choir director. I had my own region and everything and did quite well. Offered a recording contract. Directed under Mattie Moss Clark, Twinkie Clark. I remember quite well those days, this whole po' Pentecostal movement that I was in. I was even part of a singing group called The Jesus Revolution. We used to hit it. We used to travel. We'd just go to church to church to church to church. Jerry Whitley. And we sang in his group: The Jesus Revolution. And then I became a part of the Thompson Singers, and I just got kind of reunited with Gerald Thompson, who is in Little Rock, and I can remember when Gerald Thompson, Kirk Franklin guy, and a boy out of Memphis and his name escapes me. I can just see him, but I remember when we all used to go in Memphis before Kirk was who he is today. I remember singing in Yolanda Adams's church. We all loved her because she had a really cute song. Southeast inspirational singer. Honey, I took my choir down there to her church. We all sat together in fellowship hall, ate chicken, had a good time. It was like a one-time encounter. But my church days, I loved them, and I must admit that I'm somewhat disappointed that here I am fifty, and I find myself out of balance with the church. And I tried to be a part of different affirming churches, but I guess I don't like what I see and I don't like how I'm treated. Because I feel like I've put in some good church days. I've done some good churching, I mean some *good* churching, and I'm not coming in as a beginner and I don't want to be treated as such. Even if I sit in the pews, there's criticism. If I try to take some initiative and get involved, there's criticism. So, I'm like you know what? I didn't come to church to fight with nobody. I got enough fighting out in the community that I have to do. I'm not coming to church to fight. So, on Sunday, I'm curled up in front of that TV watching a western. I'm trying to rest because Pride keeps me busy. I'm just saying, considering all of this time as a young child, my adolescent years, my young adult years, my adult years, all of that is filled with church. And it don't matter to me, honey. Even when I was in college I participated in a Bible study; I led a Bible study. Something called "soul food." Can you believe it? And it ain't a scripture that you can put out there that I don't know because I understand that thing. I think I understand it really good. I really do. I think I'm pretty good.

So, those passages of the Bible from Leviticus and so on and so forth that refer to homosexuality, how do you interpret those passages?

Well, let me tell you. It's a combination of things before I answer that question. When I got saved I was in college and had this big spiritual revelation. As a matter of fact, my line name when I pledged Zeta Phi Beta was "Revelator" because I could see things; I was able to look forward in time and predict, so I believed. And my friends, it was just a big running joke all the time but every time the Revelator said something, it almost came to pass. Anyway, one of the mothers—two of them—that stood out in my mind that really left such an impression in my heart, Mother Byrd, told me before she passed, she said, "Don't you let nobody tell you that you ain't a child of God." I mean just out of nowhere. This was the sweetest little almost looked like Aunt Bea woman. Just as stout and just as fiery, and she would pull me up close, and she would talk to me and I was like, "This is a sweet little lady." And I reverenced her. She was so sweet. And the other one was Mother Bunting. She said, "I don't care what nobody else in this church say, Darlene, you are anointed and you are special in the sight of God." And that never left my heart. So when I became this out lesbian, and I want you to understand, there was never really a closet that I was in, it was more of an awareness that had to come about, and I thank God for how things progressed in my life and how things evolved—maybe that's a better word—how things kind of evolved in my life, because I got my teachings in the church, first. So, when this stuff came about the Leviticus and man not laying with man, I had to take it in the way that it was taught to me in the context that it was taught to me. This is the Old Testament. These were the rules that they had in place. Christ came not to do away with but to make it where you could fulfill the promises or you could fulfill the covenant. I mean, I don't say that it's not true. I kind of understand it in the context of that day and time, who they were talking to. And I understand that everybody who was writing in the Bible wasn't so "saved" and so "Jesus" and so "sanctified" themselves. They had their own "isms." Such as Paul. Paul took issue with women. He came into an area where women were speaking all out loud and he wasn't used to that. Remember, he was a *tax* collector, a man of power, so he took issue with that. So, he [*snaps*] silenced the women. "Put something over your head and hush." You know what I'm saying? I put things in context. I kind of understood what was happening in that day and time because that's how I was taught. This is what was going on in that day and time. It said about eating swine. It talks about blends being mixed. There were reasons why those people wrote those things. It was to govern that body of people. I don't think in that day and time had any idea that that would be used, and rolled forward in history to become the dos and don'ts of the world for those that subscribe to it. I live with a Buddhist. She don't subscribe to all of that, but I never met a more balanced, believing, affirming person, and, baby, she'll nam(u) myoho renge kyo. Right now, that's where they're gone. Somebody else is getting their gajanza today. She's going to do what they do, and I don't try to get all up in it, but I appreciate it. So, you got this big Pentecostal woman here and then you got this Buddhist woman here and you put them powers together and God has blessed us. The universe has yielded itself very favorably for us. When I used to sing that song "I Let Nothing Separate Me from the Love of God," I meant that. And I told God that when it was time to do the crossover. I said, "Let me tell you something now, if this is going to put me in hell, then I'm not going to do it." I never will forget, that was like a New Year's Eve night. That was a turning point for me. This girl had been working me. It was kind of cute. I was kind of liking it, but I told God, "Before I get too busy, I need to hear from you real clear." All I can tell you, honey, is the way the Lord spoke to me, people won't even believe. So, after I had been intimate with this woman and we were laying there, all of the sudden the radio popped, it was my alarm. And guess what was playing? [*Begins singing*] "Oh It Is Jesus," Shirley Caesar. I said, "Thank you!," and I ain't never looked back. Now do you believe that? That's the Gospel. That's the Gospel according to Darlene. I'm telling you that's how I came through because I always had a close walk. I love God. I know God loves me, and I knew that and I know that today. So I went and took some time out once I became this lesbian person. I took the time out to kind of read the scriptures and study them. And I was so fortunate that I ran into a young brother who was living in California. His name was Elias Farajaje-Jones. I love Elias. And me and Elias sat down one day and just worked it out, and he was like, "You got to understand you're on the right track. You got to understand." I said, "I don't know how to research this," and he just began to break it down to me and he became like my big brother in this movement. He helped reconcile some things just in terms of where I could talk back out to people, because in my heart I remember what Mother Byrd told me, I remember what Mother Bunting told me, and I remember how I came through. I didn't really care. I didn't care if I didn't understand it. I understood it.

So, I'm like I might not be able to tell you about it, but it's in here [*touches her heart*], and if I felt like I was doing anything against God, I would not participate in it. I don't care if I loved it. And I'm just like that. If I know, if I sense in my spirit that it's not right, I don't care what everybody else doing, I'm not participating. I'm not getting down like that. That's my little two cents on it.

Darlene begins to sing as she climbs down the rock and back into the water. The other women join in.

> *Oh, Mary don't you weep*
> *Tell Martha not to moan*

Pharaoh's army drowned in the Red Sea
Oh, Mary don't you weep
Tell Martha not to moan

At the end of the song the women re-form the circle around me, their faces taking on a bluish hue from the intensity of the moonlight. Day has turned to night in a twinkling of an eye.

Lynn

My grandmother was the mother of the church. It was the church she grew up in. My mom grew up in the church; it was our family church. Even though it was in Clinton, Mississippi, we drove fifteen, twenty, thirty minutes to church every Sunday. And when you would hear people say we were in church all day, we were in church all day. We would leave our church and go to the church where my uncle was preaching, and we would leave his church and go to night service. So religion played a major role. And my mom was coming into herself by herself spiritually, and she would try to make us read the Bible, sit in the corner and read the Bible all day . . . if we got in trouble that was our punishment. We would stand in the room with the Bible and we had to read the Bible and tell her what we'd read. I was like jumping out the window. And I always had sleepovers and all my friends, they had to suffer the consequences. But we were jumping out the window like, "I'm not reading this Bible. I'm tired of this book." During the summer when we didn't have school we had to go on Vacation Bible Study. Going into the sixth grade you had to get baptized. You sit in the first pew in the church for that whole week of revival. You sit there the whole week. Then Sunday, they prep you to get baptized and they want you to come and say, "halleluiah." I chased them out of there like "What the hell!" I've been baptized five times in five different churches in my adult life.

I went to a Pentecostal Apostolic church, I guess, and they feel like if you're crying during the sermon that this is the Holy Spirit. You should be baptized right on the spot, and I did. And I didn't go back again. If you'll baptize me, you'll baptize anybody. I went to another church where I didn't have to get dipped in water. They just come in. I mean, experienced Christian. But then I started going to an LGBT church, nondenominational. It was fun. It was fun, but it was very segregated. It was very white. And I was always felt like the token Negro in that church.

So you didn't enjoy church?

No, I didn't enjoy church all *day*. No. I enjoyed it when we ate. When they had food. I was [like,] "We going to eat today?" Or when we took communion, but as a child you didn't take communion. You had to be baptized to take communion. And I thought it was wine. They were telling me they were drinking the bread and the wine. So I wanted the wine. And like I said, my grandmother was the mother of the church, so at the time we were growing up they literally had to pour the grape juice into the little glasses. And they covered it up. And when they got ready for it, I thought growing up that there was somebody dead under there. Because they had a white sheet covering it up. You know covering. And I'm like is that a body? I was just a weird child in church. I thought someone was dead. And then they took it up and I'd get mad because everybody was going around getting communion and I can't get it. I was mad because I felt like we just poured it out. My grandmom poured it out. "How come we can't have none?" Because I didn't understand. My grandmom finally told me what communion was and stuff. It didn't stop me from not wanting it, but I felt like I was in right enough with the Lord to drink the wine.

> *Yemaya assessu, Assessu Yemaya*
> (Yemaya is the gush of the spring)
> *Yemaya Olodo, Olodo Yemaya*
> (The gush of the spring is Yemaya)
> *Kai kai kai Yemaya Olodo*
> (The Mother of the children of fishes is the owner of the river)
> *Kai kai kai Assessu Olodo*
> *(The owner of the rivers is the Mother of the children of fishes)*

Julia (Sangodare)

My dad is a Baptist preacher, along with his father and almost all of his brothers and sisters and nephews.

So, a [family] history of preachers.

Mm-hmm, mm-hmm, yeah.
　　Choir practice wasn't play, necessarily, but that was probably my favor-

ite thing growing up—was to go to choir practice and play music, listening to tapes and sing all the parts over and over again, even the instruments.

Besides the choir, did you participate in any other organizations? The usher board, for instance?

No, I didn't usher because that seemed like a lot of work. And usually the ushers were really specific. So, no, I'm not ushering, but other leadership roles, like if there was some special occasion coming up—doing speeches and so the rehearsals for that, or little skits, I enjoyed that. Vacation Bible School was always a lot of fun, particularly because kids from around the neighborhood, or sometimes around the city who didn't necessarily come to the church, would be there. Because it's free childcare, free food. So that was fun. The little boys who could do back flips off of walls, they would show up. So Vacation Bible School was a hit for me. What else in church? I think I really fully participated in the services. Usually it was my dad preaching or a relative, and once I got to the age where I could pay attention, I always paid attention and was curious about what was being said and what it meant. And whoever in the congregation that I really liked or had a crush on, like being strategic about how I could sit with them or who's got the best candy, all that kind of stuff. So, yeah, I had positive, fond memories of church.

I would like to add that I'm wearing all white because I was recently initiated in Ifá, which is African spirituality, so this is my [transition] year, and so I'm definitely in a place of transition, which is exciting and new. I feel like it's coming full circle. Sort of talk about being from the South and there's something about the South that feels really connected to both the continent of Africa and the Caribbean, and I feel like African spirituality kind of helps shed more light on that, like so many of the things that we did in church that I wonder about. I'm like, "Oh! That's where that came from." I'm excited about discovering that more and making it more visible to other people and removing some of the stigma from African spirituality or just African practices period.

So, you don't feel any tension between your Christian Protestant upbringing and African cosmology?

No, I feel like it brings it full circle. And I talk a little bit with my dad about it: "Daddy, what do you know about seers and the Bible?" "Well, you know, prophet so-and-so was a seer." So, this is the way I think about it when I think about how I want to talk about it with my family—immediate and extended family. It's like all the things that I learned growing up in church and from the Bible, I was taught that that stuff was real, but we don't act like it's real in the way we practice our faith now. So then for me continually learning, reading, and discovering, and then finding a direct connection, because Ifá is over six thousand years old, and these sort of African practices are what the people that were writing the books of the Bible, that's sort of their history, too, I think. Anyway, it's a connection. So, it's like you taught me this and this is what I'm doing. So, what's the problem? You know? The world is opening up a whole new layer, a whole new level of literacy.

> *That's interesting, because I know quite a few black queer women who have gone through this process. And some who went through it for whom it was a positive experience, wonderful. And others for whom it was not. And who kept their name, the nomenclature, but don't practice because their spiritual leaders proved to be less than on the up and up and exploited them, that kind of thing.*

Yeah, I've heard a lot of horror stories—even an elder that lives in Durham, a chosen grandparent of me and [her partner] Alexis that's had definitely some trauma and some abuse. But my godmother is really amazing. She's an out black lesbian, organizer, activist, media mogul, I would say. So, I think that's definitely a part of it. I'm learning about this tradition and a lot of other traditions, like two-spirited people, queer people, like whatever manifestation that is, like they are gatekeepers and have a connection to spirit in a way that other people don't necessarily. And when you start abusing and just making expendable the people who have some sort of spiritual power that are supposed to ground the whole community, the whole nation, or whatever, when you start chucking them out and killing them and abusing them, then that's when you end up with so much turmoil. I think that that's not a coincidence. And when I was talking about touring and the tour of superheroes, I think that that's a part of it. I think everybody is born everything, but I do think that some people maybe have a spiritual role to play. We need to get in touch with that. Everybody does. But I think queer people in particular [need] to find out your own traditions . . . go back as far as you can go back . . . tap into the spirit and get those resources back. Because I think that's what it's going to take for what seems like the way the world's ending, like if capitalism continues and multinational corporations have more rights than people. We gonna need some sort of power. [*Laughter.*] And it ain't gonna be money. It's going to have to be some other kind of power.

The river's flow picks up pace. The women drop hands and lift them toward the sky, their heads thrown back and voices filled with sound—five-part harmony, a praise song to Osun. The river rages such that I can barely stand. The women begin to fade into the darkness, but their melody lingers, echoing off the surrounding trees. Miss B. says that after the women testify, I must provide Osun with a parting gift. I bend down and kiss her. Her water is like candy on my lips, sweet and slick. I use the current to make my way back to the river bank and lie down on top of a fallen trunk. I am drunk with story, and sleep descends like wet Chicago snow.

Three

HONEYBEE
BLUES

I awaken to cigarette smoke and Missy Elliot blaring on the radio. While I was at the river, Miss B. retrieved her car from Nancy's house. I'm on the passenger side of Miss B.'s car and we're speeding down the highway as she wiggles and giggles in her seat, singing along with Missy.

> *See my hips and tips, don't ya*
> *See my ass and my lips, don't ya*
> *Lost a few pounds and my whips for ya*
> *This kinda beat that go ra-ta-ta*
> Ra-ta-ta-ta-ta-ta-ta-ta-ta.

She waves her cigarette in my face to the beat of the last line. All of the tranquility of the river is gone. I turn the radio down.

"The experience at the river was amazing. I was in such a state of peace," I say, signifying.

"Ti esrever dna ti pilf nwod gniht ym tup I," she sings puffing more smoke in my face and ignoring me. "I don't know what the hell she's saying, but it sure do sound cool."

"It's 'I put my thing down flip it and reverse it' backward," I respond, annoyed even more. "Where are we headed?"

"I thought we would have a little fun tonight and let our hair down and get some work done. We're going to a blues bar down in MS. There's a place I know called Sippi-Citi where they play the blues on Wednesday nights. The club owner is a drone I went to school with who introduced me to the life. The club used to be called Out of Sight or something like that, before it became Sippi-Citi. Anyway, I got Frederick to agree to let some of my sisters perform and let Yours Truly serve as the MC. Don't sleep on Miss B., hunty. You ain't ready for this jelly! Ti esrever dna ti pilf nwod gniht ym tup I!" I hold on for dear life as she floors it, leaving a trail of black smoke behind.

We arrive at the place a little past ten o'clock and there's only a few cars in the gravel parking lot. The club looks more like a jail than a club. It's made of cinder block painted white and there are bars on the windows.

FIGURE 3.1: SIPPI-CITI NIGHTCLUB. PHOTO BY THE AUTHOR.

"You are in for a treat tonight, Dr. EPJ," Miss B. says, getting out of the car. She walks around to the trunk and pulls out several garment bags.

"You brought your own drag, I see," I say, genuinely impressed, though wary about what Miss B.'s drag will entail.

"For sho.' And if you had a clue, you'd get you some drag, too. Bloop!" She spins on her heels and starts walking toward the club door. The door attendant immediately recognizes her.

"Well, if it ain't Miss B. The most beautiful woman this side of the sidewalk," he says to her.

"Hey Booker T. I'm surprised to see you working the door tonight. I didn't know that you were out of jail. This here is my friend, Dr. EPJ. He's a professor. A professor is someone who teaches dumbasses like you how to read and write—even in jail. Anyway, he's my guest tonight. If you get a break from 'working' the door, you should come and see the show. Toodles." Booker T. is deflated and we walk on by him into the club. Miss B. says, "I love giving Booker T. shit because he's easy prey. But he's harmless and he helps me out from time to time. It's his hateful sister, Cantstanda, who tries my patience. I got into a fight with her once and once was enough. She likened to kilt me. That girl's the size of Booker T. and then some. She is surrounded by herself. Everywhere she looks, there she is. And talk about ugly. Her mama cried the day she hatched that one. Bless her heart." I shake my head in disgust at Miss B.'s fat shaming while still suppressing a laugh.

Miss B. goes over to the bar and greets the bartender, a very handsome woman with beautiful teeth. Miss B. motions for me to join her.

"Mel, this is my friend, Dr. EPJ. I want you to take good care of him during the show. Make sure you give him that special drink you always make for me, mead and vodka with a splash of soda and a twist of lime."

"Sure thing," Mel says, in a voice so deep it rattles my chest. "Have a seat at that front table there and I'll make sure you straight."

We walk over to the table. "Wow, she has a deep voice," I say.

"That ain't the only thing that's deep. I remember losing my whole face down in her honeypot. I was down there for a good half hour before I came up for air. And then there was this butch high yellow thing that tried to work me one night. Hunty, I shook my booty about two hundred times in each direction and dropped it like it was hot and Miss Thing fainted on the spot. It was too much."

"And this is too much for me! TMI! Ewwww!"

"Don't knock it till you try it. I'm the original bee charmer, so I could teach you a thing or two. I'm going to get ready for the show. I'll see you later."

I really do need a drink to get that image out of my head. I take a seat and "Mel" brings me over the first of many strong Sippi-Citi specials. The stage lights go up and an eight-bar blues begins. Out walks Miss B. in a stunning sanguine sequined dress, her thunderous hips catching and bouncing the lights like a disco ball. She takes the mic and sings:

> Come on pretty baby take a walk with me
> Come on pretty baby take a walk with me
> I won't let nothing bother you, I'll be your honeybee

"Good evening, ladies and gentlemen, and those otherwise inclined. Welcome to blues alley here at Sippi-Citi, where you'll get to experience some of the best blues this side of the Osun River. My name is Miss B. and I'll be your hostess with the most . . . ass. Tonight, we have six of our most talented blues singers bringing to you some of their sexiest songs. First up, from right here in Jackson, MS, via Little Rock, AR, singing her megahit, "Foolish Man Blues," put your hands together for Miss Wynee!"

Wynee comes out onto the stage. Surprisingly, she is not wearing a dress but rather sporting black jeans that have clearly been pressed, a crisp white shirt, and shiny black cowboy boots. She is a dark chocolate woman with a soft butch look: short cropped hair and wearing deep burgundy lipstick. She stands at the microphone with a lit cigarette (I can't believe they allow smoking inside the club!) and takes her time to get her song started, her voice low, gravelly.

Wynee

I met this person at the hospital and I didn't know she was married and we just kind of sneaked around the hospital, a little kissing here, a little kissing there, and we'd go out to smoke together or whatever but it never came up that she was married. And she invited me to her house one day for dinner and she introduced me to her husband. What a shocker. We got along well.

You and the husband?

Yeah, we did. And sitting there eating dinner, Pauline [her ex-girlfriend] calls and she said, "While you're sitting down eating dinner with Wynee and enjoy[ing] yourself, I'm just calling to tell you she's fucking your wife."

How did she know?

I don't know how she knew. To this day, I don't know how she knew. So he hung up the phone and she [the wife] said, "Well who was on the phone?" He said, "It was just Pauline." And so she said, "What'd she say?" "Oh, she just said while I'm sitting here smiling at Wynee that y'all are fucking." Lost my appetite immediately and was ready to go home.

And he just said it like that calm?

Just like that. Hung the phone up and wasn't going to say a thing. She said, "Who's that?" "It's Pauline." "Pauline who?" "Wynee's friend." "Well what did she say?" She said, "While we're down here grinning and eating dinner and everything that Wynee's fucking my wife." They kept eating. I couldn't eat another bite. I was nervous. I was real nervous. I didn't know what was going to happen, you know. Nothing did. They wanted to watch a movie after dinner. Nothing else was said about that. So they asked to visit more often and he'd be just as excited as she was. So we all formed a friendship. We'd sit down, smoke weed, drink tequila, and everybody was happy-go-lucky. I knew his family. His brothers would come to visit. I was just a friend.

Our relationship eventually dwindled out or fizzed out or whatever, but a few years later I went to see her at the hospital. I started experimenting with drugs a little bit, whatever, so I went to see her. And she said, "Where you living?" And she said, "Oh, you mean you have an address that I can come to." I said, "Yeah." And her name was Mariska and she came by and she caught me doing drugs and she said, "Let's take a ride." So I did and she said, "I've gone through this; my husband's gone through this. I went through rehab and I don't do this anymore and I told him just as I'm going to tell you: I can't have you and you have cocaine." I stopped. Abruptly. Even though this woman was married, I was in love with her. And she said, "As a matter of fact, I'm getting you out of this atmosphere to make sure." "Why you going to do that?" "Because you're moving in with me and Ed." "Okay." They had a spare room, so I moved to that room. Him and his brothers went back and got my furniture and brought it and set it up in that room and that's where I lived. Half the time Mariska was in my room and half the time she was in her room until it got to a point that she didn't want to go back to that room. And then the issue came up that we wanted a baby.

We who?

[*Laughter.*] Mariska and I.

Did she and her husband already have children?

No. No, she could not have kids.

And was it your understanding that he actually knew that the two of you were [having sex]?

Well when you're sleeping in the other room all the time; he's sleeping there by his self. He knew.

Did they have an understanding?

Obviously, because he said, "Can I watch y'all?" What straight man don't want to watch? "Yeah, you can watch, but you can't touch me." He watched. He said, "Teach me how to do that." Why would a skillful person as myself teach another person my trade? "Naw, you gotta learn on your own." And she said, "No, up until now you said it upset your stomach. Why you want to learn now? Because I told you if you wouldn't, I was going to find somebody that would and I did." And he was like, "Well I guess you did then." I mean, that's just how calm they were. I mean their relationship was pretty open. Maybe he went out and did things on his own. I don't know, but he was quite a bit older than she was or whatever. And one night [he] told me, "Well I don't care about y'all fucking." And that was his words: "Because she loves me. You guys are just fucking."

So, then we sat down and we wanted a baby. So we discussed that and we discussed it with him. He had a good job. He worked for the railroad. I knew that my baby would be taken care of. It wasn't going to be not just anybody up off the street because even though we were her parents, she was going to want to know who her dad was at one point in her life. So it had to be somebody that I knew and could put my hands on at any given time. So the three of us sat down over some joints and tequila and discussed it. Well, he was all for having a baby. I think he was more or less more excited about getting with me, but I was smart. We weren't doing this in vain because it wasn't something that I liked. Ovulation tests, peeing on those little sticks for a sign. "Alright c'mon, tonight's the night, tonight's the night!" You know, so we got loaded and we had a threesome. I got pregnant.

How long did it take?

That time. We didn't know it, so we tried the next night or whatever, and I was pregnant. A couple months or maybe six or eight weeks we're sitting down after work because Mariska always did exercise or whatever. So I was sitting in the room changing clothes and I was like, "I could start do[ing] exercise with you because my sides are getting pudgy." And she said, "You might be pregnant." I said, "Oh surely not, surely not." We had already bought the home pregnancy test or whatever. "C'mon, do one, c'mon, do one. Let's just see." Well these were the old-fashioned ones. You had to pee on the stick or whatever and pour the solution on it. The stick turned pink before I poured the solution on it. I said, "What do you think? Are they defective?" And we would have to get some more because these are turning pink way too quick. And then she said, "No, no, no, we're just going to wait until the morning because you can really tell then. You get that fresh morning pee." I'm thinking pee is pee. Either you are or you're not, so of course wait until morning and the same thing happened. As soon as I dipped it in the pee it was pink and it gave a positive pregnancy test. I went into work and everything. I knew all the girls that worked in the lab, all the girls everywhere, but anyway, nobody was there that night that worked. They was all off for some reason or another so I went to the emergency room. I knew them, too. So, I need somebody to draw my blood; I need a pregnancy test. They said okay, and so they did. They told me to come back in an hour, and when I went back in an hour I was like, "Well?" "Go to Room 8." Room 8: that means the doctor's coming in. And he did and he said, "You are pregnant and you need to go on and start seeing you a doctor so he can put you on prenatal vitamins" and things of this nature. So I called home to confirm that the test was right and then we had it. We had a little girl.

Well, after that it was about time for him to leave. We getting about tired of him. So, she went in and put in for a divorce and he was served and he came home and he said, "Well I didn't want a divorce." "Well, we just think it's the best thing because we're going to raise this baby and we going to buy us a house." He just so backwooded. "They're not going to let two women buy no house." Two women got income, two women got good credit, I don't know why. So, we bought our first house and we stayed there a little while. And he stayed until finally we were so gracious in helping him find a nice apartment and giving him what he wanted out of the house and everything. And told him when we move out, he could move back into the house. Actually, Mariska had been to the military and bought the house with her little GI grant or whatever.

So, basically it was her house except for the fact she had a husband, but there was nothing that he could do with the house without her. So it wasn't a problem for him moving back in. That's where he is now to this day. And so we had the baby and everything. And we had talked and I told him, "This is the baby and if you want to be in her life it's up to you. I'm never going to knock on your door and drop my baby off and tell you take your baby because of this or that. If you want a relationship, it's up to you to make that relationship." And he did. They're just like this [*holds two fingers close together*] to this day. Yeah, so we're one big happy family. Mariska and I were together for about seventeen years.

Wynee takes a last drag on her cigarette and slowly walks off stage. Miss B. gives her a high-five as they pass each other at the edge of the stage. "Let's give Wynee another round of applause! I told you all you were in for a treat. Can't nobody switch hit like Wynee, hunty! She could teach me a thing or two—or three! HA! Let me stop. Okay, we're going to slow things down a little bit with our next performer. She likes her groove nice and slow. Hailing from Anderson, SC, where they raise 'em big and country, please help me welcome to the stage singing "'Pussy Juice' Bluhe!"

Bluhe slinks onto the stage. They are wearing a football jersey, jeans, high-top sneakers, and a baseball cap turned backward—not at all what I expected given the title of their song. Bluhe slowly walks downstage and picks up the mic, holding it sideways and pressed up against their lips. The musical intro sounds like the beginning of a Millie Jackson song, which seems appropriate, given the circumstances. They seductively lick their lips and then begin to sing.

Bluhe

For as long as I can remember, I've always dreamt about pussy. I'm mesmerized by the sweet, hot scent that invades my nostrils and the savory taste it leaves me with. I'm an artist, you see. Artists aren't hungry; they're just starving for pussy. Whether it's hot, wet, or creamy, I just can't stop dreaming about it. The first time my tongue tasted pussy, I knew I had to have more. Just like I'm a trick and damn, she's my hoe. It's crack and I'm addicted to the sack. As

I lick and suck, it trembles with joy and squirts all over me. My throat quickly clears the way for every ounce you see. Shit, could this be true? Pussy juice for me, for you? As my tongue penetrates your vaginal wall, you jerk and moan so fucking loud I swear I saw Jesus in the cloud. Your body spoke many languages that night. We fucked and sucked to the morning light. Your body moves to the rhythmic pattern of my tongue. Your thighs tightened up and you held on for the best fucking orgasm for centuries to come. You scream, "Leave your wife and marry me." You came so hard you passed out temporarily. Then you woke up and begged me to stop. I couldn't 'cause it seems I'm addicted to your hotspot. If eating pussy is against the law, I'm going down for the tenth round so lock my black ass up and let all the bitches loose because tonight is the night for pussy juice.

Bluhe drops the mic and does a spin on their back heels before pimping off the stage. I am clutching my pearls and in a state of shock, but the rest of the crowd is chanting, "puss–y juice, puss-y juice, puss-y juice." It's way too much for me.

Miss B. has done a costume change when she comes out after Bluhe's act. Now she is a wearing a silver dress that looks like it's made of snakeskin. It stops just at her knee but rides up when she walks. It has a plummeting neckline that leaves nothing to the imagination. I marvel at how she has been able to gather herself into it without something popping out. Her shoes are ruby red stilettos, the ones with the big toe cut out. Between the dress and the shoes, she is doing a balancing act. One false move and it's over.

"Whew! That Bluhe is something else, I tell you! I bet ya'll weren't ready for that jelly," Miss B. says, as she walks onstage out of breath. Then she yells backstage, "I'll need a little foot rub after standing in these heels tonight, Bluhe! I get off at two!" Then back to the audience. "You all don't mind me. I'm just trying to get little Bo Bluhe to come blow my horn. Y'all feeling alright?" The crowd responds in the affirmative, by clinging glasses, stomping their feet, and cheering. "That's what I like to hear. Okay, we're going to keep the show moving along and mix the secular with the sacred. How many church 'hos we got here tonight?" No one responds. "That's not a rhetorical question. I said, how many church 'hos we got here tonight?" A few folks in the audience whistle. "That's alright. You don't have to admit it. I know how you Sunday saints and Saturday night sinners are. Well, our next singer is going to blow all y'all's shit out of the water with her song "Women's Day Blues." Coming to deliver upon us a shower of blues blessings from Wampee, SC, let's give it up for Miss Lenore!"

Lenore walks out, her smile taking up half the stage. She is tall, buxom, and spirit-led. Her short, salt-and-pepper hair complements the black silk blouse that fits in all of the right places. The light catches her onyx ball earrings that seem to swing like a pendulum on a grandfather clock with each bob of her head. She's grooving to her lead-in music.

Lenore

I would go to churches, especially if I saw something that said "Women's Day." Because at the time I stopped going to church, but if I saw something that said, "Women's Day," well guess what, Lenore's going to visit your church and they were in there.

What was it about the church that said to you "This is where I could find other women who were same-gender loving?"

Well, number one, there are lots of women in there with just children. Never see them with a man. I just looked at that. Lots of girlfriends go to church and I did it, I guess, to be somewhat of a rebellion. You tell me that Jesus doesn't like me, but I want to go there and I want to stir up the pot. Maybe I tried to piss the Lord off. I don't know.

And so, when you go to these programs, how would you meet women?

They would meet me. They would come after me. You know sometimes just my name. And this might sound crazy, the name "Stackhouse," it's an unusual name. If I wrote on a nametag, that's a conversation piece and sometimes people want to talk to me just because of my name. So that was one of my experiences, and I don't know, I guess I was kind of cute, and they just want to boss me around. I find that women they used to like just want to boss me around and just tell me what to do and I would let them.

Give me an example of how this might happen. So, the service is over, you're in fellowship hall, and someone just comes up to you and starts talking to you?

Okay let me tell you; let me give you one example. I volunteered to feed the homeless one holiday. I think it was around Thanksgiving and I met this attorney. Okay? Now, she had a daughter, but she met me and I don't know, I think my personality—I might be a little funny. I made her laugh and stuff like that, and she just wanted to make sure I didn't leave until she got my number. "You make sure you do this," and "You stay right here," and I would stay. She was really pretty, so I would stay and I would just do what they tell me and they get my number and that was it.

And were some of these women married?

Mm hmm. Oh, yeah. I met one woman at work and she and her husband was having some trouble, so this one night he wasn't there. Maybe he left to go wherever he was going and I got caught in her house, had to hide in the closet and get out the neighborhood really fast, especially [because] he found out somebody was in there and it was me. So I remember backing out that parking lot, running out the house, backing out the driveway, and getting out that neighborhood. Okay? So, I've been in some situations where I could've got myself hurt I guess.

The women that were coming on to you, how would you describe their presentation? Were these feminine women?

Mm hmm. Yes. Very feminine.

Was this typical?

Mm hmm. As a matter of fact, I think I love a feminine woman. That's what I love about a woman: that femininity. It's a beautiful thing.

You've heard or you know what a church lady is, right?

Mm hmm.

Were some of these women what you consider church ladies?

Yes, yes. Yes, [Dr. EPJ]. They were church women. [*Laughter.*] Highfalutin.

Older? Younger?

Yes, older. Bourgeois.

Do you think that these women just want to experiment or do you think they had experience doing this?

I think they wanted to experiment for the most part. I think they wanted to experiment. Now there's one woman. I'm going to call her "Lady X," and she's from Charleston. We ended being together for thirteen years on and off and she just wanted me around. She loved having me around. I would baby-sit her kid when she was out of town. She was very promiscuous except that she ended up marrying a man and they called it a commuting marriage. About five or six years into our thirteen years, she married a man. I was very hurt.

Were you in love with her?

I was. I was. I think she was the first woman that I was in love with, older woman. She was the reason for my sorrow, so to speak, but there came a time where after that thirteen years I had to let her go because everybody wanted a piece of her. Everybody wanted to be with her. And ultimately, she chose to be with that man and it was hard.

I was grooving to Lenore's song until it took that unexpected turn at the end. I guess that's why they call it the blues. Despite ending on a sad note, Lenore bounces off stage in the same happy state in which she entered.

If Miss B.'s dress goes up any higher, it's a wrap. I think she's trying to be provocative, but I'm just scandalized. She peers out into the audience, holding her right hand up to her forehead, as if saluting, to keep the light out of her eyes.

"I'm looking for a new love, baby, a new love. Yeah, yeah, yeah. HA! HA! Church folks' a mess. We're going to continue this theme with our next performer. She's going by her drag name tonight 'cause she's still being chased by the stalker she's about to sing about. Like I said, you need to leave those church folks alone! Here to perform 'First Lady Blues,' give it up for Lisa."

Lisa appears onstage and I begin to think that this show should be called "soft butch blues" because all of Miss B.'s performer friends are butch women. Like all the women before her except Lenore, Lisa is wearing pants and a button-down shirt and has short hair, but it's permed. Her skin looks like cocoa under the lights. She wastes no time beginning her song.

Lisa

In '99 I joined this church: Friendship. And so shortly after that we had a Women's Day program and they asked me to be on the program. They had two services. So I stayed for the second service and I remember sitting in the back of the church and I felt like this lady was staring at me. I felt like this lady was just staring. She was in the choir stand; I just felt like she was staring at me. And I was like, "No, she can't be staring at me." So, the next Wednesday or a couple weeks after that, if I remember the time frame, I was at church again; I went to Youth Ministry. And the guy was a youth minister and he was also one of the associate pastors at the church. After church, he introduced me to his wife. Well, it was the same lady that was staring at me in the choir stand. So, I was like, "Oh, okay, okay." And so that next Sunday she said, "You know what? I need your phone number." And so I said, "Well, John has all my information; get it from John." And, you know, just casually talking. And she's like, "Oh, okay." That following Wednesday at church she asked me for it again. She said, "You know what? I don't have time to fool around with John." She said, "Girl, just give me your phone number." And so I gave her a card and gave her my number. And that next day she called me, and it was so funny or crazy because as we were talking—and I hadn't had a relationship with a woman in like over two years by then—we were talking and she said, "You know, I hope you don't take this the wrong way, but I'm attracted to you." And she was like, "I don't know why, I've never been attracted to a woman before," went through the whole spiel. Susan was a pretty bold woman.

And this was in church?

In church. In church.

And would you describe her as a feminine woman?

Very feminine, beautiful, oh my god, petite, very charismatic, you know, and had a voice out of this world. That woman could sing, oh my god, mm-mm-mm. She had it all. She had the total package. She had the *total* package.

So, you met her somewhere?

She came to my apartment one Sunday after church and we spent the whole day together just kind of talking, playing around. And then the next day she came back . . . because I didn't go to work that next day because I was so just kind of messed up in the head. And she came over after she got off work and we ended up having sex. And I'll never forget Susan telling me—and this was so true—she said, "Once we do this, we can't go back." That's what she told me. And needless to say, God, almost six years later is when we ended our relationship.

Oh wow. And she was still married?

She was still married.

Did she have children?

Yep, three kids. Three kids. Her son was in college . . . 'cause she was forty. I was twenty-seven at the time, and she was forty. And she had just turned forty right before we met. I also felt years later that I wasn't her first like she proclaimed I was 'cause she was just too good at it. You know what I mean? And Susan was a survivor. You know, she grew up on Ninth Street in Jackson. She was a survivor. And so she was going to do whatever it took to survive. I just felt like I wasn't her first. But the masquerade that we started . . . charade, rather, we had was that we were best friends. So I was always at the house and the kids loved me. You know, when he [Susan's husband] had surgery, I kept the kids. I was taking dinner over there. Crazy as hell. [*Laughter.*] You know, crazy. Need to be happy we didn't get shot, really. Need to be happy we didn't get shot.

You don't think that there were other people who suspected?

I'm positive. Since I've been here, one of her close friends has called me a couple of times just to kind of see how I was doing and everything. And she told me that Susan told her. She told me that Susan told her. So I'm positive that a lot of people knew and suspected because we were just so close. I know her mom suspected.

Oh really?

Yeah, her mom suspected. And so, you know, yeah.

So, you think she was a player?

Yes, God. [*Laughter.*] So, let me tell you why. Okay? To tell you how far gone I was, Susan lost her job. I headed up housing for the city. I had a secretary's position open—I hired her. It was awful. She did no work. She did no work—none. She didn't do any work. But in the midst of her working for me there was this guy, a developer I was working on a project with. And I knew they were getting close, right? But I really didn't understand how close they were getting. But I knew they were getting close. At the same time, there was this other guy that was paying her a lot of attention. So, I was like, something not right. Something's going on. Well, her husband called me one day and her husband said I think Susan's cheating on me. I got nervous. I got nervous as hell. Talking about, "Oh, shit." He said, "I really think so." He said, "I went through her phone and she has this number on her phone." And so, it turned out the number was the developer that was working with me on a project. It just kind of messed me up because I'm thinking, she don't even give a damn about me enough [that] she's trying to jeopardize my job. I'm doing a deal with this guy. But then more than that—damn, she's cheating on me *and* her husband! You know? She's cheating on both of us. And so shortly after that she got a job at the post office, which was great. So she ended up working at the post office at the center where they do all the mail distribution. And there was a supervisor there, which the supervisor was a white woman, June, and her and June are friends to this day. I'll never forget, John called me one night and he said, "I'm gonna kill her." And you know, I'm still paranoid. I'm like, "You're gonna kill her?" He said, "Yeah, I'm gonna kill her." He said, "I don't know what she doing." He said, "I don't know if it's man, woman, child, what, I don't know." So, I got real nervous now because he tells me that his son heard her tell somebody that she loved them. And I said, "Okay." He said, "You know, maybe you just need to talk to her." I said, "I don't think so." He said, "Well she's not answering my phone." And so I said, "Well, let me call her." I called her; she didn't answer my number either; she didn't answer my call. And so I'm sitting outside on my patio drinking. I'll never forget, I was drinking some Grey Goose and cranberry juice, smoking a cigar because I'm thinking, this shit is fucked up. And I was saying, God, if you get me out of this, you ain't gotta worry about me. Just get me out of this one. And so Susan ends up coming by my house. Ironically, I bought a town home maybe three blocks from where she lived, okay? And so, she came by my house and she said, "I need you to go home with me." And I was like, "What?" She said, "I need you to go home with me." I said, "What's going on?" I said, "First of all, where you been?" And she said, "Well, I was with June." So, now I'm pissed 'cause I'm thinking, "Okay, you're dealing with [the contractor], you're doing God knows what; now you're with June. What the fuck?" And she said, "Well, I think John's gonna try to hurt me, but if you go with me he won't hurt you." And I'm thinking in my mind, "*I* want to hurt you."

You know, the whole time we were together I didn't have a relationship with a woman until after she did all that stuff. I always dealt with men. But she used to get so jealous even if it was guys. I mean, she used to really act out if I was with somebody, and so it was as if she wanted me just for her—you know what I mean?—while she's doing God knows what.

So, I went home with her, and true enough John's livid, the kid's livid, she's fussing at her son saying, "You started all this by telling your dad that. This is all your fault." John is such a calm-tempered person. I had never seen him like that before. And I ended up spending the night over there, sleeping at the edge of the bed, although I didn't sleep. He stayed in the kitchen the entire night in a bar seat. She was the only person that slept that whole night. Everybody else up. She slept real good that whole night. I was like, "You know what? I gotta leave this girl alone. This is just not gonna work for anybody." And so John forgave her. They tried to keep their marriage together.

Now, that was quite some tale. How scandalous to be turned out and scammed by a "church lady"—and a preacher's wife, no less. Who knew such shenanigans went on in the hive?

Miss B. has saved her best dress for last: a strapless, black lace fishtail with the tiniest of gold beads sewn all over it. Even though the dress is lace, nothing is spilling out or over. Her shoes are black patent leather pumps with a gold-plated toe and heel. She is stunning. She looks over at me and winks.

"Lisa, Lisa, Lisa. Girl, you know you sang that song. Now, that's the blues. Ain't nothing like a my-woman-done-left-me-but-I-love-her-too-much-to-let-her-go blues. But we gonna shift gears once more as we bring on a fairly new-comer to the scene. But don't sleep on these young folks. They're a quick study and will teach you a thing or two. Singing her new single 'First Time Blues,' let's give it up for Miss Monika!"

Monika is a force. She bum-rushes the stage and takes the microphone off the stand but then just stares at the audience. She has a mane of fiery locs that droop like branches of a weeping willow over her shoulders. Jeans and a T-shirt complement her b-boi aura. She is clearly younger than the other performers, but I don't know by how many years. The musical intro plays for what feels like an eternity before she sings.

Monika

My first experience was with the girl that moved to North Carolina. When she came back, me and her hung out all the time. And then one night in particular, we had went to the movies. And I drove my stepdad's car, so we went to the movies. So we were just sitting there talking and talking. And that Keith Sweat song, "Nobody," came on. That was her favorite little song or whatever. I was like, "Well, when this song's done, I'm gonna go." So, when the song was getting close to the end, she just leaned over and kissed me. And it scared me at first because I'm like, what she doing? But then I kissed her back. So I still was tripping about it. And so, after it was over, she got out and went in. And I sat there in the driveway for a minute, just tripping. I'm like, "I just kissed a girl," it blew my mind. So, the whole way home, I'm just like, "Wow, I kissed a girl." And I felt some kind of way about it; I felt like I wasn't supposed to be doing it, but at the same time, it was different but it felt good. After the little situation with the kiss, I was ready to explore. So, the female who actually [this] first happened [with], she played basketball, too. In the summertime we used to go play basketball wherever we could play—Lawson, Montevallo—anywhere where females were playing. We used to drive to Montgomery sometimes to play basketball. Anyway, this [woman] had told my home girl that she was feeling me or whatever. I'm still new to it, so I'm still kind of shy and I don't know or whatever. So we ended up talking on the phone. We had went and played basketball this day, me and my home girl and her. We went to Montevallo that day. And she stayed in Montevallo. But I had drove my car and my friend drove her car. So, [my home girl] came on back to Birmingham, but I stayed at [this girl's] house [in Montevallo]. She stayed with her mom and they had just like a small apartment. It was a one-bedroom. So her mom had her bedroom, and then she just slept on the pullout couch. We was all watching TV and her mom fell asleep on the couch. So she was telling me to come on in the room. So I'm like, "But your mom," and she was like, "Just come on." So I go on in there with her. So we were just watching TV. So I'm sitting up there. I'm nervous, because this is something new for me. And then [her] mom in the other room. So anyway, one thing led to another. We kissed and all this. And so, she gets to like pulling my clothes down. So I'm still like, "Your mom, but your mom." So, she was like, "Don't worry about it." So, she did her little thing. I mean, I couldn't believe it. I don't know, it was like some crack. You know what I'm saying? I just wanted to keep on, keep on doing it. After that, I had the experience with a guy. No guy had ever made me have an orgasm. That first time with a female, it just happened. Like no-brainer. So, I was hooked. I'm like, okay, I'm doing this with this guy and . . . he's getting [his] but I didn't get mine. With the female, it was like every time, every time, every time.

"That's right, Monika! Every damn time! Push the button if you wanna come in, baby! Don't you just love the young people? I had this little young thing sniffing around me one time and when I showed her all of this, it was too much. I was like, "Little girl, grass don't grow on the playground! Fish or cut bait, baby! Whew! Let me move on before I get in trouble." The audience is eating out of her hands, bent over in laughter. I'm clutching my pearls.

"I have saved the best for last. This next woman needs no introduction. You all know her from her military days, but I know her from her clubbing days. We used to funk until the break of dawn back in those army bases. Tonight, she's closing the show with her hit 'Turned Out Blues.' Please give a round of applause for the one, the only, Joy."

Joy walks out, dressed in a white linen suit, a white shirt, and sporting a white fedora with a black band that matches her black sneakers, whose rims are as white as her suit. Like Wynee, she is giving soft butch realness, but with a twist. She peers over the top of her glasses to scan the audience while she takes the microphone off the stand and moves downstage to begin her song.

Joy

I just liked playing sports. And when they were saying, "Oh, that bulldagger or that dyke" . . . those were fighting words for me. And I had a boyfriend and everything in school. My senior year, Michelle Harris was a student teacher for my history class. Nice-looking black woman and stuff . . . it was something about her—she dressed real nice and all that stuff, and there was just something about her. I would be like, "She's really nice-looking." And I would look at her in class. [*Laughter.*] But I never acted on it. So, she started coming to my track meets. She was married and everything, but she took a liking to me, and so she started coming to my track meets and my basketball games. On Saturdays, she would come and get me and we would hang out and all this stuff. And come to find out, her sister was two years older than me, but played at Eisenhower High School, which was in our district, and I remembered . . . she told me who her sister was. So we started hanging out, me and her sister.

Around prom time, me and my boyfriend go to the prom and we go to Galveston and we hanging out and we laying in the bed, and I was like, "I miss her." And I'm like, "Girl, you crazy! You know, you thinking about another woman!" I had never approached her, we had never . . . it was nothing. We would just hang out and go play basketball, go play volleyball, you know, just hang out, she would introduce me to her friends. And after I graduated, we still hung out and everything, and it was like we played in a basketball tournament and I was real sore. And she was like, "Well, you can stay all night over at my house." This was the sister, not the teacher. And one thing led to the other and I just turned over and we started kissing and all this stuff.

So how did you get the gumption to make the first move?

Well, she told me that she wanted to massage me. She was like, "You sore? Take your shirt off." So she's on my back and rubbing and all this stuff. And I'm starting to move and she said, "Flip over." So, she's laying on top of me. So, I felt like it was that connection by then.

Joy takes a bow, which no other person before her has done, and stays onstage as Miss B. comes out singing in what I can only surmise to be a parody of Anita Baker: "'Cause *you're the finest thing I seen in all my life. You bring me joy! Myyyyyyyyyy Joy! Myyyyyyyyyy Joy!* That's right, Miss Thing! I'm signing up for a massage right now so that you can bring me some Joy, Joy! Give it up one more time for Joy bringing us some Joy!" The audience applauds as Miss B.'s theme song starts up again:

> *I'll make you honey in the morning, I'll make you honey at night*
> *I'll make you honey in the morning, I'll make you honey at night*
> *I'll make you honey three times a day, if you treat me right.*

"I sure hope you all enjoyed the show. I know I did. Stand to your feet as I bring them all back to the stage for one last round of applause—Miss Wynee, Miss Lenore, Bonita/Bluhe, Miss Lisa, Miss Monika, and Miss Joy." They join her onstage and sing along with her:

I won't let nothing bother you, I'll be your honeybee.

There is thunderous applause from the audience. Miss B. walks down the steps from the stage and over to my table.

"Did you enjoy the show, Dr. EPJ? But more importantly, did you dig my sartorial performance?" She pushes my shoulder.

"You were alright," I say, trying not to be too complimentary.

"Why, thank you! I think you genuinely mean that. Now, let me run backstage and get out of this drag. It took two girls to get me in this thing! Plus, I need a cigarette like yesterday. Hold tight. I'll be right back."

I find it interesting that there are so many drones in the club, some who are dancing with each other, and some dancing with women. Gender and sexuality seem to flow in multiple directions such that I can't tell who's zooming who. The DJ puts on some house music and the folks run like roaches to the dance floor. I watch bodies grind, trancelike, to the music. I'm reminded of my clubbing days when I would travel to DC or Atlanta to hear this one DJ, DJ Sedrick, mix gospel and house music. The house remix of Shirley Caesar's "Hold My Mule" was the one song that would send the place up. It was the closest thing to catching the holy ghost in the club when DJ Sedrick spun that mix combined with his commentary about how grateful we should be that we had been spared from AIDS. My friends and I, sweaty, tipsy, horny, and perfumed to the hilt, would take refuge in the sexual spirit moving through the space and on the dance floor. This moment in Sippi-Citi evokes that same energy, but my friends are not here. In fact, as I look around this scene, I realize how out of place I am. These are not people that I would party with—or even be friends with. They lean a bit too far outside of what I thought was my high tolerance for "otherness": their costumes, vernacular, movements, genderfucks, and bad weaves are a real test of my own ability to see another way of being in the world that isn't prescripted by my own need to be liked, to fit in, to be in control, to . . . be. And in this moment, I realize that what I'm really feeling is envy.

While lost in my own revelations this . . . person . . . walks up to me and grabs my hand and pulls me onto the dance floor. The DJ is jamming "Follow Me" and the place lights up. This person I'm dancing with has on a baseball cap turned backward and sunglasses so that I can't see their face, and surely, they can't see too much of anything with those shades on. There is something really sexy about them, though, and I'm trying to remember that I got a husband at home—one that should be worried sick about where I am. Just as things are about to get a bit more uncomfortable because of this person's grinding their crotch into my ass, Miss B. steps in between us and begins to twerk. The person walks away and begins dancing with someone else.

"You're welcome," Miss B. says to me as she continues to dance.

"For what?" I ask, both messing with her and relieved that she intervened.

"This is Sippi-Citi, where you don't know who's who until you do, and then it might be too late. Honey, that was Hot Rod, a Butch Queen who walks the balls in the Butch Realness category for the House of Hymenoptera. I saw Hot Rod sweatin' you and I *knew* your little naïve tail didn't know what time it was."

"I'll have you know I have a former student who wrote a whole book on ballroom culture, so I know a Butch Queen when I see one," I retort, embarrassed by my tired and nerdy response and by the fact that I've never actually *attended* a ball.

> *I'm hoping to see the day*
> *When my people*
> *Can all relate*
> *We must stop fighting*
> *To achieve the peace*
> *That was taught in our country*
> *We shall all be free*
> *Follow me . . . Follow me . . .*

The music intensifies and Miss B. and I are getting our life on the dance floor. The DJ's voice booms over the bass of the music. "Are you ready to make some noise! I said are you ready to make some noise! There's a challenge on the floor tonight. Yes! There's a challenge on the floor tonight. The house of Hymenoptera against the House of Aporcrita! And the category is . . . VOGUING FEMME!"

I'm not sure what's happening but everyone starts to "ooh" and "ahh" as they divide along two sides to make a runway similar to a soul train line. All eyes turn to one end of the makeshift runway to the DJ's platform as five people walk up the side steps of the platform and sit behind a table next to where the DJ is spinning. They are all dressed in over-the-top costumes—some with sequined capes, feather boas, and big costume jewelry. They wave what look like church fans in the air, but they have single numbers on them—6, 9, 5, 10, 7.

Miss B. leans over to me and says, "I guess you've never been to a ball, huh? Well, tonight, Dr. EPJ, you're going to witness Miss B. decree her category!" And then she vanishes.

The DJ commentates:

show/me/show/me/show/me what/i/wanna/see

i/wanna/see/you/voguing/for/me real/cun-ty

cun-ty hun-ty

cun-ty hun-ty

cun-ty hun-ty

show/me

show/me

show/me/watcha/got

you/can/only/really/show/me/if/you/really/got/a lot

that/beast/that/ho/that/Nefertiti

that/bitch/that/serves/the/ball/community

The crowd goes up as this slender, fair-skinned woman appears at the opposite end of the DJ's booth. The DJ says: "Awwwww, shit. Representing the House of Aporcrita is the bitch that slays just by entering a room! The delectable, the divine, the face that launched a thousand tricks, Miss Insecta Animalista!" Miss Insecta begins to do pirouettes while her three-foot ponytail takes flight. Out of the pirouettes she drops to the floor on her back, one leg tucked underneath and the other straight out. "HA!" the crowd yells when she drops. The DJ commentates:

givealittethis

givealittlethat

kit ta kitkit ta kitkitkat

backtotheback

backtotheback

backtothebacktobackbackback

Miss Insecta does a low duckwalk while giving a stunning hand performance, her head cocked to the side while her ponytail drags the floor. She drops again to her back. HA! And moves into a helicopter spin with her legs. "SLAY, HO!" "WERK!" The crowd encourages.

The DJ commentates:

"MISS INSECTA ANIMALIIIIIIIIISTAAAAAA! The judges are playing poker face tonight. What say you!" Ooooooooooo, the SHADE of it all! Is there is room? Is there is room for the House of Hymenoptera to snatch the trophy from the reigning queen? It's gettin' muthafuckin' hot up in here!"

The audience begins to sway and swoon to the pounding bass and throw shade at the house mother of Aporcrita. Then all eyes turn to the top of the runway where Miss B. has appeared in a black-and-yellow striped catsuit.

The DJ commentates:

oh/wait

oh/wait

oh/wait/oh/wait/oh/who/could/it/be

it's/Miss B./lookin'/mighty/cun-ty

cun-ty hun-ty

cun-ty hun-ty

cun-ty hun-ty

I am speechless as I watch Miss B. take to the runway to perform. She begins with a dizzying hand performance while duck- and catwalking the length of the runway. She then goes into a series of spins and death drops. Pop. Dip. Spin. HA! Pop. Dip. Spin. HA! Pop. Dip. Spin. HA! She makes her way back to the top of the runway and begins to twist her body in positions like a contortionist.

The DJ commentates:

oldwayoldway cha-cha-cha

oldwayoldway cha-cha-cha

live (the old way)

work (the old way)

pose (the old way) cha-cha-cha

"Miss Thing is dancing OLD WAY, Hunty!" "Did you see her duck walk and her hand performance?" The people around me can barely contain their admiration for Miss B., who ends her performance on her stomach with her chin in her hands, her legs making a scissor motion.

The DJ commentates: "Awwwwwww, shit! Mother has schooled the children tonight! Don't sleep on the grand dames! Judges, what say you! Judge 1, Miss B. Judge 2, Miss B. Judge 3, Miss B. and it's a wrap, bitches! Miss B. from the House of Hymenoptera has snatched her tenth trophy!"

Miss B. is bum rushed by admirers as she raises her trophy into the air. I do not join them. Instead, I slink to the side of the club and observe from a distance the world I'll never be a part of.

Folks take back to the dance floor and Miss B. spies me off to the side and begins to head in my direction, beaming from ear to ear. Before she reaches me, we hear a commotion and see folks scattering. On the opposite side of the club a fight has broken out but it's hard to see who's involved. Miss B. and I run in the direction of the commotion but we can't see through the crowd. When a few people peel off, we can finally glimpse that a man is on top of a woman, who is kicking and screaming, but no one is helping her. "Beau Willie Drone," Miss B. hisses. Before I can blink, Miss B. turns her back to the scene, crutches, and lets out a blood-curdling scream.

Eeeeeeeeeeeeeeeeeeeeeeeeeeewwwwwaaaaaaaaaaaaaaaaaaaaahhhhhhhhh!

Ninu oruko Osun ni mo ba o wi!

(In the name of Osun, I rebuke you)

The walls crack. Floor rumbles. The drones cover their ears and screech. A circle forms around the two bodies—the one on the floor that lay limp and the one that has taken to the air. There is no sound. Only vibration. There is no light. Only darkness. As Beau Willie's body levitates, all eyes are on Miss B., whose two tendrils of hair are erect like ancient statues. Her back is still turned to the circle of bodies gathered around Beau Willie's flight. There, in midair, like an old washrag hung on a clothesline, his body floats. Everyone, even the drones who have now taken their hands from their bleeding ears, are stunned into stillness by the sonic intervention of Miss B.'s scream. I feel faint but manage to steady myself against the courage of the others keeping time with the vibration of breath.

Miss B. is crying and breathing heavy. I try to put my hand on her shoulder to comfort her, but she recoils from my touch. "Don't touch me," she says in a half whisper. She rises to her feet and walks under Beau Willie's *still-floating body* to attend to the young woman still lying on her back, staring up at Beau Willie hovering over her. She's most likely in shock, but snaps out of the trance when Miss B. caresses her forehead, her cheek, and cups her chin. "Hive minded," Miss B. she says, which seems to be a code for something as the drones move to the edge of the club and Miss B. helps the young woman to her feet. The other women, while still formed in a circle, turn their backs to Beau Willie. Once the attacked woman joins the circle, Miss B. begins to speak.

"Beau Willie Drone started messing with me when I was just fourteen—grabbing my breasts, my ass, and pulling out his dick. And when I went to the Queen Mother at the time, whose name I won't call, she said she couldn't do nothing because that was her son and if he was coming at me, it must have been cause I was being fast. Well, last I heard, only Queen Mothers can solicit *that* kind of attention, and she also knew that my honeypot swung the other way. Still, I had to put up with that for years. How many of you all standing around me have had it happen to you and you didn't say anything? We need to speak up. Right here, right now. And you drones up in here—even you Butches and Butch Queens—need to hear these stories, too. If you want to be an ally, you need to bear witness so that you know what we've been through. So, come on, my sisters, speak your truth. We'll hold the space for each other." The woman beside me pushes me outside the circle, as all the women join hands, their backs turned to the floating man. Then, one by one, various women begin to tell their stories.

Almah
....

The first incident that I remember was when I was five. But there was a picture of me growing up . . . I remember when I was a kid, people would talk about this picture. It was a picture of me that people liked to pull out because it would make me cry. I guess it's the idea that you push a button, the child cries for some reason. And years later when I saw that picture, I think I know why I cried, because my father is holding me in a way, and I was like one year old. And his hand is in my crotch in a way that seems like it's not just about the way you're holding the baby. And so, I'm uncomfortable looking at the picture now, so it makes me think that it started early, it started earlier than five.

And continued until when?

I would say thirteen. Because I remember being a teenager and putting on makeup. Like a preteen. The reason why five is so vivid is because I kind of went through the court system at that time. And there was a period of time I had to go to court and testify and stuff.

Oh, against him?

Yeah.

Oh, because you told?

I did tell.

Okay. That's an important part.

It is important, yes, I did tell. I did tell. And it was weird because that particular incident, which I'm in no way condoning sexual abuse, it didn't feel bad, it felt weird. It felt like, "Oh, he's asking me to do these weird things." And I remember it happening, getting out of his bed. He asked me to come to his bed on my way to see cartoons. And I went to see *Woody Woodpecker.* It was like, it was kind of strange. And so, I shared it with my mother. I'm like, "This weird thing happened." And I remember her reaction was so grim. It was so grim but no comforting of me. Like, "This is wrong." But I wasn't really clear if I had done something wrong. And so, this kind of grim machinery of telling millions of people what happened. I got so tired of it. I even told her, "I wish I had never told you," because it wasn't a big deal to me. So I lived with my aunt in response to this. So, the idea was I could never be alone with my father for a period of time. It feels like a long time, but it's hard to know how long it was. And I had to stay with my aunt.

But your mother stayed with your father?

Yeah. And for me, I think that actually is one of the most traumatic things. It's not what happened but consistently, I feel like she's chosen him. And there's been many more examples. Because it would be nice if this story ended here. But I came back and it continued to happen. And I told her. And that time, she told me to—I'll never forget this. She was washing dishes and her back was turned to me. And she said, "You should talk to your father about that." Yeah. So you know how that went over. So I went to my father. And my father grew up in a large sharecropping family where there was a lot of food to go around, but not a lot of affection. And he definitely cast himself as a victim. I'll never forget what he said. He said that he didn't have much affection and he needed it. And that's when I thought in that moment, as my mother, she was useless to me. I'm just like, "Okay, you're not on my side, I'm on my own." And so, from then on, the abuse continued and I never told anyone about it. I told her again at thirteen. And again, she betrayed me and said, "You're old enough now that you can do something about it."

I remember my father finally sat down and talked about the birds and bees. It was like, "Are you acting like I've never seen your dick before?" It was kind of crazy. Like we're going to do this performance in front of everyone? Like you're not telling me anything I don't know. Something that I haven't read or something I haven't experienced with you. And so, that was weird. It was like, you know what? Adults are just so—they're on something else. Like this fakery, you know. But my mother, I remember when my period started. I told her about it. And she came to my room, opened the door, and put a book on the bed that was very dated. And it was white women. It was so weird. And she left. And thankfully, I had already read Judy Blume and stuff like that. So, I knew what was happening. But my mother acted like, "Oh, my God, you're on your period? Oh, I can't deal with that." And so there was that. But it's hard to know what's like my southern upbringing and what's the fact that both of my parents are incest survivors themselves. And they have a lot of sexual wounding that is unhealed. But, you know, both my parents come from a certain era, like my father grew up a sharecropper's son. He started working with sticks on a farm in Tennessee. And my mother [is a] rural Kentucky farm girl. And they're products of their time.

How did you find out that they were incest survivors?

My father, I found out because he said one day that he was abused by his aunts. And he wonders how it affected him. [*Laughter.*] It's like, "Oh, wow." And that was one incident. I feel like he mentioned it at other times but I'll never forget that, because I was like, "Oh, my suffering is invisible to you? You have become a perpetrator." Because he also abused my sister, too. Even though my sister is not his biological child. And my mother, I found out because when I moved to college and started to get concerned that younger girls in my family might be abused by my father, I wrote her a letter and tried to talk to her about that. And she was like, "You know, Vaughn," it's what they called me at the time, "You know, it happened to me, too, and I got over it." Which is so not true, but I come from a family that if you go into work every day, you alright. There's a million ways to not be okay and still be kind of a functioning member of society. So, they both told me. They both told me. She told me who her perpetrator was, and he told me, too. But I don't know which aunts did it. I don't even know the aunts in question.

The woman I was standing beside who forced me out of the circle begins to sob. My thought is to try to comfort her. Remembering Miss B.'s reaction to my touch, I squash my impulse. I'm not the enemy, I think to myself. I'm not the enemy. Another woman testifies.

Diane

I was molested by a family member from nine to fifteen, so from nine to fifteen it was just day in, day out the same thing. It was like clockwork, you know, as far as this person. They would come in, do what they need to do, then leave out.

Did you tell anyone?

[*Shakes her head.*]

No?

I didn't tell anyone because it was actually my brother. I didn't tell anyone because of the fact that my sister and I were adopted into this family, so the first thing I was thinking if I would've said something they would've took us back. So, I was really trying to protect my sister, not so much myself, trying to protect my sister knowing that she need the stability that we were getting, I just didn't say anything. I didn't really say anything until about three years ago.

Oh wow. You confronted him?

No, I told my mother, his mother, our mamma. I didn't say anything to him, but I told her, and I guess for me it was, I guess I was looking for something when I told her and . . . she was like, "okay." [*She begins to weep.*] . . . Stop. [*long pause*] . . . Okay I'm back.

Take some minutes. [Long pause] Do you think you'll ever confront him?

[*Shakes her head.*]

No? So, how will you deal with that pain?

I really haven't. I think I would rather leave it where it is. I would rather leave it where it is. I just . . . it's kind of like under the carpet and that's where I want it to stay.

You don't have a relationship with him now?

We speak. We're cordial, but other than that it's not like [a] big brother and little sister relationship.

Does he have a family?

He has a daughter. He's not married, but he does have a daughter.

Do you think he's doing anything to her?

She's eighteen, nineteen years old. I don't personally think he has. I don't think so. But those were my thoughts at a point in time. Like, "I'm your sister," you know, not so much as him doing anything to her. "What if someone else was doing the same thing you're doing to me to her. How would you react?"

So, with being adopted, being sexually abused by your brother, that really clouded your experience as a child.

It did, but a lot of people think, a few people that know the story or know some of my history, ask me was that the reason why I became a lesbian. I'm like, "No." That doesn't have anything to do with it. And at the end of the day I'm at a point in my life where, to be honest, I could care less if he live or die, and at some points of time in my life, I was just like if I get in my car and run him over, would I go to jail? I mean, just being honest, I really do. Those feelings I like to keep dormant. I don't like to think about it. I don't like to bring it up.

It's like for me when I see him . . . no feelings. No nothing. It's like, "Hey bro, what's up?" I'm done. Next conversation. I don't like really to be around him. He does not like my lifestyle, period. And that's fine with me. I could care less.

Do you think your mother has had a conversation with him?

No.

Or your father?

My father doesn't know, not unless my mom has told him. I personally don't think he knows and that's the way I want to keep it.

Because you're afraid of what your father might do?

What he may do or what he may say. I'm not for sure because the reaction I got from her was "Okay," and that was it, and then I don't know per se what he would say or do, so I don't know. So, right now I just want to keep it the way it is, leave it the way it is. I don't like to talk about what happened. I don't like to relive it, and I bet that's one of the reasons why I don't go to counseling. I don't like it. I'm this tough person on the outside, you know? I'm a big girl. I don't like to feel emotions. I don't like to feel pain, I don't like to feel hurt, I don't like to feel bad, I don't like to feel anything that's not good. So, to be the person that I am now it's like I have an electrical fence, not a wall, mine's an electrical fence. You touch it, you're going to get shocked. I don't want anything in there. I don't have the energy to deal with it, I just don't. I don't have the strength, the energy. I want to leave it dead even though when I talk about it, I get emotional and I'm still hurting, but it's like I want it to be dead where it is. I just want to leave it dead. I want it to stay there and bury it all.

The testimonies seem to spring out into the darkness of the space. Only deep breaths and sobbing disturb the story and the drone hanging in the air. A vibratory vigilance passes through shoulders touching, heads bowed, elbows bent and praying to some other god beside the one who said let *his* will be done, bonds these women in unholy matrimony. They seek refuge in one another—and speak.

Felicia

....

When I started going to Huntsville in the summers I very clearly remember one time there had been this incident during the school year where I was in the choir. This little boy liked me. And I think we got caught kissing in the bushes or something and someone called my aunt, which was my dad's sister. It was like, "Dude, I think your niece was getting it on in the bushes." And I'm like, "No, we were just kissing." We may have gone there, but you know—and so I remember him asking me had I truly, officially had sex. And I told him no, but I had. And I was thinking, "Oh my God."

How old were you?

At that time I was thirteen. But I had had sex at eleven, but that's another story . . .

With a guy.

Yes. So, for me it had been two years, but I'm thinking, "Whew, well at least they only know or think that I kissed this boy in the bushes." So I remember my father asking me, "Have you had sex?" And I was thinking, "No, I haven't." And my dad knows when I'm lying because believe it or not, I'm a lot like him. And so I knew I would get in trouble. See, my dad's philosophy was you don't get in trouble for things that you do that are not stupid. But you get in trouble for doing stupid things like getting caught. If you're going to do something, at least don't get caught. So I remember him asking me and I said no. And he said, "Well I'm going to check and see." I didn't think anything. I'm thirteen years old, thinking, "Oh my god," because I'm thinking I'm going to be discovered. So to check he had to physically look around. I didn't think anything of it. Well, when I came out of the room I remember [my sister] asking me what did he do? I'm thinking, "He checked." And I'm still not thinking that nothing was wrong because I knew that she had played around with a little guy, too. So, I'm thinking maybe she's asking me because she wants to know—maybe we need to get our stories together. And I remember her being like very upset and still I didn't get it. But it took the actual occurrence for me to put two and two together and say you know what, he's doing this to her, too. And so, I had an option of not going every summer but I felt like I was protecting my sister.

Because he would never do anything to both of us together. He would have to isolate us. And so I had a bedroom. She had a bedroom. But I never slept in my own bedroom. I always slept in her bedroom. So it went on for years, and I left to go to college. I had my dream scholarship to go to Auburn.

So even through high school this was happening.

When I was going just for the summer.

But what was his excuse then? Not that he was still checking you to see if you were having sex.

No, then I knew it was wrong. Then I started to know it was wrong. And my last two years I didn't go there. I was sixteen and seventeen. I didn't go those two years because at sixteen I had gone to a program at Tuskegee University. It was a minority introduction to engineering program for up-and-coming smart people, whatever you want to call it, interested in engineering. So I went there my eleventh grade year, and my twelfth grade year I went to a similar program at Auburn. And went to college right after that. So I didn't have to go back. So it was really those three years that, you know, I would go back and be in the line of fire during that summertime.

So you never told your mother.

I told everyone. I was twenty-four years old.

What was her reaction?

She was very quiet. And my mom is the kind of person that doesn't get loud. You don't really know how she's feeling. But I know her well enough to know that if she is quiet, it really bothered her. And because this is one of the only men I've ever seen in my life that she dated. And I know she loved him. So I told her. Well, we tried to get him arrested before that. When I went off to Auburn I felt like, "Okay, I abandoned my sister" because she was now a sitting duck. I'm not there to protect her anymore. So I confided in my track coach and I said, "Hey listen, I have to ride with my father to go home. I don't want this to happen." You know there are other things happening. I had gotten pregnant and, you know, I had to confide in someone. And so—

You were pregnant by your father?

Yes.

Did he know?

Yes. And so I told my track coach and I fell out on the field. He just said, "I wish you would have told me, but I'm here now." I'll be your father basically. So he made sure I got the abortion. He made sure I was safe. He got the resident assistant involved. He put a restraining order out there. So he basically did everything a father would do for me in that situation. And then it sent off a wave of getting involvement back at home because those kids were still minors. So they had to come in and take them out, remove them from the home temporarily. My stepmother left him temporarily and he didn't try to lie. He agreed that he had problems and issues.

Oh really?

Because it came out and we found out that he had been a victim also, and not only him, but four of his other siblings as well. And so he agreed to counseling and those types of things. So by the time my sister was graduating she was able to leave, and over time my stepmother eventually came back to him, but she was gone for a while. But to make sure that I didn't have to rely on him for anything or anybody for anything at that point, I left school after my freshman year at Auburn and I went into the military. Because to me that was going to give me stability, money, a car—things that I would need so that I would not be a sitting duck or a target. And so I did that and never looked back.

Did your sisters and you talk about what had happened?

My oldest sister and I did. We talked about it as kids. We used to—before we told on him we used to write letters back and forth for years and he started intercepting our letters. And I still have those letters to this day so I would know when it happened, what had happened. So that became evidence in court. So, yeah, we talked about it. But there was the point in time where I got angry with her about it. And it was when I told her that I had decided to start dating women. And she basically said to me something of the sort, "Well, that's not right" and blah, blah, blah. I said to her, "Listen, how dare you tell me anything?" I said, "I protected you for years and shielded you from a lot of things putting myself in danger." And I said, "You know, but you never thanked me about that. You never thanked me for those choices I did not have to make. But you're trying to be upset about a decision that I made. Don't do that. You can't. There's nothing you can really say to me at this point." And I'm pretty sure she's gay. But she lives under the radar. She would never come out and say it. But she hasn't dated a man in a hundred years. And it's only been girls around, and you just don't take an Olan Mills portrait with someone that you're not sleeping with, and there's two beds but there's one unmade. So the difference in our lifestyles. But you know, even though my father was the one that did these things, there were things that I learned from him. And, again, I'm a lot like him in that I'm a fighter. I'm not going to give up. I choose to be happy and I won't let people hold things over my head.

And he's a minister?

He became a minister some years ago. He was not at the time.

Oh, okay. Have you interacted with him? Has he apologized for what he has done?

He has not apologized and that's a problem that I have. He said things to allude to an apology, but I think that I am owed an apology. I have forgiven him because it will eat me up if I don't. I mean, and I don't feel like I should behave like a book says. The book says you know if these things happen you act like that. Well, that's not my character. That's not those seeds that were implanted in me, so I'm not like that. My thing is that if I forgive you, I can move on and have a great life and I've had that. What I have learned is what I'm not going to tolerate, what I'm not going to do, and I'm not going to put myself in those situations. And I'll never *trust* him now. Forgive is one thing, but forgetting is another. If I ever have children, they would never be around him. He went to counseling, but I just don't think people who have true issues are never really healed.

I feel myself getting weak in the knees. I know that I can't listen to too many more of these stories, and I am concerned about how long Beau Willie can stay in the air like that. I find a chair and take a seat. I bend to put my elbows on my knees and bury my face in my hands. The stories continue.

Nora
....

From fourteen to fifteen, I really heavily relied on the Bible, church, spirituality. [One of my dad's] nephews raped me, and so I was really jacked up in the head. So, I held on to that and that really got me through.

Did you ever tell your father about what his nephew did?

Oh, yeah, I did.

And what was his reaction?

I was fourteen or fifteen. I remember I was at Eisenhower High School, and I would stay after school a lot because at the time we didn't live by the school. We used our old address so I could go to that school, I guess so my mom wouldn't feel so guilty for sending me off to my dad's. And so, I'd stay after school awhile to wait for the bus or for my mom to pick me up. I was always in the band hall, and I walked out to the pay phone back when there were pay phones, and I called my dad at his job, so it was an 800 number, and I told him. And he pretty much [*laughter*] didn't believe me. It was just like, "Uh, okay, I'll talk to him." And he said that he would talk to my grandmother, too, 'cause actually my mom sent me to my paternal grandmother's 'cause I had a summer program at Rice University I was accepted into, and then to my dad's in Allen. So he talked to my grandmother, 'cause that's where the stuff started. I don't know. That's why I'm guessing he talked to her.

I used to feel really "ugh" about telling people 'cause I had just turned thirteen and he was already fourteen. But he was tall, he was already, like, lifting weights and stuff, and for a while I felt like that kinda invalidated everything. But I feel like I learned very well from watching my mother that whatever a guy wants, he's gonna take it, and that's how it goes. 'Cause that's how it went with every relationship in my mom's family. But my dad called me back I don't know how much longer like that, but he said that my cousin denied it and said that it was consensual, and he said, "And I just told him just never do it again." And I was like, "But that's not true that it was consensual." And he was like, "He's like a son to me. When a kid makes a mistake, you tell him 'Hey, that it was a mistake' but you still love 'em." And I was like, "But I'm your actual child." And then a few weeks later he invited him up for a barbecue.

So you had to see him again?

Um-hm. I mean, by this time, I was back in Houston, but I would go over to my grandmother's and, yeah, I had to see him.

Did you tell your mother?

Yeah, I told her around the same time, fourteen, fifteen, yeah, I think I was probably fifteen. I was doing our laundry, had a little laundromat in the apartment complex. I was in and out. And so, what I did, when I went to go take another load, I wrote it on a piece of paper, "One of my cousins raped me." And I came back in, she was laid out on the couch, just with her eyes closed and her hand over her head, just like holding it. And she was like, "Was it Boobie?" which is her nephew, my oldest cousin. I was like, "No!" I was like, "And it's not even on your side." And then I told her who it was, and it was like I just broke my mom down even further and made her feel even more guilty for sending me up there; she felt my dad didn't protect me.

But she believed you?

Yeah. She did. And it got to the point where I was so depressed and suicidal that she finally broke down and took me to a psychologist, 'cause you know, in my family and a lot of black families, it's like psychology, they're quacks or "That's the white man's thing," you know, "We don't get therapy, we don't go to shrinks." But I mean, it got to the point where it was just so bad, like, she did take me, and that became our little weekly bonding time. It was weird.

So she went with you to the therapy?

Yeah, she went with me. I went in there alone; sometimes she would come in the session with me, but most of the time I was alone. But she'd wait and then we'd go to Exxon gas station and get a little Starbucks Frappuccino in a bottle, and that was like a treat, 'cause it was expensive, and we only got two for the two of us and drank that on the way back home. So yeah, my mom believed me.

I can't see Miss B. but I can feel her presence. Given what I just learned about her own story I know that hearing these stories for her is like pulling a scab off of a very old wound that won't quite heal. But she knows that there is healing in the telling, if only for the scab to be scraped off again.

The stories are beginning to overlap, and I want them to stop. Surely, there can't be more. Where are the stories of a loving touch? A tender touch? A healing touch? I need to intervene with a song, a prayer, a chant—anything to lift the energy in the room. But one last woman beats me to the punch with her testimony.

Michelle

As my life began to kind of transition, I began to become really rebellious and I was angry with my father because he's the one that initially fondled me and inappropriately touched me.

And you never told your mother?

No. How do you tell? I would say this started about seven or eight. So how do you say that? You don't know what to say. I didn't know. I know one time she walked in. He would always come down the hall early in the morning and he would lay in the bed with me and my sister. And he would let us touch him. Oh, I know I would touch him and then he would have an erection. Well, I'm too young to still understand really what's going on. Well, she walked in on that one morning. Later on, she said, "Well, that's how little girls get pregnant by their fathers," and this, that and the other. She said that to me.

As time went on and he'd make me come sit on his lap and he'd have his fingers all up in my stuff and I began to be rebellious. Out of that came rebellion and I was rebellious towards both of them. First off, because you violated me. Secondly, you didn't protect me. You know? Later on, in my life I used [drugs] behind the hurt and the pain that came from that for years. I used that as one of the reasons that I got high. Because what they didn't teach us coming up was how to appropriately deal with emotions and feelings. You stuff them. You can't go ahead and cry about it. Even down to spankings. If you get a whipping, well, then you need to shut up. They gonna whip you until you shut up. Well, this is crazy. How you gonna do this? What is going on? You know? They never taught us how to deal with emotions, how to grieve—they never taught us these things. Somebody die, you cry, you'll get over it. You know? It was nothing about a healing process. When I look back I think they did the best they could with what they had, you know? I don't hold it against them. So, now it's my turn to break the curses, you know?

Did you ever have a conversation with your father about his molestation?

We haven't to this day. I'm gonna tell you how good God is, because I've had to come into my own with some things as it directly relates to my years of active addiction, when I really realize it was a reason why I'm using.

Did it move beyond marijuana and alcohol?

Oh yeah, it escalated. When I got to A&T [University] I was drinking and found the connection over here in Winston [Salem] where you get the nickel bags. And it was a game for me. I became one of the biggest weed connoisseurs. I needed to have so many different kinds of weed, it begot friends. Because at that time I was dealing with self-esteem issues. You know, I'm a big girl, molestations, I didn't feel good about myself, inadequate, and I always found myself trying to live up to my dad's standards and, no matter what, it was nothing ever good enough. And then I was always called names, you know. "Water buffalo" and "tank," "tubby," all kinds of things. So, nothing that was motivational or a builder. There were always things to break you down and so, needless to say, my self-esteem was shot to hell, it really was, if I can say that. It was shot. But I have done some work on myself. And that's why I opened with I'm a molestation survivor, because he fondled me. My uncle molested me. My mother's sister's husband went and he fully molested me.

And how old were you then?

I was a teenager. And my latter years in my active addiction I would use that as a form of getting my way. That was one of my ways and means. I was already connected to him, so it was easy for me to trick. And I felt nothing for it because I hated men for doing that. I hated them. Even though it hurt me in active addiction to be with this man, that one, that man, this one, that one or the other one, and the other one and another and another one, as my ways and my means. It was nothing to me anyhow because they were nothing to me. And it was almost like a way of getting back at them. Because all that you can do to me has already been done to me. You can't hurt me.

So, in a way you were sort of using your sexuality against men.

Mmm hmm. Mmm hmm. And then at the end of that, then I get what's on the other side of it so that I could support my habit.

Oh, so you were trading sex for the drugs.

Absolutely. Absolutely. Ways and means.

Right. And because that sex didn't mean anything to you . . .

Having sex with men didn't mean absolutely nothing. My uncle took me to liquor houses and introduced me to other men and things of that nature, which, in turn, would become my sugar daddies, that kind of stuff.

And you were in college by this time?

Uh, yes, or out of college. But see, I was in college when it escalated to cocaine. And we were snorting powder then. They didn't have this rock and crack and stuff. I came up on rock, they got crack now. But I was introduced to powder.

Hmm. So what was the turning point? What was the "come to Jesus" pivotal moment for you?

That got me to the point I am now?

Mmm hmm.

I've just been in a thirteen-year relationship. Raised kids. When I got in that relationship I was thirty years old. I don't have any biological kids. I wanted kids, had boyfriends, had a fiancé. Anyway, got in a relationship with Lisa. She had two little kids and I was clean. Had been in recovery for a minute. And never been in a relationship with children. And she said to me, "How would you have this relationship if you could?" I said, "If I could have you without them, then that's how it would be." She said, "Well, okay, we're a package deal. Now you can take all of us or you take none of us." Well, she was really the first woman that I had been with. So, I thought to myself, "Self?" and myself said, "What?" "Maybe you need to try this." And I tell you. Did I try it? We went through thirteen years. All of it wasn't bad. But when you're dealing with someone with even deeper levels of brokenness than what you are, it can be challenging. And we were truly raised from two different sides and just our viewpoints were totally, totally opposite. Even down to how we raised these children. And so, it was an in-and-out relationship. A relationship full of fighting and using. When we were on, we were on. And when we were off, I tell you, we were off. I was the one that was consistent with trying to be in here and made a promise to you and da-da-da-da-da. And she was just in and out, in and out. She'd catch a whim, she'd be gone. Every three, six months. Boom. Gone. In and out. But I loved her. How sick. I didn't love her; it was codependence and it was still me in my sickness. Relapsed. We broke up one good final time. Every time that we broke up the hole was gaping. She took three people when she left. She left my heart in such an ache that I couldn't hardly make it. It would just hurt to beat. And so, I relapsed. I just said, "F it. I don't care anymore." I've taken all these years, and by this time we had been in the relationship six, seven years now. I said, "I've given all I can, and I gave so much of me, I gave all of me, that I had no me left." So, when I needed me, there was no me there to show up to hold me or to help me in any way, form, [or fashion]. I was emotionally, mentally, and spiritually bankrupt. And when you get like that you're in danger. When an addict gets like that they're in danger.

At that time . . . I call them bids. I did seven years of dealing drugs after that point. The turning moment was I was at a point I couldn't *not* use. Hunty, I couldn't *not* use, I had to have it. Thing would wake me up in the middle of the night calling me. I was a slave to the rhythm, baby. And hunty, I ran that crack, you hear what I say? I ran it. I had probably a $500 a day habit and did what I could to make sure that I kept my habit. I would drink five forties [forty-ounce beers] and if I could get liquor in between, would. If I could get wine in between them five forties, I would. But I definitely had to have five forties, at least a dime bag a week that I could lace with some of that crack. And that was every day.

On March the 7th, 2004, I was sitting in my backyard [*begins to weep*] . . . excuse me . . . it's still real. I was ready to blow my brains out. I had three options. I gave myself three options. Either I can go take another hit and I can blow my heart up, either I can go get that gun and I can blow my brains out because I'm on the cycle and I can't stop right now, or either I can try to get some help. The third one seemed so far-fetched. At that time, as I began to stand up to go and get that gun—because I needed it to end, because I couldn't end it myself—I heard this voice speaking just as clear as I'm speaking right now. And it said, "Not yet, my child, I'm not finished with you, I'm not through with you yet." And I know today that that voice was none other than the voice of God speaking to me.

It was just after tax season. I owed the dope man $1,700. He was giving me $100, $200 a day on crack. He was giving me that on credit because I told him that my income taxes is coming. And by that second week my income taxes hadn't gotten here. And he said, "Nigger, I'll kill you if you don't give me my money." Well, I'm gonna jump bad. "Nigger, don't you never threaten me. I don't give a fuck how much I owe you, don't you never come for me like that. What you got, I got." I was scared to death, shaking in my boots. Shaking in my boots, child. My money finally came in, and I called him and I met him, and when I got there to him to pay him that $1,700 he bought me a knot like that [demonstrates the size of the bag of crack cocaine]. He knew I couldn't resist. Set me right back up again. I couldn't resist. So, after that run right there, I looked like walking death. When I got out of the shower, went on to the hospital. I called Dad, I said, "I . . . I can't breathe and . . . and I need some help. Can you meet me?" That one that violated me, the one that talked bad about me, called me names, all kinds of stuff, was the one that met me. And I said, "I need some help, Dad." He said, "You want your mama to come?" I said, "No, don't bring her. I want you here. She can't take it." So, they checked me in. On March the 8th was when they got me upstairs, but it was late night. When I finally got up to the psych unit, it was March the 8th. So, my clean date is March 8, 2004. And by God's grace and mercy I'm eight years clean.

I've had to learn in this healing process that the ones that violated me were just as sick as I am. So, through this growing process I've had to learn to forgive. So now I humbly serve my father, I humbly serve my uncle every day. I still take care of my parents, and I take care of my aunt and uncle faithfully. Every week I go get their medication, their groceries, and anything they need in between. My mother and father, I live with them. When Lisa and I got married, a year and a half later it was over with. We were divorced. I was homeless. So I moved home with mom and daddy. This November will be four years, and in that four-year time period my dad has had to go on dialysis. I couldn't get a job; I don't care if they threw it in my face. What I found out in this healing process and growing process was what happened with Lisa. And it was supposed to happen because I'm on assignment and have been on assignment with my parents. God put me in that place and humbled me so that I could learn how to serve. And I needed to learn how to serve from a place of being violated. I needed to learn how to serve at home so that I could serve his people here and do it with the spirit of God.

There is a sorrowfulness in the air—a suffocating stench. The bit of light shining on the disco ball refracts the light onto the wall and floor. Every now and again, the reflection of tears on the silhouetted faces in the circle gathered around Beau Willie's *still-levitating body* play peek-a-boo to this tragic scene. I am overcome with guilt, but the guilt is too deep, too rich to will away. Absolution is not to be found here.

I get up from my chair and walk back over to the circle of women. My heart begins to pound and I can't quell my urge to cry. What begins as a steady flow of silent tears turns into a weep, and then an inconsolable wail. I collapse headfirst into the bosom of the woman who earlier withdrew from my touch. I'm heaving and snotting into her cleavage, my arms wrapped around her midsection. I feel a sting. Miss B. is standing next to me with her hand rested on my right shoulder.

"Enough," Miss B. says.

She pulls me off the woman.

"I'm so sorry. I didn't know," I say, trying to compose myself.

"You can keep your sorry. We've all had to put our big girl panties on and deal—and you have to do the same. Living is a part of the burden of life. Your gender is your burden—and mine is mine. I just ask that you don't make my load heavier. Remember what I told you in Prentiss?"

"Yes, I remember. I get it. I really do," I say, snot about to spill over to my lips.

"You do, huh? We'll see about that. Somebody give this boy a tissue," she blurts, frowning at my face in disgust. A few of the women hand me a tissue and I pull my face together.

Miss B. turns to the women in the circle.

"Now that we have shared our stories, we must now change the energy in this space," she says, pulling a cigarette from her cleavage. She walks over to the DJ's booth and grabs a lighter and walks back to the circle. She lights the cigarette, but instead of taking a puff, she begins to walk around the edge of the circle of women holding the cigarette in the air, leaving behind a trail of smoke. My sadness turns to annoyance at the thought of cigarette smoke filling the air, when I'm taken unawares by the most beautiful scent. Hints of vanilla, sandlewood, mogra, musk, and Jasmine fume the room. Miss B. chants in a low hushed tone.

> *Pa aaye yii mo ti gbogbo nkan ti o je ibi.*
> *Pada isokan ti Ile Agbon yi pelu ife, alaafia, ati idunu.*
> (Cleanse this space of all that is evil. Restore the harmony of this hive
>   with love, peace, and happiness.)

She walks around the circle with the cigarette chanting until the cigarette is almost gone. She takes a long, exaggerated tote on the square and as she exhales, Beau Willie's body descends slowly to the floor. At first, he doesn't move, and I fear the worst. Then he begins to come to, sits up, and looks around the club somewhat dazed. Very few folks are left in the space except Beau Willie, the DJ, Miss B., the bouncer, Booker T., and me. Beau Willie and Miss B. lock eyes momentarily before Beau Willie drops his head. Miss B. turns to Booker T.

"I think there's some trash you need to take out. It's been a while since we've given Osun an offering," she says, as Booker T. walks over to Beau Willie, grabs him by the collar and drags him across the floor and out the door. Miss B. then turns to me.

"You sure you alright?"

"I'm okay."

"Then come on, let's go hear about love." She takes my hand and we vanish.

Four

HONEY LOVE

For as far as the eye can see, there is color. We are standing in the middle of a vast field of wildflowers. The tangerine of African daisies, the faded denim of baby blue eyes, the yellow and lavender of forget-me-nots, and the pure red of red poppy, among others remind me of a Monet. The beauty is dizzying. Miss B. is standing with her hands on her hips, surveying the land. She seems pleased with herself. She pulls out a pair of sunglasses and puts them on. They make her look as if she has two sets of eyes.

"Where did you get those?" I ask.

"Oh, this is one of many. These are my favorite pair, though. Vintage Dolce and Gabbana," she says, trying to impress me. "Isn't it gorgeous here? I come here and spend hours on end. I thought it a befitting setting for you to hear some love stories. After the club and Beau Willie's shenanigans, I figured you needed a change of scenery!"

"You got that right."

"The women are in a clearing a little ways down. Now, I have to warn you that these sistahs are talkers—and strong willed. You ever met anybody who just always has to have the last word?"

"Uh, well. No, I don't know anyone like that."

"So, what you trying to say?" she grins. "Come on before you get yourself in trouble."

We walk for about a half hour in the field until we come to a huge clearing that is in the form of a circle. There, in the circle, are twelve tree stumps of varying heights with women sitting double-dutch on them.

Miss B. looks annoyed. "These heifers couldn't follow a direction if you handed it to them in a bucket. Now, ain't nobody told them to bring their other half. I gave them explicit instructions for just one in the couple to show up. You really in trouble now, Dr. EPJ, 'cause you ain't gonna be able to count on the one being quiet while the other one tells the story. This is going to be a hot mess. Oh well, they here now."

The couples are holding hands and looking like the cat that ate the canary, like they are holding some secret they can't wait to tell. Miss B. goes to the center of the clearing.

"Good Morning, Ladies. I wasn't expecting *all* of you, but thanks so much for coming today. This is Dr. EPJ, who I told you about. He's good people and you can trust him with your story. He's a little sensitive, so keep it light, or he will surely go into the ugly cry," she slaps her leg and starts to laugh, and the women join in. I smirk. "Seriously, he's a sweetheart. By the end of the day, you'll be asking him to perform your wedding ceremonies—once they make it legal down here. It will be very important, however, that as tempting as it might be, that only one of you tell the story of how you met. Okay, Cherry?" The woman nods, but Miss B. rolls her eyes while walking back over to me.

"She lying. She ain't going to bit more sit there and let her wife tell that story," she says to me, shaking her head. "I'm going to go visit with one of my smoking buddies while you talk to them. I'll be back a little later on. Try not to let them work your nerves too bad." I walk to the center of the clearing and have a seat with my recorder.

"Y'all have fun and don't tell too many lies! Remember I have the real dirt on all y'all," she says as she walks off digging into her yellow basket for a smoke.

Shetikka
....

[I met my partner] June 5th, 2009 [at] a women's meeting group. I don't think it was necessarily lesbian. But it was a once-a-month meeting group for women to talk about women's issues. And actually, it was funny because my friend at the time, a really good friend, kept trying to get me to come out to meet this person who was running the meeting. And I was like, "No, no, no, no." And so, I had just broken up with a girlfriend about a month ago maybe. And it was a Friday night because it happened to be the first Friday of the month when this meeting was . . . it was just me, her, my friend who invited me, and the person who was running the meeting. And the reason my friend told me to come, she was talking about my partner and she was like, "Yo she's got a booty on her." And then she was telling me about this girl. She told me how attractive she is to her. She said, "Just come out to the meeting. It will be fun to get out." Because again I'm sitting home brooding over this broken heart. I'm just not going to spend another Friday night alone watching movies over and over again so I don't have time to think about it. So I went to this meeting. And when I saw my friend, I was like, "Wow." I see she's gorgeous. But again, my friend is interested in her, so I'm just happy for my friend. I don't have any reason to be anything but just at the meeting and doing whatever the meeting is supposed to be about. So we end up having a discussion about relationships or something. I can't even remember what the conversation was. But I know at the end of the day she [her partner] did not like me. We argue that that's not the way it was. But she said she did not like me. I was just saying stupid things. I don't think they were stupid at the time. I think they were genuinely how I felt about the situation that we were discussing. I remember one of them being about if an ex gives you a call after ten should you take it? And my philosophy was if we're just sitting there watching TV and she calls then I can pick up the phone and answer it. And I think she was like, "No, that's crazy." Like that's disrespectful. I'm like, I'm not going to interrupt the conversation to answer the phone. Like if we were talking, then she's going to wait. Or I'll talk to her tomorrow. But if we're just sitting there watching TV and we're not even in the same room when she calls, yeah I can talk to her if I want. I was stupid. She was not happy with me. She was not nice to me. Well, I left the meeting and I was talking to my friend about how great looking she is, and I was like, "Man, good luck with that." Again, my friend liked her, so I wasn't trying to step into that arena. And so eventually they got on a date and it didn't go well. Well, my friend considered it a date. To her [Keturah] it wasn't a date. And she backed it up with her proof that it was not a date. But it was a date for my friend. And my friend came back [saying], "Oh, she was a bitch" and "She was horrible." And I was like, "Oh I'm so glad you went on that date and I didn't have to go through it." Because she was like, "Oh, she was picky," she was this and . . . "She didn't want to see a picture of my kid. How rude is that?" And I was saying like, "Yeah that's rude." And I knew how my friend felt about her daughter. She had graduated from high school and she was very proud and she was like, "Want to see a picture of my baby?" And Keturah was like, "No. I don't want to see no kids." And so, I was like, "Oh, I'm so glad that was you and not me." So, from that point forward she was eye candy. I'm like my friend went out on a date; it didn't go well. She don't like me either, so I'm just going to look at her for a while and enjoy my once-a-month Friday meetings just looking at her. So, that's what I did for a good year and change. We didn't ever go out on a date, I think—she invited me to her birthday in August of 2010.

So, what changed? Was it the group? The group dynamic?

She won't tell me what it is. Because I had girlfriends throughout that process. I even had girlfriends going to the meeting with me. They didn't know that this was my girlfriend at the time. But I had girlfriends going to the meetings with me. And I don't know we kind of started walking, which I don't even know how that started. But I think she initiated walking. We'd walk once a week. And then I wasn't very forthcoming with my current girlfriend, off-and-on girlfriend, and so she kind of gave me an ultimatum. And so, I'm like, "Hey we can't walk anymore" because of my current person I was with was a little jealous of her. So, I was like, "We can't walk anymore." And so, we went for a while and I think she invited me to her birthday and so we started talking again. And then we started dating. I was dating someone at the time too, and we started dating, and then she was like basically "I think I like you." And then it just started from there. I don't know what happened. Whatever it was, I was thankful. I was thankful because I had been watching her for too dang long, too long.

And how long was it before you moved in together?

I think it was a year. The first thing that clicks for me [is] the financial piece. She was someone who split things 50/50. Groceries, toiletries, it was like we're going to share this. Like, "I'm going to pay half. If we're going out to dinner, I'm going to pay half." I'm not just sitting there waiting for the check to get there and then looking like, "No, I'm not paying that." And after five minutes and the person is "Are you ready for me to take this?" And there's nothing in there, [and] you're like, "Oh I guess I'm supposed to pay." Okay. And so, I'm paying for everything. So, she was the first one who was about splitting things equal. I was like, man, I hate this about her—like you're going to treat me to the movies? Because I might have treated two weeks ago. She was like, "I've got this." Love it. That just blew my mind. And so even while we weren't living together, we started spending a lot more time in each other's place, and it was things she did for me to make me comfortable. And then there were things that she needed for me to have in my house. So we weren't traveling with bags in the car. I'm going to stay at your house but I need my certain this, this, and this. She's a very avid tea drinker. I was like she brought a tea contraption and all her stuff. Okay this is what I need at your house but it stayed at my house. It wasn't one of those things, "Oh I've got to bring this with me." So and I realized we had stuff in each other's houses. "We should just be living together." And so, we did.

And who asked whom to marry?

Oh, that's funny. So, the technical version is I did. But I have to admit that it was so off the cuff that if she probably would have took me up on it I'd be like, "Oh my God now I've got to go forward." But she asked me first. She asked me for the ring first. Like I said, [my proposal was] off the cuff. We were in Vegas, passing by a chapel. And I was like, "Hey, let's get married." But she asked me—I want to say it was a year later.

Did you say yes immediately?

Yes, and this is the funniest part about the story. She always makes me tell this part. It was the last day of school, I think, and I was trying to get her to go out. And she was like, "No, I just want to go home. Let's just go home." And the Beyoncé song "Should Have Put a Ring on It" came on. And I'm in one of my moods because I've got to go home again. We're not going to go out. It's the last day of school, so now you don't have to go to work and you're off for the summer. That's no excuse. So, she was like, "No let's just go home." So the song comes on. I'm just like, "Well, I should put a ring on?"—just being annoying. And so, when we get home and I don't remember the details of this part, but I think she wanted a cherry pie. And I can't remember if she bought it or I bought it, but there is a cherry pie in the house, and she's like, "Do you love me? Take a bite of it" and I'm just like, "No." Because I don't eat fruit pie. I don't eat cooked fruit anything. And I'm just like, "No, no." And she's been asking me for the longest time to try this pie. She's like, "It's so good," and I'm just like, "No. No, I'm not going to eat this. You are not going to make me eat this. No." And she just keeps going like, "You don't love me." I'm just going back and forth like, "Why do you equate love? Why do I have to eat this cherry pie?" "Just if you love me you'll take this one bite." Under duress, I eat this piece of cherry pie. And I mean it wasn't even big but it was still like too much for me to eat. So, I eat this piece. She was like, "Okay let me take your plate." And I'm sitting here like what's all this extra and I'm not getting it. And she's like, "Turn around." And I turn around and she's got a ring. And I was feeling like such an ass. I was sitting here feeling like an ass, [like] "You are the biggest ass. I should have put a ring on it." I'm going through all this with the cherry pie. And she's, "I wanted to see what you would be willing to do." And I'm saying like, "Oh my God, imagine if I wouldn't have ate that cherry pie." Oh, I would be crying. Nothing wrong with eating that cherry pie, that could have been just like the end of my relationship right there. All based on a piece of cherry pie. But yeah, she proposed first, and we were at home by ourselves. And I was just like I had to go to a club that night. I'll eat a whole cherry pie if you ask me to. I was like, "Yes." So that was great. That was awesome.

And when did you get married?

December 12, 2012. 12–12–12. Stone Mountain. There is a resort at Stone Mountain. She's good at surprising. I like surprises. I can never surprise her, though. So she tells me she's going to take me somewhere. I can't even remember how that came to me. But she's taking me somewhere and I'm realizing that we're going to Stone Mountain. I'm just like, "Where is she taking me?" Because we're going to eat. And we get there and it's this buffet thing they have and it's supposed to be really nice. So we get there and I'm like, "Oh, I'm excited." I'm enjoying the buffet. And I'm liking my dessert, a chocolate cake. I love chocolate. So, I'm about to really get into this. And she's like, "Stop. I need you to go to the car and get something. Get the camera like right now." I'm like, "Right now?" I was just about to put that bite [in my mouth]. "Yes, stop now!" I'm like, "Oh my God! I can't finish this? We can't go get whatever it is when we get ready to leave?" She's like, "Stop now." I'm like, "Oh God." So I'm upset, leaving to go get whatever it is she wants me to get out of the car. I was going to make myself like Charlie Brown. And I go to the car and she tells me it's in the trunk. I go to the trunk and I pop the trunk and it's cold as a matter of fact. This is December, remember. So, it's cold. And I open up the trunk and I'm looking in the trunk like, "Why are my clothes in the car?" And I'm looking around. Am I punked or something? Like what is this? What's going on? And then I get my phone in my pocket and it vibrates and it was like, "Grab the bags and come on, meet me at the elevator. Fourth floor of the elevator." I'm saying, "What the hell is going on?" So, I get the clothes and I'm like, "Oh, this is an overnight bag." It's coming together and I come up in the elevator and she's sitting at the top of whatever floor we're on. And she's like, "Okay, just follow me." And we're going down the hall and it said, "Haywood Suites." What? So, we walk in and the room is fabulous. It's got a fireplace. It's got a table—a dining room table that seats eight. It's got a little kitchenette. A living room. It's got two rooms, a bathroom, jet tubs. I was sitting here like, "Where am I? Who is watching me?" I had to pinch myself. This cannot be real. Champagne, chocolate-covered strawberries, and I'm like, "What? This is amazing."

So, I have to be a kid because I am a kid at heart, and so I'm running to both rooms, jumping on the bed, like this is just the greatest thing in the world. She's like, "We're gonna stay here." So I'm excited. She said, "Yeah we've got a late checkout." I'm like, "Okay, great." So I'm enjoying it. I'm not going to work the next day so I'm just like, "Hey, let's just leisurely get up. We've got a late checkout." I'm strolling and she's kind of rushing me. And I'm getting agitated because she's like "Hurry." I'm like, "Wait a minute. They ain't closed nothing up." So we got massages. So, I'm having massages and I'm relaxed and we have them together. And it's all just like this is awesome. And then she tells me, "Go put on your clothes. It's Stone Mountain we're going somewhere." I'm like, "I can't put on my sweats? Why do I have to put on clothes?" And she's like, "Yeah you have to put clothes on." And then she tells me we're going to have a private ceremony on top of Stone Mountain. So I think she does tell me that. It's just going to be me and her. We're just going to go up there. She makes me write my vows. And I'm like okay. But I'm like, "Really? I've got to get dressed for that? It's just me and you on top of Stone Mountain. We can't wear sweats?" So I'm getting done and I think the next thing I hear one of my favorite songs, "At Last," and I'm like, "Why is that playing?" And so we come out. Cameras everywhere. It's decorated in the living room. Her sister is there with her niece. My sister is there with my niece and nephew. I'm all about to cry. It was beautiful, it was amazing. So, we had our ceremony there. And it was just like people I love was there.

I know for her one of the things is her parents possibly saying no to coming or being there. I'm okay with my mom not being there. If my dad doesn't come I'm still going to be okay. But I already know my mom is not going to be there. So for me those weren't important pieces. I wanted a big wedding. She kind of shied away from that. So for them to have to be there for that commitment ceremony for us was like—I was like at the end of the day this is all. And it was funny because she asked me to marry her first but I actually asked her mom before I gave her my ring and her mom was like, "It's not a relationship—it's not something for us. It's for you and her and the spirit." So it was kind of one of those like blessings and it was like at the end of the day you're right. It's just between me and her and what we have committed to each other. So she's good. It's awesome. I love her. I'm over happy. I'm ecstatic.

Tommye

Actually, I met Phyllis here in my house. On the very first time that *Essence* had a party . . . the *Essence* Music Festival. I have so many friends all over this country. I had friends calling me from New York saying that they were coming, friends calling me from Chicago saying that they were coming, LA, they were coming, Detroit, they were coming. They all had hotel rooms. But all I knew is that I couldn't see them all in a three-day period. That was impossible. So I decided what I was gonna do was to have a party. So I had a little pool party and invited them all here. They, of course, came to town with friends of theirs. Okay? So, of course, when you invite friends, then their friends, so I ended up having, I guess, maybe about seventy women here inside and out. I have a little pool out back, and I'm the hostess, so I'm busy, busy, busy. And there was this woman who came up to me and tried to have a conversation and it was Phyllis. And she says, "Hey, my name's Phyllis, I'm from Atlanta." And I just said, "Hey, how are you? You must excuse me now." And that was it. I didn't have a lover or anybody, I was by myself but, still, I was the hostess and I gave this party by myself, which grew a lot bigger than I thought it was gonna be. So this was on a Saturday night and, at any rate, finally, as the night wore on, I never got to talk to this woman. I was going out the back door, and I had something in my hand. I don't know what it was. I think it was a tray of food. But this hand just grabbed my arm and I looked down at this little woman and she said, "Look, I'm tired of following you around all evening like a puppy dog. If you want to talk to me, I'm in the pool." That was my first time seeing her, and I saw her, and I said, "Oh, okay," totally unaware that she had been following me around and stuff like this. Anyway, forty-five minutes later I finally got a break and I saw her in the pool and I got into the pool and I said,

"Hey." And she says, "Hey." And I said, "What did you say your name was?" And she said, "Phyllis." And she says, "Well, gotta go."

And she was gone because her friends were ready to leave, you know? They had already been there about three hours. And by the time I got out of the pool and then somebody else called me and by the time I looked around she was gone and that was it. And the next day, which was a Sunday, I said to myself, "Did I miss my blessing?" And so I got on the phone, calling all my friends to find out who is this girl and who is she with? "Who is she staying with? Who is this woman?" And finally I called Kim, and Kim said, "Oh, that's Phyllis. They're staying at the Hyatt." And I immediately called and I said, "What's her last name?" and she didn't know. So I just called the Hyatt and I said, "I'm looking for Phyllis um . . . [snapping fingers] . . . can't remember her name," blah-blah-blah, and the girl at that time, she said, "Johnson?" I said, "Yes, Phyllis Johnson." And when I called, Phyllis answered the phone. And the thing about it is I heard this, "Hello?" And I said, "Hello, may I speak with Phyllis?" "This is she." And I said, "Well, Phyllis, this is Tommye," and I heard this [gasps] and I said, "Whew." I heard her go like [gasps], I took her breath away, and I remember smiling to myself. And I said, "Well, I'm very sorry for my rude behavior," da-da-da-da-da. "I was wondering if I can take you out to lunch" or something like this. And she says, "Well, actually, I'm leaving today and I'm on my way to the airport." And I said, "Well, look, can I come and take you to the airport?" And she says, "Actually, the car is downstairs, we're about to leave." I said, "Okay." She says, "Well, give me your number and I'll call you when I get back to Atlanta." And I gave her my number and she left and that was it. About eight that night the phone rang and it was her. And then we talked for about three hours and then the next night we talked and continued to talk. And then we talked about every other day for maybe about three weeks and then finally I invited her to New Orleans and she flew in and we had a wonderful time and she left. And so, three weeks after that encounter in the pool, we finally meet the first time.

This is 1996. And then I go there and she comes here. I go there and six weeks later she moved. And she had her own barbershop and salon right across from Morehouse College in Atlanta for years. And she closed up her business and she moved. And that was almost nineteen years ago.

Lindsay

[My partner] is an engineering major and I am a chemistry pre-med major so we don't really have classes together, but I happen to be friends with a girl who was in the anime club at the time. And she dragged me to this anime club meeting . . .

So I went to the meeting and I happened to run into a dude who was in a class with me. So I sit there and we're talking for a minute and of course all of his friends come over and, somehow, we ended up in a very warm-natured debate between him and all of his friends and me. And I'm meeting all these people, when along walks this girl who's apparently friends with him. And she comes up behind me and I know now, I couldn't hear it at the time, "Hi," to which I responded for about five minutes, at which point she then said, "Okay bye" and walked away. So, I blew that, but over the course of several months following that we became friends and she was dating someone else at the time. She actually started dating someone else shortly after this first interaction, so I just really blew it. But she was dating someone else at the time, and I had to get to know her more on just a friendship level first, which I appreciate now, best friends forever. But we didn't start dating until the spring semester. This happened the fall semester my freshman year and we didn't start dating until the spring semester . . . because I was at home over Christmas and she had recently broken up. And I called up my friend from high school and I was like, "So there's this girl," and she stops me and she goes, "Okay pause. Is this one straight this time?" And I said, "No," and she goes, "Okay continue." And I said, "So there's this girl and she's really pretty and I like her a lot," and she goes, "Okay pause. Does she like you?" And I said, "I don't know. Stop asking me questions so I can tell my story."

It was right after Christmas, right before New Year's, and my grandmother always said that Christmas wishes mean absolutely nothing. It's the New Year's wishes that mean something. When you make a wish at midnight on New Year's that that's the most powerful of all because you're starting a new year, you're starting a new time, and if you actually work toward that wish, you put in some effort, then it's more likely to come true because it's turning over a new leaf. . . . So, I, of course, then made a wish at midnight on New Year's that I would get to know her better and that we could have some kind of relationship, and lo and behold six hours later, at 6 a.m., she decides to text me about whether or not I watched the Twilight Zone marathon. And we had never actually contacted each other through texting or phones or anything because we had each other's numbers but hadn't actually talked on the phone. So, I'm like, "Yes, I always watch the Twilight Zone marathon on New Year's," and we just started talking. We started talking nonstop for two days until we got back to school, and it wasn't until a week after we got back to school I was like, "So, what are you doing on Saturday?" And I took her out. I didn't have any money. I was a very broke college student and I wasn't getting a full ride at the time . . . so I decided what's the most romantic thing you can do on a budget. Let's have a picnic and go bowling at the campus bowling alley. So, I was running late because I do laundry to have something to wear. So, I'm running to Walgreens trying to find bread and peanut butter to make sandwiches. I'm running really super late, so I decided to buy some ready-made sandwiches just in case, so I had Coke, some Oreos, bread, peanut butter, jelly, all the stuff I needed, and I couldn't find a picnic basket. So I made do. I ended up having to make sandwiches because she was also running late and texted me. She was like, "Could you come at 2:30 instead of 2?" So I was like, "Yeah okay, that works out great for me." So I made sandwiches and shoved it all in Tupperware in a plastic bag, and we get down to the bowling alley and it's closed because for some reason the bowling alley wouldn't be open on weekends. So I, of course, smacked myself over the head repeatedly and decide to just go ahead with the picnic, and we ended up sitting there for six hours just talking. And bear it mind it does not take long to eat peanut butter and jelly sandwiches and some Oreos. We were sitting there down by where all the picnic benches are on campus for six hours just talking and we only stopped because I made myself say that I was going to get her back to her dorm by a certain time because it was a first date. And I was going to be respectful because both of my parents instilled in me very, very chivalrous tendencies, especially when they found out I liked girls. So both my parents gave me all these rules to live by. . . . And seeing as I asked her out, I was going to take the lead on the date. And so I was determined to get her back to her dorm at a certain time, and . . . walked her back and we just started talking and dating. It was actually interesting because we ended up having sex before our second date but not after the first date because that would be improper. We just, it's been snowballing ever since and it's awesome.

Sharita

I met my partner on Myspace. She sent me a message, saying, "Hey I was browsing profiles and I see that you're here and you seem like a really nice person." And I thought, "Oh okay." So, we talked for a while. And we talked over there, and so she sent me a message, and she was living with her ex-girlfriend. She said they were no longer together but they were still living in the same apartment because they had been together for like five years. And so they were still living in the same apartment . . . but the computer was in the room that her ex-girlfriend was using, and so she was like, "Here's my number. Text me." I said, "Okay." And so we started texting or whatever. And one day I was leaving class and it was before I had to go to work, I said, "What you doing?" She said, "Nothing. I'm at home, lying down on the couch watching the rain" because she didn't go to work because she was sick that day. So I said, "Well do you want to meet me?" And so, she's like, "Yeah I'll come and meet you."

This was going to be your first meeting?

Yeah. So, we can do it anywhere. In a public place in this case. So we picked a parking lot—a church with a big, open parking lot. I said, "Okay you can meet me there." She said, "Well, okay." So she got up, got dressed or whatever. And she was getting off the interstate and it so happened that I was coming up the road that she was turning on. "Are you in this black car?" She was like, "Yeah." I said, "Well, I'm behind you." I said, "I can see you." She said, "Oh no, oh no, oh no. Oh my gosh, I can't do this, I can't do this. I can't do this. No, no, no, not right now." I said, "Well, I can see you now already so it's not a big deal." We're just meeting as friends. It's not a dating thing; we're just looking for friends. We wasn't looking to date. Because she just got out of a relationship. I just got out of a relationship and I was trying to build this world of my own so I wasn't looking for dates. I said, "Oh, okay, well I already see you." "You're right down the street, just keep going and I'm already behind you." "No, what if you're like a killer?" "I'm not a killer or anything. Just come on." I said, "If I was a killer I wouldn't have told you I'm following you." So we got there. I got out of my car. I got in her car and we sat there and talked. And despite us not looking for anything there was already this connection between us. That's what I wanted. Talking and stuff, and I guess she pointed out to me that I was growing facial hair the first time we ever met, and so she leaned over in my personal space with her tweezers to pluck my hair. I was like, "Girl, get off of me." And she was like, "No. You've got facial hair." And she felt obligated to pluck it. And as she's plucking my facial hair her face was in my face and we already had a common attraction, giggly and all, like two people do—two little kids and when they meet and they like each other, and her face was in my face and she kissed me. I said, "Oh we kissed." And so, we kissed. I said, "Oh my goodness."

And how long ago was this?

Six years ago. We kissed and we kissed again and it was like, "Oh I've got to go to work." And she was like, "Oh, okay." I said, "Okay, I've got to go to work" and she was like, "Oh, we've got to leave and I don't really want to but I've got to go." So I eventually get out of the car and leave. I called her on the phone, and for her that was like a desperate plea or something. She made a call. And I'm like, "No, I just wanted to talk to you while I was on my way to work." She was like, "Oh well," so we talked or whatever. She disclosed this later on. She was like, "I didn't know what to think. You just called me again. I'm like definitely making sure you get where you were going and I was going to get to work." And I was like, "Well what are you doing later?" And she was like, "Nothing." I said, "Well, Destiny [her daughter] go to bed about seven o'clock, eight o'clock. I think about eight o'clock. Destiny got to bed at eight o'clock; you can come over. Come over about then."

So she knew you had a child.

She knew. We were friends. And, well, the friendship lasted like two days.
Yeah the friendship lasted about two days. And so she came over and we talked. We talked in her car until about two, three in the morning. We talked; we kissed. I believe that might have been it, maybe not so much, . . . so she left. I think her roommate called. Her roommate called, "Where you at?" She's like, "Oh I'm out studying or something." "Studying? If that's just your roommate why you got to lie?" "Well, we've been together five years, and I don't want her to feel like I just moved on like she didn't matter." So she's like, "I was studying" or whatever. I'm like, "Okay." The next day she came back. She came over the next day with her best friend. And she was like, "Oh I want you to meet her and da-da-da-da." And I'm like, "Who is this?" And she's like, "Oh that's my best friend. I just wanted her to meet you; you're so cool da-da-da-da." She obviously was feeling me, right? She wanted to get somebody else's point of view on this person that I'm talking to. So, we all sat over there and

talked and stuff. And from that moment on it was like every minute she got extra she was in my apartment. And in the morning time she'd go to the gym. She'd say, "I'm going to the gym." She would leave home early, five o'clock in the morning. Tell her roommate, "Well I'm just going to go to the gym." And she would come to my apartment. And it rapidly grew into a relationship. About a month later we were like together and she was at my house or I'm at her house. She'd met my daughter. She had two nieces and that's how the kids met. She had two nieces—three that she would have all the time. And I thought, "Well, okay we can meet downtown," and so we all met downtown. We all played around and stuff and so that's how my daughter met her. And she always had nieces that were my daughter's age. And so one of her nieces and my daughter are exactly the same age, so they always hit it off, and so that all kind of went well. Probably about two months in we were living together in her apartment because it was like either one person lived in that or the other person lived in another apartment. I'm like, "Hey look, I'm cheap. Why are we paying all this in rent?" And after that first week or two were over, I started going to her apartment because my apartment where I lived they had raccoons. She is scared to death. She said, "Oh my gosh, these raccoons out here. I can't get out of the car." "The raccoons aren't bothering you."

This is in Little Rock?

Mm hmm. She said, "No I can't do this. No." So, we ended up going over there once my daughter had met her and we all kind of hit it off. We would go over there and spend the night or the day. Spend the night and the day, days and weeks. I'm driving my daughter to school from her apartment and stuff. And then I'm like, look, you're paying this much rent and I'm paying this much rent. If we're sure that this is what we want, we can just go ahead and move together and we can save that extra money that we're spending on an apartment that's not going anywhere. I'm relationship oriented. She's more of an "Uhhhh, not so much." I don't know; she's more leery of things. I'm like, if I'm going to commit myself, I'm going to commit all that I have to the best of my ability. I'm not perfect or whatever, but I'm going to give it all.

And so we ended up moving together. Before we moved in together she had an extra key. Her ex-girlfriend had moved out by this time, obviously. Because there were times when she hadn't set her down and told her she was dating someone else. And so she was like, "I don't want her to find out by seeing us together." I think one time we were out and ran into one of her ex-girlfriend's cousins who called and told her that. And she's like, "Nah that's just my friend da-da-da." But by that time they had sat down and had the conversation that I am dating somebody else and we are pretty serious. And so they was like, "Well, it's probably best that I move out." And so the ex-girlfriend moved out. And I was over there at some point and I helped. I'm like, I don't have any hard feelings against her. It's just a relationship that ended. But I'm not going to treat her any kind of way because she was dating my ex. We all have a past. And I'm not a jealous type person. So, after she moved out I had had a key. I would go to her job for lunch. And I had lunch before she had lunch. I had a split shift so I would be already off and she would meet me for lunch. And she would want me to sit outside. "I'm not sitting outside the job every day waiting for you to get out for lunch. I need a key." So she gave me a key. She says that I got the key and never gave it back. But she never really asked for the key back. And so, after that incident of the key situation, she gave me the key; I didn't take the key. We moved in together and then so it kind of went from there. We've been together—I mean it hasn't been perfect, but we have been together for these six years.

And so you got married.

We got married. September the 24th was our anniversary of us dating and I was looking for an anniversary gift. And me and Destiny went to the store for an anniversary gift. "What do you think about I want to marry Shayla?" She didn't really care. And so I said, "Okay." We were out looking for an anniversary gift. It wasn't planned. I said, "Oh let me just go in here and look at rings." So I went in there and looked at rings and stuff. And it hit me this is what I should do. I bought her an engagement ring and took it to our anniversary dinner. We were talking about Build-A-Bears. Destiny has a Build-A-Bear. She goes, "I've never had a Build-A-Bear." It's a store and you can go in there and you build your own bear. You pick out the bear you want. You watch them stuff it. She stick a little heart in there. You build your own bear; you direct it however you want and stuff like that. And I'm like, "What? You never had a Build-A-Bear?" So, in my mind, "Perfect. This all comes together." So, we, Destiny and I, got the ring. I said, "I need a Build-A-Bear." So, we went to Build-A-Bear. I picked out the bear. I thought it was perfect, cute, something she would like. And I let them stuff it, but in it I put a personalized message in it. Because how you push the button and it talks. I picked a personalized message. And so I said a personal little thing. And I said, "Well happy anniversary. Will you marry me?" And then I had them put that in the little bear hand and they filled it up and I dressed the bear in a wedding outfit. And so for our anniversary we went out to dinner and she seen this box. She was like, "Oh, what's that, what's that?" and I'm like, "Nothing, nothing, nothing." She said, "I see that box." And I said, "Yeah it's nothing." So we ate, and I gave her the Build-A-Bear. In her mind she probably expected perfume or something. Oh, I got some perfume. No. I got her a Build-A-Bear, and it talks, too. You push the button; see what it says. She's like, "Oh that's so cute." She stopped and looked. "The bear just asked me to marry it." I said, "Oh yeah." I said, "Do it again; let me hear." So as she did it again, I pulled out the ring and said, "Would you marry me?" She's like, "Oh yeah." So, we got all that stuff started and we had our ceremony in DC.

Pat Hussain

It was in Huntsville, Alabama. It was '85 . . . '84. I was being transferred to take over a new store, Toys"R"Us, and I asked why. I had been engaging in a series of meaningful overnight relationships [laughter] and had included in that a number of women who were married. I wonder if it was deliberate? I didn't want someone for myself. I wanted someone for now. I just want to borrow someone nice. "She's a nice woman. I really like her. Thank you. Until next time." And I had had some brushes . . . with men who object to that type thing. I asked the legal people. I said, "Why are you going to send a dyke to Huntsville?" I said, "It's a smaller town. It's a toy store, for God's sake. This could be a real problem." They said, "There won't be a problem." I said, "Well, if you say so, but I don't know." Atlanta's a pretty big place. Huntsville, not so much. They said I'd be fine. I said, "Okay, alright. Y'all got me, right?" Okay. So, I went, wallet in my back pocket, and the suits were there for the tour and the managers getting to meet them and we're in the front of the store and they're introducing me around there. Cherry breaks through them and walks up, shakes my hands, and says, "Hi. My name is Cherry, you're going to love me." They said, "Oh that's Cherry; don't mind her. She's one of the employees here. You'll get to meet her and now this is so-and-so." And I thought, "Wait until you find out I'm a dyke. You just wait."

So it escaped them what just happened?

Yes . . . I'm presuming that she's just talking off the top of her head. And I thought, "Yeah, I'm going to love you, really? Do you know I'm a dyke? I'm a lesbionic?" And I thought, "Wait until she finds out. If she doesn't know already, when she finds out she'll say, 'Oh my God did I say that to her?'" Yeah, but I was just tickled. I thought, "Okay, you got it." And that's the first thing she ever said to me, "My name is Cherry and you're going to love me." And I got in and tried to get settled. "We're moving right into my blackout season, the holidays. Don't talk to me. Don't call me unless someone's died." Now it's time to make money. Now it's time to make that bottom line beautifully black, like a laser on there and work we did. And coming out of that I realized that I had a girlfriend in Atlanta.

Cherry [interjecting to warn Pat]: Don't say her name.

Alright. I liked to go out with straight women or presumably straight women. A friend of mine and I would go out, a guy, a straight guy. He's really disgusting. He was really disgusting. My buddy, he would go out and meet women and tell them, "Yeah I'm gay and I've tried to change and if I could ever meet the right woman, someone who was woman enough to . . ." He got laid so much with that horrible line. I told you he was disgusting. Anyway, we would go out and we went to a bar. See a beautiful woman sitting there, walk in the room, and he'd say, "Alright, I'm going first." I'd say, "Go ahead. Go talk to her and get her phone number or something." [He was] shut down. He comes back and I said, "Alright, let me show you how it's done." And what he didn't know is that I would go over and introduce myself, "My name is Pat. The gentleman that just came over and I are together and we had a bet to see who could get your phone number, get to sit down and talk to you, and I want you to know that I'm very, very much interested in getting to know you. You're a beautiful woman." I said, "If you say no, you're not interested, I'll still have my fantasies, even though I hope you don't. But I would like for you to assist me in ruining his evening. If you could just give me a big ole hug or a kiss on the cheek or something, it would just be perfect." Woo! I got kisses. I got full body hugs. I got phone numbers. I'd go back over to him. I said, "Thank you very much, and I will call you." "What did you say?" I said, "No, just watch and learn." So I was a little predatory. So you might say when I got here I had a girlfriend, and once we got through the holiday season she was asking me out. "Let's go out and have a drink." I thought she was married. Not only married but children. I said [to myself], "You're in Huntsville, girl, and she's working for you. Slow your roll. Put a big fence around this. No." I liked it. She was bothering me at work. She was so nice. She packed up my Christmas presents for my girlfriend and sent them off on UPS because I had done apparently really badly and she had to do them so they could go. She would bring me fruit and little Hershey's chocolate kisses, and she's a hugger. She always wanted me to hug her. And one day she said, I think we were at the break room, and she said, "You hug other people. Why won't you hug me?" I said, "I just really don't want [to]." She said, "But I saw you hug so-and-so and so-and-so and so-and-so." I said, "okay" and I hugged her. I gave her a giant hug, a meaty shoulder. The room got quiet. [*Laughter.*] She got quiet. I hugged her alright. Mm-hmm. Yeah. Then she said I kept putting her off, but I was going out. "Where are the gay bars?" "You mean the gay bar?" The people that worked for me were saying, "Are you going to park your car in front of the bar?" I said, "I'm going in it. Yes. Yes, I am." None of the women there transferred out. I was going home for Easter. I go home to see my girlfriend every chance I got. She was a straight woman, escorting her. My brother-in-law thought that was hilarious. And she gave me an ultimatum. She said, "This is the last time I'm going to ask you out. You go or you don't, but this is the last time. I'm not going to ask you anymore." And I thought well, this is the mouse that roared. She said, "I can come to your place. I can cook breakfast for you." I said, "Oh, you got it. You got it." As soon as I get back from Atlanta, I think it was going to be on a Wednesday, I think, and I said, "You got it, you got it. Not a problem." I said, "But you have a week to change your mind." No. She said, "Oh yeah, I'm going to set up the time." Okay, you got it. I went to Atlanta and saw my brother-in-law. My brother-in-law and I used to go out. My sister stopped us from going out together. He said I always introduced him to too many women. "Too many women, nope. That's over. I can't run." I said, "There's this sweet little thing up in Huntsville and I've been stepping around her but she married and got two children. I'm not trying to get myself in any trouble in Huntsville, but she gave me an ultimatum, and when I go back, the predator will be on the loose. I can't wait." He said, "Okay." I told my girlfriend who would not come visit me. It was a one-way street. I told her, "I'll get you a plane ticket. I'll get you a bus ticket." She didn't like to drive; I knew that. It was one way. And she said to me, "Well can't you just be an adult? Be an adult and be by yourself." I said, "No, I'm not going to do that. I'm going to start going out." So, she said, "You going to be having sex with other people?" I said, "If the opportunity presents itself. Yes, I'm tired of being by myself. If you want to stay in Atlanta, stay in Atlanta. I'm not a 'hear about it' kind of girl. I will tell you."

So I came back. I was looking forward to it, and I was exhausted from the trip, went to sleep. The phone rang. She said, "Oh did you change your mind?," and I said no. And I had just slept too late, sleeping like the dead. I said, "Give me just a minute" because I had to get up and get myself collected, and I did. I let her in. She brought in the food she was going to make. She was going to cook. When she came in I said, "Hey, how you doing?" Went around me, put all the stuff down in the kitchen. I said, "Don't I get a hug?" Nope. I thought, well, and she then was so skittish like the cat in the room full of rocking chairs, and I thought, well. And she cooked a delightful breakfast of omelets. We ate and it was just wonderful and I had to go to a meeting. I said, "I'll go to the meeting and I'll meet you back here." She needed to go work. I said, "Do I get a hug before I go?" And she kind of gave me a hug but she just kind of shot out the door. I thought, "Shit, okay." I went to the meeting and got back to the apartment and I was late. I got back there.

Cherry [interrupting again]: A friend had to call me at work.

I called a friend of hers that I knew that worked with her. I said, "Would you please call Cherry?" because she had two jobs. "Will you please call Cherry and tell her I'm running late but I'm coming." She said okay and she did because I didn't want her to leave thinking "Ha ha got you to come back." And we went into the apartment, but she was so jumpy in there I thought, "Well maybe, let's go out." We went to the park and we laid on the grass in the park and I was just rubbing my head on her and we had talked and talked and talked and then she kissed me. [*Whispering*] Oh, and it was on. It was on. That's how it began.

The women all walk off in different directions, holding hands and giggling. I remain in the center of the clearing and lie on my back and take in the Carolina blue sky and scent of lilac tickling my nose. The love stories form concentric circles around the stillness of the clearing. Daydreams of Stephen descend around my feet and work their way up to my lips. I miss him. We haven't spoken since I've been on this trip. I know he's worried. Probably has the police looking for me.

"I sent word to him. He knows you're alright," Miss B. blurts, pulling a drag on her fag. "You worry too much. We only have a few more folks to talk to. You'll be back in your sweetie's arms in no time." She starts to throw the cigarette on the ground, looks at me, and then walks over to one of the tree stumps, puts the butt out, picks it up and drops it in her purse. "What? I was not going to litter!"

I shake my head.

"I'm going to take you back to the interior of the hive to the public square. There's a forum tonight on art and politics. Some of our most famous artists and activists are going to be in conversation. I've arranged for you to moderate."

"Will some of the women who performed at the club be there?" I ask, excited about the possibility of meeting some of them since I didn't get a chance to at the club because of the fight.

"Unfortunately, no. But you'll meet some other very talented folk. And this time, you don't need to hold my hand to be transported. You can get there on your own. Just close your eyes and imagine the square as you remember it when I first took you there."

I close my eyes and do as she instructs. I open my eyes and I'm standing in the public square, but I don't see Miss B.

"I'm here. You just can't see me. Don't worry. I'll catch up with you later," a voice says in my ear.

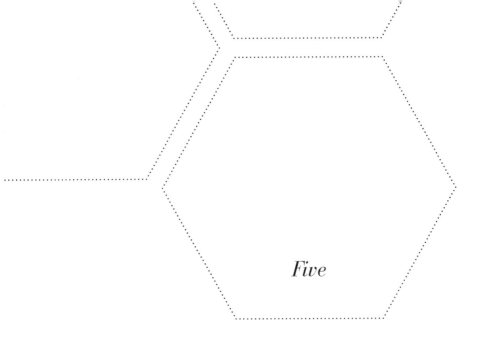

Five

BEEBOP
AND BEESWAX

Just as before, there is lots of activity in the square: children, old women, and a few drones milling about. To the right of the square is a building that looks very official—like a courthouse. There is a long queue wrapped around the building. This must be where the forum is taking place. I join the line. It's a very eclectic group of folks waiting to get in. A gaggle of young girls with purple hair, body piercings, and tattoos are speaking to each other in some foreign slang I've never heard before. They don't look like they bathe—on purpose. There are some older women in front of the girls, who clearly disapprove of the girls' "sartorial performance," as Miss B. would say. They are dressed much more conservatively—like they are headed to church rather than a forum. One of them is even wearing a hat, the brim beaded with flowers. She has to cock her head back and tilt it to the side to see her friends from underneath.

The line moves pretty quickly and we're all inside in about fifteen minutes. The room is an auditorium with thrust seating in the form of a hexagon. Down in the pit is a long table where six women are seated—three on either side of an empty chair, the one for me as moderator, I presume. Miss B. said she would meet me and introduce the panel, but she is nowhere to be found. Before I start to worry, in walks Miss B.

"What did I miss?" she says, walking past me reeking of pot and descending the stairs toward the table where the women are seated.

"Are you high?" I whisper, following her down the stairs.

"Boy, what I tell you about staying out of grown folks' business? I need a little something to help with my arthritis," she says between her teeth, walking up to the podium and pointing me to the chair in the center of the women. I greet each of the women and take a seat, and Miss B. gives a welcome.

"Good evening and welcome to our annual art and activism forum. As in years past, we have invited three artists and three activists to have a dialogue about art and politics in Hymen. We'll hear, in turn, from an artist, and then an activist. I know that in our advertising we announced that Alicia Garza would be here, but unfortunately, due to yet another incident of brutality by the ashies, excuse me, I mean the police, she had to cancel and is headed to Ferguson, MO. We hope to get Patrice Cullors next time. Moderating our panel this year is a very special guest from Chicago. He is an authority on all things artistic *and* political. Reverend Dr. EPJ. There will be a reception immediately following the forum in the propolis lounge." Although she's high, it's the clearest I've heard Miss B. speak.

"Shonda"

You started writing early on . . . well, you started reading early on. Talk about how you developed as an artist and how being a southerner and being lesbian influenced your work.

Hmm. I think probably listening to the music of the language was a big influence. Listening to the way people talked in the church, the singing and the . . . it was very theatrical, actually. You know, the ladies shouting, their hats falling off, kicking over the benches, and the minister shouting, and he had these verbal tics that felt like they were designed to wake me up, when I'd fall into a particularly deep daydreaming. So, the music of the South, the food of the South, I think all those things influenced my writing. And also the ways in which people make community and make family, all these different kinds of families, I think. I wanted to capture that, I wanted to catch that because all the people that I grew up with, they died very . . . I lost a lot of people early on and I wanted to catch that because I felt like . . . I hadn't read it and I hadn't really seen much of it. And I thought, okay, well, here's your opportunity . . . to catch that and show some love to the people that really gave you the kind of love that made you think that everybody must have love like this, that this is the way the world is.

And what about lesbianism?

Um . . . how has that affected my work? I think that I tend to write a lot . . . write about sexuality in my work in a very organic way. It's a part of life. It's not the biggest part of my life, but it is a part of my life. And that's the way it's been for me. For some people, it's like that is their identity. When you meet them, you see them, they talk about it, they live it, they love it, it's a beautiful thing. And for me, it's one part of my life. And so I think my desire in writing and kind of in the way that I write is to put all those kinds of ways of living and being and loving and all those ways that one can have family, I try to put that in my work, too. So, that's been the effect of that.

And what genre are you most comfortable with in your writing? Is it play-writing? Is it fiction?

You know, I'm really interested in challenges, and the last thing that I wrote was a noir for a . . . because I lived on Staten Island I was asked to write a noir piece. I'd never done one before, so I was like, "I'll try it." And so, for me, I like the challenge of different forms. And I am equally ready and willing to tackle something new and different, but I'm a storyteller. And at the end of the day I tell stories. And so I'm most comfortable telling stories.

When I'm working on a novel, I'm a novelist. When I'm working on a screenplay, I'm a screenwriter. When I'm working on poetry, I'm a poet. And I incorporate all of the elements, all of the genres. When I'm working on anything, all that comes into play in a way. All that information, all those ways of being. You know, a little bit of noir might find its way into my next novel. Music is always there. The visuals . . . the screenwriting, the elements that one uses in screenwriting, so that you can see something, I try to incorporate all the senses in my work, too. And so it's all there in everything I put my hand to.

Iris

Talk to me a little bit about ZAMI. How did you get involved with it?

I had visited New York and many places. And had met a number of other lesbians. So by that time, I was probably first identifying myself as such. I was not closeted, but I also was not out. I made sure the people who mattered knew. So that included my mother, my father, who I'd gotten back in touch with. I never told him, but he just sort of knew. So by the early '80s I was doing certain things. I hadn't really so much joined a group as it was I would go to certain events where I could meet other people. I met a few lesbians. Not a great number of them. So, I guess towards the late eighties, mid-eighties, there was a group called Sisters, I believe it was. But they didn't identify as lesbian. They made a point of not identifying as lesbian. They were identified as women loving women, much like the subtitle of your book. So we did some interesting things, mostly social kinds of activities, that kind of thing. And I met a couple friends in that group. It still wasn't really doing what I wanted it to do. It wasn't really saying what I wanted to say. So one of the books that I read in the mid-eighties was *Zami*, by Audre Lorde, what she called her biomythography. And it touched something in me so deeply because some of the background was familiar because her family was from the islands as well. They were from Carriacou and immigrants to the United States. Although she lived in New York and, obviously, a whole generation before me. But still, it was some of the things I could just see, you know. And just the way she wrote and the language and all that and the feeling, so much so that when I did my doctoral studies at Emory, I used it for a paper, a long paper.

So, I went out to Colorado in '89 to do a fellowship out there. And when I got back in 1990, there was a group that was already meeting at the bookstore, at Charis. And it was called, oh, my goodness, I forget the name, Mary Anne probably remembered the name of the group. But there was an arm of the group called "women of color," that was an arm of this group. And so when we started meeting, I just felt it important, and some of the other women did, that we concentrate on issues that affected just the women. Because like with a lot of other stuff, a lot of times, like she said, "You start out and you're saying we're going to work on both men's and women's issues, but a lot of times, it gets co-opted, much like the book did." That's a part of the larger culture. That's just part of a lot of socialization of many men and women. So

I just wanted something for the women. And once we started concentrating on that women of color group, we started talking about it. And I said, "Well, you know what? Do we want to be—are we going to call ourselves—is it going to be for black women? Or is it going to be for women of color, which is very different than African American women or women of African descent." And after a lot of back and forth, because by this time, you may have to come back, because I had gone to London by this time, in '87. And that was a whole 'nuther experience of dealing with, you know, perceptions and definitions and names. Because when they said "black," that was something very different than when we say "black." That included very often Asian women of the sub-Saharan continent, like Indians. So, in just a few years, I've had a lot of different experiences—not just personally, but socially and politically, as well, and culturally. So, me and a couple of other people were very insistent on saying "women of African descent," that our issues would be very different say, than white women's or even women who are from Asia or women who are from the Spanish-speaking Caribbean. And we got ZAMI because we really were trying to come up with names. And again, I had been so influenced by Audre Lorde's biography that I just sort of threw it out there. I said, "Well, you know, *Zami*," and she described it as a Carriacou name for women who live and work together as lovers and friends. So I said, "Well, it seems like that's what we want to basically embody in this group." So, you know, so most people hadn't heard of it, some people had heard of it, a couple other women had heard of it. And so it was almost like instantly and very much overwhelmingly, "Yes, let's do that." And I don't think there were any other names that were put out there once we got that. It just seemed to fit. It just seemed to really, really, really fit.

And how many were in the group?

The original group was about, I think it was about maybe ten, fifteen women. Because the group was very much changing. Some came in, some came out. And we really started as a more social group. But we were also doing certain things that were social, as well as political, and we would have discussions every week—every month at the bookstore. And some of them ended up being discussions of coming out and that kind of thing. Because you always had people who had this process. And then as we started doing more and more things, we moved into other things, like we did celebrations on Audre Lorde's birthday. And so, in the fifteen or so years that the group existed, it went from discussion, social, to like advocacy and that kind of thing. One time, we had a little meetinghouse. We went from that to having drawing parties and that sort of thing to raise money. And then towards the early '90s or so, we started—several people started getting burned out. I was one of them because that always happens when you have a few people trying to do a lot of things. So, at that point, it was when really Mary Anne decided, okay, you know what? Why don't we just move into another direction? And that direction was with the Audre Lorde scholarship, where that was the primary purpose of the group. So, not so much social anymore or what have you, but really about raising money to give to out lesbians and colleges and universities. And then that became—that went from that to just lesbians and gay men who . . . basically had the spirit of what we thought somebody like Audre Lorde would have espoused.

I can't remember what my actual title was. I don't remember because I was never too much into all of that title stuff anyway. But like I said, when we were up and running, we really, really, really did do some very, very, very good things. And many people, I would hope, were helped, not by just the discussion groups, [but also] sort of pushing people in the way we thought might help them, if they had a specific need, that sort of thing. But it was a quite significant part of my life. And I really, really, really enjoyed it. I enjoyed it. I also enjoyed the years I worked at that same bookstore that I started visiting way back in the eighties.

You started working there?

I worked there from '92. I worked part-time from '92 to '94, because I was also teaching at Clark Atlanta [University] then. When I got back from Colorado in 1990, I had started working at Clark, I was teaching at Clark Atlanta. And I actually just started working there part-time. And really nothing, not so much I needed the money, it was really more to have access to books and all of the other types of items that they sell, but mostly the books. And, in fact, when I was working on my dissertation, I was able to get access to many books that I ordinarily would not, because I was working there, and I can get them at a discount, you know. So, I really enjoyed it. And then in '94, I didn't go back to teach at Clark, so I worked there full-time really from about, oh, '94 to like '98, I guess. And, you know, at that point, I said, "Okay, well, I really got to go back to teaching. I really need to make a little bit more money now." You know, because I was never really paid a whole lot. The owner talked about becoming a partner. But that really wasn't what I wanted to do. I liked working there, but I didn't really want to so much own a store, and that's really the only retail I've ever done. I don't really like retail. But I could do that because I love books and because I knew books. I had no problem with somebody coming in and saying, "What's a good book? What's a good biography that just came out by so-and-so?" And so I could do that. But because I liked books.

Q.

What's the relationship between your art and your sexuality? And if you want to throw in the South, you can throw in that.

I call my art "activism through art" because just by me being onstage it's an activist or an activist act or a political act just by my body and the way I present and my energy being on that stage is already activism. I feel like people seeing me onstage in whatever I'm doing, it just allows them to broaden their mind as far as, you know, art and entertainment. My show that I'm doing right now, the main character is a woman-loving woman, but that's not what the story is about, that's not what the show is about. And so, I feel that by just me being onstage and people being able to connect with my character, it brings down barriers. Eventually some of the other things that I'm gonna do artwise aren't gonna have anything to do with sexuality or being queer. Only thing that would have to do with it is just Q. being onstage, and that's part of who I am. And I think that that's revolutionary because a lot of people are just used to seeing a certain kind of person that presents in a specific way and is depicting a character in a specific way. So, just me being onstage transcends all of that. It fucks everybody's world up. So I like to say it's activism through art because it's just by the nature of me doing it is revolutionary. And other than that, I think that's the only thing that really lies at that intersection. I do feel like queer people are extraordinarily creative, and so I appreciate how open I am and how free I am and that I don't have any inhibitions or hesitancy around creating anything because just me getting up and putting on my clothes and going outside every day is revolutionary, you know? Whatever I'm gonna have to encounter on that day. And so I reflect that in my art. It's like no fear.

Does the South play a role in your art at all? Can someone look at a film you made or one of your shows and know that it's southern?

Definitely my show right now is based in the 1920s rural South. [*Laughter.*] But as far as films and other art, I guess you could say yes, just by the nature of how deep I like to get into people's psyche. I don't know if that's specific to the South, but I feel like taking the time to really talk to somebody and asking those questions to really get a feel for that person, you kind of have to have that southern mentality. Like I'm not in a rush. And yet I want to get what I want to get, and I want to enjoy my journey to that destination. And so I know that's definitely reflected in my work because I'm not trying to rush to get it done. Because I'm actually invested in getting the highest quality. I'm invested in reaching that person at their highest. Yeah. So, you can't rush when you do that. You can't . . . you can't . . . yeah, you can't rush when you do that, you have to be patient.

What genres of art do you work in?

. . . I want to say film, [but] nobody uses film anymore. . . . Mainly video and graphic design online, and then performance art. But I fuse it all together, and a little bit of photography. I started out as a photographer, so that will always be a part of my aesthetic. So, I like to put all of it together, so performance, visual art, and video. I don't know what you call that. "Interdisciplinary" I guess is the academic term. I don't like to be limited, you know? People say I'm not a theatre artist, because I'm not. And I'm not just a filmmaker. I don't know what it is in me and always being something other that has not been defined. That's just it. . . . You can't define what I do. I'm at a point where I'm tired of being categorized. I'm tired of being in a community just because I fit that mold. I've been really getting into internal art forms here recently, the past six, seven, eight months. Tai chi, yoga. I guess I could officially say I'm a yogi. And in those communities as well as [in] Buddhism . . . people just accept you. And when I'm in those spaces, I'm just Q. and I really enjoy that: just being Q. There's so many different things that come along with being Q., but being that I love women doesn't need to be stronger than everything else. And for a long time, it's been that. And now that I'm really starting to navigate away from that, I just feel so much better and so much lighter. And so, I'm just enjoying being Q. and everything that comes with that. Yeah, I'm black, yeah, I love women; I'm also an artist, also love football. I'm a foodie, you know? So, I like being all of me all the time and not having one particular thing being heightened because that's what people want to heighten. So that's how I feel.

Joan
....

In 1989, Maynard Jackson, former Mayor Jackson, appointed me as a senior advisor to the lesbian and gay community. That was my entry into politics. I had just started twisting [my hair], because I had locks for eight years. Just started twisting. And I was his out black lesbian liaison. He had two white guys and me. And I remember my friends here telling me, "You don't want to be conspicuous." Oh, and here I am being conspicuous, you know. And there are only like a handful of us who are willing to be out and be ready for the "Donohue Show," you know, all of that. [*Laughter.*] I was like, yeah. And so I was thrust into this role, where I was being political in a city that was predominantly black.

And you had your middle-class black folk that I had to interact with. And part of me had fear about that. Because I know where it came from and I know what people think. But while I had part fear, I knew that I had the mayor backing me up, who was taking a big chance. And he was like, "Okay, yes. I put her here. So, yes, she belongs here." And then there was the other part of me that was like, okay, but I'm not from here. So, I don't really have a whole lot to lose, because I'm not really from here. I don't have the "Who's your mama? Who's your daddy? Where did you go to school? Where did you go to church?" I didn't have that. "Where do you go to church?" "Unitarian." "What is that?" You know? So that helped me get through. But it helped me see.

And what I learned was the more comfortable and confident I felt in who I was, because when I came out, it was like, "Okay, this is who I am, y'all. I'm a black lesbian, this is who I am." But then I had to back down, because other people had gone through their coming-out process, and we would try to organize political LGBT stuff for the black community. And we'd get twenty-five people. But then you'd have a party over here at Texas and you'd get five hundred black lesbians out there . . . [and] we weren't out. And so it was difficult because you didn't have that support from your community. You had a handful of folks who were there. But even then, you had to be careful, because everybody was not accepting. But when I waivered on being comfortable, then I saw that doubt in other folk. And it was like, okay, I need to not go there. So you had to work through your fear and just know that you stepping out here and not everybody's comfortable with it. And even today, even though I'm out, I ran out, I don't have any secrets about it, I still get people who will say, "Well, what do you think so-and-so will think about the gay issue?" "What do you think?" And a lot of it comes from my people who are saying, "Well, what do you think so-and-so, the gays on the south side of town, think about the gay issue?" Well, what about the gay issue? I go out, this is who I am.

But the church thing is real—it's very strong here. It's so prevalent, especially with your choir directors, you know stereotypical. And people in church, even in the pulpit. And we've got a minister here in town who came out a few years ago. He and his wife are head of the church. He came out. She was devastated. They have grown kids. She worked through her issues around it, realized that there was more to their relationship than this. She's worked through it; she's accepted it. She's still part of the church. She understands he has his life. But they're no longer married, they're divorced. But she has joined him in their dedication to bring the truth to ministry around homosexuality. And they are really challenging other ministers to do the same. But people resist it. And so I've found that you've got folks here who are in high places who are very closeted, will not come out. And I've had people say to me along the way things like, "Well, you do what you do." "Gotcha," you know. And it's okay. And I've had people say to me, "Well, you know, I am part of the family but, you know, I've got to like . . ."—it's like, "I got it." I respect people where they are. I don't out people. But once you're with me any more than fifteen minutes, you'll know who I am. So I don't have issues with that. And I realize that I go in and out of a lot of different places, a lot of different circles. But I know that I do not have roots in the traditional solid black community here. I don't. And when I look around at who my network and support folks are, they're white lesbians.

So, do you think that that is an Achilles' heel, in terms of some of the things that you want to get done in your position? Or do you think it's a benefit?

I have never looked at this as an Achilles' heel. I think that I've gone through phases in my activism. I've gone from being the new out lesbian—"Oh, this is so great!"—to being, "Okay, now I can relax," because I grew up during the height of the civil rights movement. In fact, fifty years ago, I wanted to marry a politician because I wanted to tell that person what to do around policy, because I knew this was critical stuff happening in the nation's capital and in the capitol. So, that's where I was fifty years ago. I was like, "Yes, Dr. King, I'm going to marry a politician, because I'm going to tell that person what to do." And so, I don't lead with that. I look at healthy communities and that's A to Z, that's everyone. And everyone benefits when everyone is healthy and has access to health and resources. And so that's the way I lead.

I always have to go back to growing up. There was all kinds of people that grew up with you in your neighborhood. So I can go down into south Georgia or north Georgia, or city of Atlanta, and I feel that I can sit and listen and hear what people need, because bottom line, we all have the same basic needs and we all just want to be heard and we all want to make sure that we have the same access that everybody else has, to have a decent quality of life. That's what I'm about. That's my agenda. I can remember becoming the director of the Fund for Southern Communities, which is a social justice fund, part of a national network. I think I must have been the first black executive director. I had black folk from South Carolina saying to me, "What? Do you think people going to give you money because you're black? Because you're gay?" I had other people saying, "Well, do you think people will think this is now a gay fund?" "Why, because I'm gay? It's like I don't represent other issues, as well?" And it's like, no, I realize that I'm black, I'm a woman, I'm gay, I'm old now, something's wrong with my foot so, you know, there's an ability issue. I had to bring all of me to the table. This is where the intersection and the connections and the intersectionality of issues came front and center for me. So, it's like I can't just advocate for gay issues. I have to advocate for feminist issues. I have to advocate for health issues. I have to advocate for employment issues, housing issues, it's all related. Gay people were being denied housing. I have to look at the total human being and where we fit in that and bring all of that. So I used my being gay as a platform to further social justice and civil rights. And so that's kind of how I see it and how I've used being gay. So I never let that stop me. I saw being gay as an entrée to sit at the table that we were never invited to. Because like I said, if you're going to be with me more than fifteen minutes, you'll know. And I took that charge very seriously.

> There's been a lot of discussion back and forth between the gay and lesbian community, primarily white gay and lesbian community, and the black community about the comparison between the gay rights movement and the civil rights movement. As someone who grew up in the '60s, in DC, who's an activist and a politician, what are your thoughts about civil rights and gay rights and those movements?

Yeah. See, I look at them all as human rights. I try to look at everything from the sixty-thousand-foot level and then breaking it down. And, you know, there are differences in our cultures and in how we behave, and where we come from. But when you look at our sexuality, being LGBT people, we're just a microcosm of the whole society. And so yes, black folk fighting for civil rights, we want to be heard, we want to participate, we want access. Gay folks, yes, we are fighting for the same types of things, but at a different level, or on a different platform. Because for the white gay folk, you already have access. You already have resources. You are the ones who made the rules to the game. And so now that you have come out in terms of your identity, you're experiencing what it means to be denied, to being discriminated against. As black folk, this has been part of our history since we got here, so we have had to live with that. So you can't make a direct comparison. And the way that I look at it is, where is the intersectionality of it? Where can we meet on a common ground about it? And please, you need to go do your homework, just like I had to do my homework about who you are and how as a black person I have to live in this culture, in this country, in this society, I have to know everything about you in order to be able to survive. You have to go do your homework. You need to learn about justice. You need to learn about the civil rights movement. And you need to be willing to advocate for me, because I'm willing to advocate for you, when I go in a room that is not an LGBT room, I am willing to bring your issues along with my issues as a woman, as a black person in this culture.

And so I look at it as not a comparison. And I can't compare my life to someone who's had a disability. Honestly, even with, you know, I have an issue with my foot, I cannot. I can't. However, I know what it feels like to be discriminated against. I know what it means to be denied access. I can take that. That's where I can go in and advocate for you, because I understand that. And I hope that you again will understand that. But I don't get into the let's compare. First of all, I don't think there's any hierarchy of oppression. We're all oppressed, because if you're the oppressor, you're affected because I'm being oppressed. And if I'm oppressed, you're being affected. And so there is a synergy there that we've got to realize and that we've got to acknowledge. But don't compare yourself. And it's like I tell my partner all the time, we get into this and she's like, "Oh, woe is me, woe is me, woe is me." And I have to stop and say, "Look, okay, I get it. I understand where you're coming from and I respect where you're coming from. But let's broaden it a little further. You do have access." And we have those kinds of conversations with each other. And she's learned a lot from my perspective. "Oh, I hadn't looked at it like that."

And she tells a story, and she'll probably kill me for this, but she says she tells a story about how the first time she saw a black person with a golden retriever. As simple as that. She was young. She was like, "I saw a black person with a golden retriever and I had to like stop myself and go, 'Well, why wouldn't a black person have a golden retriever?'" Because she'd never seen a black person with a golden retriever before. And she didn't think that black people owned golden retrievers. And so, she was like, "You know," she said, "I had to stop and say, 'What kind of thinking is that?'" You know, it's the little things like that. So I don't get into the whole comparison. Because until you walk in my shoes, then maybe we can do some comparison. But the fact that I haven't walked in your shoes, you haven't walked in my shoes, however, we are both being targeted and we are both being denied and we're both being discriminated against. So let's look at where we have some common ground and see how we can move forward.

Just like with the decisions that just came down from the Supreme Court for gay folks. It's like yay, DOMA is no longer legal and we've got momentum and we've got more states that are recognizing gay marriage. For black folk it was like, hey, we're saying that Section 4 of the Civil Rights Act is no longer constitutional. It's like, okay, here is an opportunity for black folk and gay folk to come together because neither one of you have made it to the end yet. You still got work to do. You still got work to do. Here is an opportunity to look at where is the commonality and where can we gain some traction and come together and advocate for one another. And perhaps we'll have more of a momentum to get what we want on both sides. So I kind of look to see where you've got some commonality.

And that's kind of how I approach my work as an elected official, as well. I kind of look for the common ground. I know that some schools kind of look for the differences and where we can be different. I kind of look to see is there common ground. Because, again, for me, my agenda is how can people get access. I don't care who you are, because we got just as many poor white people as we got poor black people. We got just as many poor gay people as we got black, white, people who still don't have access. You know, and the whole health piece, the whole AIDS piece. And that was my entrée again into the movement and understanding. . . . I was a member of the first dinner committee for the HRC here in Atlanta. I was the only black on the committee. And my charge was to go out and find the black community. Up to that point, I hadn't really come across a lot of black gay and lesbian people, so I didn't know where they were. And I went to this organization called AALGA, African-American Lesbian Gay Alliance. And I was like, "Oh, my God, I felt like I've come home. Where are you? How come you're not participating?" And then I had to learn. It was like, okay, so here's my family and my family had my back as I was out there. And I went back and I was like, "Look, I am not going to go do your work." They do not want to be brought in, paying all this money, and not get any benefit back. And so that's just the deal, and I'm not going to be on this committee anymore. [Laughter.] You know, so I went to the first dinner committee. And then I was like I'm not doing this again. I said, "You are an elitist group and you're being exclusive. We are not going to come." Of course, I continued to participate but, folks were like, "We're not spending that money. We don't have that kind of money to spend," especially when they were not out. So, you know, it's those kinds of things.

Talk about some of your other involvement in community activism and leadership here in Atlanta around LGBT issues.

Okay. I first started out working on—Michael Lomax, who was the former chair of the Fulton County Commission decided to run for mayor. And I had a friend recruit me to work with his campaign. That was kind of my first entrée into getting involved into politics. And then joined the primary. I think he decided not to move forward, because Maynard Jackson was running again. And then I got involved with Maynard Jackson's campaign. At the same time, I was starting to work for the Fund for Southern Communities, which is a social justice fund. And that group was actually the first to fund social justice issues in the southeast, small grants. And I was involved with AALGA. So, with Maynard Jackson running the election and making me the liaison for—one of the liaisons for the gay and lesbian community, that means I had to keep my eye on what was going on in the gay and lesbian community. I was by then probably a cochair of AALGA, and so I was involved locally with black gays and lesbians. And then I was funding gay and lesbian issues as part of the funding for Fund for Southern Communities, so I had to know what was going on across the board in the metro area in North Carolina and South Carolina around gay communities. So all of that was happening at once.

So, Maynard Jackson then appointed me to the License Review Board. And one of the city council members at the time appointed me as cochair of the Public Safety Committee for lesbian and gay issues for city council. And so I was getting involved on a political level on boards and commissions, representing the gay and lesbian community, representing the mayor, and then also actively engaged in AALGA, working with the African-American lesbian and gay community. And then funding lesbian and gay issues, as a funding area. So all of that was happening, and on the local level. I got involved with national funding for lesbian and gay issues as a member of the board of the Fund For Lesbian and Gay Issues. But I was doing all of that around the same time. This was from '90 to like—yeah, '99, 2000. And so, by then, my reputation as a lesbian activist—oh, the other thing that happened in the mid- to late '90s was I was one of the cofounders of Southerners on New Ground, with Pat Hussain and Mandy Carter, Suzanne Barr, Mab Segrest, and Pam McMichael.

That's when I really started looking at this whole intersectionality and interconnectiveness and started looking at the political ramifications of gay, lesbian, bi, transgender, queer, all of that, because I was working with some heavy hitters here. I was in the movement but I was mostly funding the issues, representing the governmental entities, the local, not coming at it from the hardcore feminist work that my colleagues [were]. And I was like, "Oh, God, I'm a real lightweight right here." But I brought a different perspective. And so I was doing all of that during that time.

And what was your role in ZAMI?

Okay. So, ZAMI had a couple of iterations. When I was with AALGA [African American Lesbian and Gay Alliance] . . . Sabrina Sojourner, I don't know if you've run into Sabrina Sojourner, she's in DC, she had come from California. She came to Atlanta, made a big splash, politically. She'd bring that California energy, and then from DC. She was the one that actually helped me sort of get my footing. We started a Woman of Color Caucus in AALGA. Because we were not getting the women to come out to the AALGA meetings, it was mostly male. It was male-founded, male-driven, -dominated. And there were a few of us women who were willing to participate and be there. And so we created a Women of Color Caucus. And what we did was we met separately, like on a Friday night, it was a potluck. And we would invite other black lesbians that we knew to come over to Sabrina's house. And we'd sit and get to know each other and network. And we'd have these five or ten minutes where we'd go around and talk about an issue, let them know what was going on, invite them to come to AALGA. And so we did Women of Color Caucus for about a year or so. And then we started getting more women who were coming in. And then people started wanting to do something different. And you have some who want to do something over here, want to be real political. Others who just want to be social. And then you have folks who just want to kind of be middle-of-the-road, and so there was a split. So Women of Color dissolved. And then we had another group, and it was called ZAMI. And that was the first iteration of ZAMI, this was pre–Mary Anne. And that didn't last because it was more social. And then there was a group who wanted to be the womanist forum because Alice Walker was doing her womanist thing. And that lasted a hot minute. And then Mary Anne came along and there was still a couple people who were part of the initial ZAMI. And then I think Mary Anne might have been part of that, as well. And that's where ZAMI came, ZAMI that we know came together. And by that time, I had sort of backed off, because I was more interested in the whole political piece and we couldn't get a lot of traction for that. So I participated in some of the early ZAMI meetings. But then my energy was more focused on a lot of national work and more of the governmental and neighborhood kind of stuff.

Laurinda

Talk a little bit about how you became a writer.

I had to put it somewhere. I mean whatever I was going through I had to be able to put it somewhere. The ability to alter the truth played a huge factor in it, but when I started trying to tell the story at first I couldn't tell the story by making it up. I had to put part of me in it. And I realized once I started putting a little bit of me in the story it was easier for me to tell the story. And what I found when people started reading what I had written, I wasn't alone. Or this character wasn't alone. They had experienced that. So I guess when I saw the impact it had had on others and how, of course, I'm not the first black lesbian writer. But I'm the first one to really not hold my tongue. So the point of being able to say everybody in the church is a hypocrite, you know and mean it. So, those writers after me, like Skyy, I remember seeing them at book signings. I had to get to the point where I wasn't feeling intimidated by their presence. I had to feel like, "Hey, but you're where they came from. You made them feel like it's okay to talk, to write." And so it's a place for me to vent and hide the truth about certain things and certain people. I can put it in a book. And if you see yourself, you see yourself. If you decide you want to sue me, you ain't going to go to court and tell people that your husband is a homo. I've enjoyed it because it allows me to see the world through a whole other set of eyes that I don't share with everybody. I can't wait to cry about all this, my experiences. Evil eyes. I can't wait. I cannot wait.

And then you've done plays as well. How do you see the relationship between your fiction and your plays? What can you say differently in those genres? Or do you see them as just different ways of saying the same thing?

Just different ways of saying the same thing. When I did "Walk Like a Man" my vision was to be able to see my character. I wondered what it would look like—I wondered what it would be like to hear this character say this, this character say that. I always wondered what it would be like to see them onstage. Always, if I say I'm going to do something, I do it. And I mean six weeks later they're onstage. We opened in DC in 2006. I had no idea—I saw a textbook. I was working at a school system as a grant writer, and I had gone by to train this lady on how to write a grant or something, and I looked in the textbook and they were talking about writing plays and how much it would cost to do a budget and what goes in a budget or whatever. I said, "That's all it takes?" So I sat down and turned my attention to it.

Putting a play onstage. I didn't know how to write scripts. The first day of rehearsals I gave them the manuscript. "Here you go." Gave them the book. "Just read that story." And they said, "What are we supposed to learn?" "Just read that story." And then I said, "So, what do we do now?" [They said,] "We were waiting on a director." "Oh, okay." So we sitting around and I said, "Who's the director?" [They said,] "You." "Oh, that ain't what I want to do." And then we were called to check on venues and they asked about the producer's name. And my ex was like, "Who's the producer?" [I said,] "I don't know, ask what a producer does." So, I go to the phone, [and learned that] the producer pays the bills, "Oh, that's us." Then she gets on the phone and I'm like, "I didn't want to do all that. I just wanted my stuff onstage." So over the years I had to do all of that. Be producer, be director, be writer. And [on] any given day, I'll tell you I'd prefer to be the writer.

Priscilla

What is your involvement in the gay community?

Beyond involved. Unfortunately, I live, love, and work in the same place, which I work for a queer people of color organization in town. It's a community-based organization. And I've been there fourteen years. And so a lot of my socializing happens there, because we do community events and activities. But it's where I get paid from. And it requires me to work with the white people on some level. But because we are an autonomous queer people of color organization, that's safe and home, for the most part. But then when we got to go out and interact with people from white culture, then we actually have to come home and debrief.

Is that because there's tension between the white gay community and black gay community here?

I think it's because they don't have some of the same priorities that we have but that they also are racist and don't think that they are. Because everybody thinks Austin is liberal. And I'm like, its liberal white. Let's be clear. It is liberal here, but it is liberal white, which is very different than being liberal. Because everything moves from a white perspective. And so, yes, there's tension, because there are also, you know, some of the more—and I don't necessarily call them mainstream because I feel very main and very stream. And so, I call them the white people, because that's who leads them and that's—their priorities are very reflective of white peoples' priorities that we don't get invited. I mean, the organization I work for has been around longer than every queer organization, lesbian organization, gay organization in this town, and still doesn't get the respect. It's been around twenty-seven years. And sometimes we get—many times, we get left out of shit, until you need some faces. Then we're brought in. So the table is already made and half the time, they done ate half the bread. And then they're like, well, next time, we'll bring the rest of the bread and then y'all can come, right? So it's always like we're always coming in as an afterthought. Except when there's something that goes down with people of color. Then we get called to be in the lead. But what we talk about is we still people of color. And that by you taking that position, you're not recognizing the intersections. We black and queer. We Latino and queer. We are people of color and queer. And those are synonymous. One don't come before the other. But they always feel like the queer trumps. And so when black folks do something that they would consider homophobic, then they want us to go after the black folks. But you don't ask us to do that when it's something else, when it's white people. You'll take the lead and claim the credit and do everything else. And so it's rough being involved to this level.

And that's the visible queer community, what I would call the "visible queer activist" sort of community. Because there's a whole 'nother group of people who are not involved in any of this, that I have the privilege of being in a relationship with as a lesbian, who don't do the more political or who don't even come to allgo. And that's because I'm from here. So I can go to a black lesbian party and see all different people, which is what I did before I got involved with allgo. I mean, allgo has been there twenty-seven years, I didn't know about it, even though it was a Latino organization before. I went to an event in '92, didn't know it was the organization. Didn't know it was the organization I'm working for now. Friend of mine said, "There's a gay dance in town," we went to it. I didn't know that it was the organization I currently work for. Didn't have a clue. So when I went to apply, they were like, "Well, who are you?" Because they'd been in the community twelve, thirteen years, and they were looking for a case manager to work with HIV-positive, black, primarily black folks, somebody who was from the community. I show up and they were like, "Who—where you come from?" And they're like, "Where you grow up?" I said, "East Austin." They were as shocked as I was that I'm from East Austin, they don't know me, have never seen me, and I don't know them. But we supposedly in this community. I'm hanging out with all these other people.

So, for me, there's like multiple communities here, depending on what's happening and who you're talking about. Because what I know is that people that are from here are really not involved in allgo. And some of that is, I think around the politics, that allgo is political and is out and is that's not all we do is social-cultural things, but it's a political place, right? It's a place to also learn about racism, and it's also a place where black and brown people have kind of come together. And these folks tend to be more segregated in like black, right? So all the people I was hanging around with were black lesbians. Never at a club. Out every weekend at somebody's house, playing spades. [*Laughter.*]

But there's a part of me that can't be me, because living, loving, and working in community is rough. You're always on. I can't go to a poetry reading without somebody saying, "What's the next thing at allgo? When's the next event?" And I'm like, "Did you get the newsletter? Call me on Monday." I'm one of the directors. And I've been there the longest. Like there's no board member or staff that's been there longer than me. And so I hold a history, all fourteen years of history that has kind of come and gone through the doors, right? And so I'm overly involved. [*Laughter.*] Because I also host events here that are the organization's. We ain't got a lot of money, so what that means is that sometimes we need a space to have a brunch for an artist that we bringing in. Well, this lovely space, which I don't mind because I feel like this is an abundance of space for two people, right? Like this is a four-bedroom house [*laughter*], it don't make no sense to me. So, when people come to town or the artists come, okay, then all these rooms and all these people, right? And so, in that way we get invited to everything. We get invited to speak. I'm constantly a lesbian. It's a good thing that I'm out.

The work I did at allgo for the first—so I started there in 1998, and we had a case management program for people of color living with HIV up until 2006, so I provided direct services to people living with HIV and AIDS. And I was also the supervisor of that program. And so some of what happened in being in a community-based organization is that people I grew up with were my clients, which is this social work dilemma, right, around what's ethical and what's not ethical. But recognizing that we were the people—we were the organization that served people of color. What did that mean for them not to be able to get services there because I'm there? Some of what I have to think about is . . . how culturally that's not . . . ethical to send people other places because I'm there, right?

And so, there are a number of people that I grew up with who have died, men and women. And it has turned out that some of those clients—they're related to me. I didn't know this at the time, right? I didn't know when they're sitting in front of me. So I'm talking [about] people that I went to elementary school with, who became my clients as HIV-positive people. And then some folks' parents being my client. I suspect that there are a number of people in my family who are HIV-positive, who are much closer to me, who I just don't know are HIV-positive. When I saw my aunt's husband in a picture, I said, "He's HIV-positive." I said, "Mama, who is he?" I said, "What he do?" She said, "He on disability because he has a back injury." I said, "He's HIV-positive." I just knew it. Had never seen him. He didn't look ill. He was six-feet-four, muscle-built, and I looked at him and went, "He's HIV-positive." And, of course, it came out later that he's HIV-positive, but at the time, and he wasn't a client of mine, I just sensed it, right? And I think working in the HIV field has led my family to have a much more open conversation about HIV and AIDS, because some of the stuff that they've done around people who they thought had been HIV-positive, I've had to be like, "Excuse me, you don't need to wash the plate. You don't need Clorox and we'd all have it. And I would be HIV-positive. Do you understand this? That I have sat in rooms with people, I've drank, of course we all have drank after somebody, you know." So in that way just knowing the number of people who are impacted by it.

But also, I sit on a planning committee of women living with HIV and AIDS and have been on that committee since I started at allgo. And so it's this interesting mix of like being in the lesbian world, being in [the] gay world, around where I'm immersed in it and where I'm holding all of this knowledge about peoples' status, that other people don't know, but I know because I'm a case manager and I know because I've been to the clinic with clients. And I've seen people at the clinics, where other people don't even know where the clinic is.

The other thing that it does is that I believe HIV has robbed me of having black gay men, particularly in my world of a certain age. And so when I'm with black men who are twenty-something, thirty-something, and they're having birthdays, I have to remind them or I have to ask them to please don't be ashamed of their age. Because black gay men got this thing around being old queens or being old. And reminding them that I want to grow old with them, because they're it. That all of the men my age and older who were out and black gay men are not here and I don't have them in my world. And that it's important that they know how important it is that they're still here. And so, in that way, I'm always craving black gay men, particularly black gay men. Because I just don't have them in my world. And I wonder what it would have been like over these last twenty-three, twenty-four years, if I had been around black gay men and black lesbians. So when I think about Ebony Connection, which was a black gay men's group that was here, that was part of allgo, that all those people are gone, like what would it have been like. And I was here and I was out but I just didn't have the opportunity to be around them because they were in the more political world and not in the communities in which I was moving in. And so I feel like I always crave that and want that.

"They something, ain't they?" Miss B. says as we rise to leave. "They asked me to be on that panel instead of introducing, but you know I get called to do so many public events that I had to decline the invitation."

"Which side of the table would you have been on? The artist side or the activist side?"

Miss B. shakes her head. "Did you just really ask me that question? Did you not just sit for over three hours and listen to these women talk about how the artistic is political and the political can take the form of art? You call yourself a scholar/artist, huh? If you say so. Since you don't know, I would have been on *both* sides of the table. You know I'm bi . . . lingual." She winks at me. "Let's go across the street here and get something to eat and then I'll take you on one last stop to talk to some special ladies."

Six

ALL HAIL
THE QUEEN (BEE)

We walk across the street to a diner called Honeychild. Their special today is honey fried chicken and two sides. We get the special; I get the honey-glazed carrots and biscuits with honey butter for my two sides, while Miss B. gets honey-sriracha brussels sprouts and honey apple cake for hers. We splurge and have two glasses of mead to wash it down.

"Umph, umph, umph. Sue sho'll did put her baby toe in this food today," Miss B. says, licking her fingers of the bits of fried chicken. "I've been coming here for years and it never disappoints. It's one of the few places in the hive where you can get downhome cooking with a twist. Most everybody goes outside the hive to eat these days, foraging for the next 'it' place. But I don't care what nobody says, can't nobody hold a candle to Honeychild."

"It certainly is good," I say, taking the final swig of my drink. "So, you said you were going to introduce me to special women. Are they close by? Or do we need to go on another road trip? You left your Lexus at Sippi-Citi."

"I called the club this morning. It'll be alright. Besides, we won't be taking any more road trips. The women are close by. Let me get the check." She gets up, goes to the counter, pays the bill, and then comes back to the table. "Okay. Let's step outside so I can have a smoke and then I'll introduce you."

We're standing outside of the restaurant while Miss B. lights up. Her face becomes pensive, like she's plotting some grand scheme. She begins to hum what sounds like the old Walter Hawkins song "Be Grateful."

"Are you humming 'Be Grateful'? That's one of my favorite songs."

"Umm humm. It was my mother's favorite, too. She used to play it all the time. Even before she passed and didn't quite know who I was, she'd look at me and say, 'Sweetie, could you play my song?' She had an old record player that still worked, and I'd pull that record out of its worn jacket and put it on. I had to put a nickel on top of the needle to keep it from skipping. I remember it would skip every time Lynette Hawkins would get to the vamp 'be grate . . . be grate . . . be grate . . .' She could never get the 'ful' out." Her laughter turns to tears. "Mama finally just taped the nickel on the needle so she didn't have to worry about it. Oh, how I miss her." I grab her hand.

"I bet you're a lot like your mother, Miss B. Fierce and feisty."

"You got that right," she says, wiping the tears away. "We don't have a lot of elders here in the hive. That's why I want you to meet those who are left. These are our queen mothers. They are the matriarchs of the hive and are responsible for our very existence. We have one reigning queen and five former ones here in the hive, which is rare. Typically, not more than one queen mother can exist in a hive. In fact, I remember when I was a little girl, they chased one queen mother out. Rumor has it she was always keeping up drama and was jealous and felt threatened by her own daughters. Nobody has been put out since, but that is because we in Hymen voted to change the rules so that former queen mothers can stay in the hive after they step down, as long as they don't meddle in how the new queen mother rules. So far, it's worked."

As Miss B. and I head down the road, "Be Grateful" is stuck in my head and I begin to sing. Miss B. joins in, harmonizing her alto with my tenor.

> Beeeeeeeeeee graaaaateful
> Beeeeeeeeeee graaaaateful
> Beeeeeeeeeee graaaaateful

"I bet you didn't know that I can sing, too!" I state proudly.

"You alright. I guess I'd sing with you again," she chides.

In the distance, I see a big white house with a long porch. The yard is dotted with trees, but there is a huge weeping willow closest to the house, its branches scraping the ground. There are five women sitting in rockers on the porch, but I can't make out what they are doing.

"This house we're coming up on is called the House of Queens. It's where all of the former queen mothers live. The reigning queen mother lives a bit up the hill in her own house and she don't interact with the former queens that much, but the oldest queen mother, Queen Mother Aida, is still alive, and you'll get a chance to meet her today. The queen mothers know you're coming, but they didn't want to talk to you one-on-one. Every Saturday they gather on the porch and do their thing: snap beans, grease heads, quilt, dip snuff, sing, and, most importantly, gossip. They said that you could just come and listen to their conversation. I thought that would be a good idea, too, because once they get going, they can spin some amazing tales—stories you might not get in a one-on-one."

"Okay," I say, a bit confused about how all of this is going to work if they are having a conversation among themselves rather than talking directly to me, but I go with the flow. When we are a few feet from the porch, the women come into full view and they are all beautiful but in different ways. They represent every hue from deep chocolate to café au lait and seem to range in age. I would not be able to tell who's the oldest or the youngest.

"Good afternoon, queen mothers," Miss B. says in a fake proper voice that reminds me of the one my mother used when I was child when she answered the phone. It was always amusing to us kids because just before answering the phone she might be chastising us in black country vernacular. The dramatic switch between the two was always comical—boy-ef-you-don't-get-somewhere-and-sit-down-I'm-gonna-jerk-a-knot-in-yo'-head [*phone ring; throat clearing*], "Hellur." I chuckle to myself at the memory as Miss B. continues in her proper voice. "This is Dr. EPJ. He'll be taking down your stories."

The women all look up briefly from their business at hand and once me over. They all give me a look of welcome and pity all at once.

"Hello, queen mothers. It's nice to meet you all. Thanks so much for allowing me to listen to your stories. I used to listen to my grandmother tell stories all the time. I even wrote my dissertation on my grandmother and write about her in my first book and . . ." I don't finish the sentence because I can feel Miss B.'s eyes burning a hole in my head.

"He's young and easily excited, but he'll be fine," Miss B. says, trying to smooth over my awkwardness. "Now, EPJ, down on that end is Queen Mother Aida. She's the oldest living queen mother. Next to her is Queen Mother Cherry. Then there's Queen Mother Lori. To her left is Queen Mother Ida Mae. And closest to us here is Queen Mother Mary Anne. The current queen mother won't be joining us. She's too busy with her duties."

Rather than speak, I simply nod after each introduction. The women turn back to their tasks, and Miss B. and I take a seat on the steps of the porch, where there are rags burning in flower pots to keep mosquitos at bay, I presume. The oldest queen mother, Aida, begins talking, but I can't understand what she's saying. She's speaking in a different language. I just assume it's another language spoken in the hive. Miss B. leans over to me and whispers, "Miss Aida is actually not from Hymen but a little island south of the hive called Puerto Rico. A long time ago, the ashies put out a rumor that queens from PR were overly aggressive and should be disqualified from serving as queen mothers. Of course, this was all a plot to sneak as many ashy mining queen mothers in as possible. Not to be outdone, Queen Mother Aida campaigned to get on the ballot and proved them wrong. She is one of the most beloved queen mothers to this day. She'll start speaking in a language you can understand in a minute. She speaks her native language as much as possible so that she doesn't lose it."

Miss Aida's other language sounds like a song—melodic and high-pitched. She is a caramel-colored woman with closely cropped hair, her lips evidencing the slightest bit of red lipstick. She has a bowl of papayas resting on her lap in the dip of her skirt and, seemingly to the rhythm of her own words' musicality, she peels the fruit, cuts it in half, and scrapes the seeds out in another bowl sitting on the side of her rocking chair. Watching her work with the fruit and listening to her native language is hypnotizing. No sooner than I begin to go into a trance, she begins to speak in a language I can understand.

Aida Rentas

My childhood was not being able to fit anywhere because when I was four, my parents left Puerto Rico and moved to New York City. My mother and father didn't speak English. Of course, I didn't speak English. We were in a no man's land. They didn't know the rules; they didn't know what was going on; in 1938, they didn't understand. I was one of the first Latinos in the States, and so there was no training if you didn't speak English. You just went to class and got all D's to the point where I told my mother "D" was "delightful" because she didn't know no better. "A" was awful. She caught on to that when I was about ten but it was very frustrating until I decided to go into my own world because I couldn't see and no one knew that. I needed glasses. They discovered that when I was nine years old. So, [I] was just lost all around. Always been a leader, so that helped a lot because I had my own little cliques of friends, but you wonder what would have happened if you grew up understanding at least the language.

I'm the oldest of eight. And my mother had [taken care of] one, like I had four brothers and then two sisters. The sisters are eleven years apart, but the boys came one after the other, so I went to school and came home and babysat and took care. I was mamma. I tell her to this day *I* raised those boys; *you* didn't raise them boys.

I left home when I was eighteen, but I got to girls' camp because everybody thought I was not listening. I was a bad girl. Bad girl didn't understand what the hell was going on. But it was a wonderful thing. I became a lesbian in jail because, hello, it was only girls in there, and so I discovered another sexuality. I think I was straight. I had boyfriends and then I went away and I'm a Scorpion and so I started weighing the two. You have to cook for these guys and do this and do that, and I think I'd rather be a lesbian. And it was a choice that I made, which of course gave me a hard way to go again. But it was okay. I made the choice and I was willing to do whatever it took and I met wonderful people, older lesbians, older guys, that took such good care of me. I always say thank God for the community, because when we see someone lost, we usually take them under our wings, and that's what happened with me. I've always loved people because people have always been very kind to me.

They used to call me half-breed. "Where are you from?" "Puerto Rico." In 1938, Puerto Rico was like, "Puerto what?" [*Laughing.*] "You're a what?" And so, the African American kids didn't understand why I had good hair, why I spoke another language, and was I trying not to be black. They didn't know any Latinos. I was their Latino, so I adopted the African American culture heart and soul because it was easier to blend in. Years later somebody said to me, "Are you in the closet about being Latina?" I never thought of that one. And then I became more Latina because I didn't really know the customs. I didn't. And it's funny, I missed out on both sides because I didn't know American fairytales. Because who was going to tell them to me? But I didn't know Spanish fairytales. I had a lover when I was twenty-eight give me *America's Greatest Fairytales* and I sat for I would say a month and it was like, "Oh this is Humpty-Dumpty. Oh!" But you get joy and all the sudden you understand what people were talking about. So I always had a positive attitude. I don't know how but I always made things. "Hey, I'm the only one then I'm number one," because I was the only Puerto Rican in town. So, it was like okay, I'm top daddy. You all can't find another one like me.

My mother was twenty-one when she had me, and we lived where I live now, Sábana Seca. It's a little town now, but then it was the sticks really, and she went to San Juan to work, and my father came from Ponce and went to San Juan. He was a gardener; she was a cook. My dad is white with red hair. My mother looks like me, but they're both Puerto Rican. And when my mother got pregnant, you couldn't stay in Puerto Rico in 1938 when you weren't married and you were pregnant from a white man. My mother was going to get rid of me, and my dad was like, "Oh no you don't." So what they did was they got an apartment in San Juan, and somebody was helping them. My dad went to New York, got a job, and sent for my mom. That took four years because I went when I was four. Because he was white he met up with some Jewish guy who taught him ambulance chasing because Puerto Ricans didn't speak English, didn't trust people, and there was a big need. So my dad always wore a white shirt, black pants, and had more money than any other dad because he was an ambulance chaser. At the end he was almost like an attorney. He was with Lithkowitz for so many years; he knew the laws, the regulations. Didn't read or write, but you couldn't beat him out of a penny.

But my mother, if it couldn't go in the washing machine or if she couldn't wash it by hand, because she didn't have a washing machine, we didn't use it, so in the winter we had cotton clothes with sweaters piled on. Now Latinos are more connected. There are programs. But in those days, you would see most Latin families with a big heavy winter coat and cotton clothes because they couldn't afford the dry cleaning. They didn't really understand wool, so I ended up explaining everything to my mom. Like, I had an Italian friend and I used to go to her house and her mother cooked spaghetti and meatballs and stuff like that. I was like, "Can I take some to my mother?" And I would say, "Mom, this is what they eat." And she would say, "What did you tell them? I don't feed you?" I was like, "No mom, but I told them I was going to bring them some rice and beans and they would give me this food for me to show you." Lima beans? There wasn't no such thing. We ate red beans with color and flavor, and this lady gave me lima beans. I was like, "But they don't have no taste and they don't have no color." I was like, "You need to put something in them." She said, "These are lima beans, and if you want to eat here, you've got to learn to eat the way we eat, too." So I took ham hocks and lima beans to my mom. "Mom, look, this is what my African friends eat." So she started indulging me and cooking, like, spaghetti and meatballs, but my dad always had to have white rice and some colored beans with some meat. People would come to our house and we would be serving spaghetti and meatballs and rice and beans. There was always rice and beans in my house.

So the blacks and Latinos interacted with one another?

Well, to be honest with you, someone had told my dad that black people would hurt us, so he tried to make us not have black friends, but we went to public school, and my best friend had to be the biggest blackest girl in town. And I told my dad if he didn't like black people, why did you marry my mom? I always made those questions that shocked him. And I somehow found out about protection of children. I think one of my teachers gave me the number to children's protection agency, and I called them and told them that my dad was telling me not to hang out with black folks and he was going to hit me and throw me out the house. So, they said that's a very serious accusation and you would have to go to court and say that. I was like, I'll go, because I wanted them to take me out of my home and put me in one of my friend's homes. That's how my family is, going nowhere real quick, and I had to take care of kids and stuff. So instead they put me in, they used to call them "girls' homes." Saint Ann's, Saint Philomena's, Saint Germaine's, because my mother was Catholic, then girls' camp. This was on and on from when I was nine until I was sixteen. When I was sixteen this Oriental woman said, "She has done nothing." I was the baby of the camp because people knew I was there with murderers and everything else. I had done nothing. So whenever I came back they were like, "Oh she's back" and they would make my life wonderful, then I didn't want to be home but they looked out for me and they taught me a lot. And this woman said to me, "I'm going to take you out because if you stay after sixteen, you're going to go to Bedford. That's a woman's prison. Then you will have a record. I'm going to take you out, but you've got to live with your mom. You've got to promise me that you will do everything necessary until you're eighteen because I took you out." Word is bond. I learned that there. So for two years I went to school, I did whatever, I saved. I tell my mother, "What hour was I born?" Seven thirty in the morning. Seven thirty, November 14, 1956. I had my friends outside waiting. I had an apartment, a job. I made more than my dad. I had my connections. I found the gay clubs on 125th Street. I was eighteen and I was free. You know?

And what did your siblings—what happened to them since you were taking care of them?

My brothers loved that I was gay when I came back out. They would take their suits a size bigger because I came out [as] a daddy, okay? They would get their suits bigger so that I could fit in them. They were very proud because I told them you never judge people by what they are because I knew I was a lesbian and they were going to start hearing that so I kind of trained them that everybody has a right. My brothers cook and wash laundry. They take care of themselves. Your wife is not your slave. She's your partner, and partner means you share. So these women nowadays, they're like, "Aida, thank you." My brothers are fifty-fifty or more partners in anybody's life. When you visit, you bring a bottle [of wine], flowers or something. People have invited you to their home. So everything I was learning from being away from my mother, which I say was a good thing, because I got an education at an American institute called a jail, but who cares? We had no television—none of that. And when I went away I had all of that, so I learned. And in jail there were all these cases that we knew because we knew the girls. So I learned early about if someone accuses you of something, there's a court system and you don't have to accept it and get your reputation ruined. You have a way to fight. I grew up in that system. So I was always a leader. "Go tell the principal. Don't fight her. Kick her ass later, but go to the principal."

I would come out of school at 3:00 p.m. and have to be home by 3:15 p.m. or I would get beat, because my mother decided that that's the longest it should take me to pick up my brothers, collect all these kids and bring them home.

In fifteen minutes?

Yes. And it could be done, but I used to talk to my friends and I would always be late. Milk used to come in glass bottles. She would half fill them with water, kneel me on rice, and if the bottles fell, I was lying or whatever she wanted to accuse me of. I became very strong [*whispering*] because I ain't dropping these bottles. I don't care what she said. It was my mind over her mind. She believed in witchcraft. She took me to a witchcraft woman to get rid of this boyfriend I had, and I told the woman, "If I lose my boyfriend, I'm going to come and kill *you*. You better hope he stays with me forever." And my mother was kind of crazy, the things that she would do. She had the iron cord, the cord from the iron, and she would say, "Okay you did this, I'm beating you twenty times with this cord, and if you raise your hands, it doesn't count." "Ma, I didn't do it!" She said, "You did it."

They used to take me to the gynecologist all the time to see if I was pregnant. I was a virgin until I was eighteen but she decided in her head because I had all these boyfriends, they were friends, that I was having sex. In her mind—she's a sexual deviant, too—in her mind, she imagines I'm having sex. My niece right now will lock the door to her room to our apartment with a friend in there. My mother [would ask], "And why would you lock? Okay . . .

you're a pervert." [*Laughter.*] And so she would insist I did this and I did that, which I had not done. And I refused to let her think that she was fooling me. I was like, "Hello? I know what I did. I didn't do it. I don't care whose Saint you burn or what you do, I didn't do it." So after a while I got used to the beatings, know that something, she's always had this [saying] "mejor tu mano herida que tu corazón" (better your hand hurt than your heart), so she whipped you. It didn't faze me anymore. I said, "You know what? I am rushing home with these kids to get them there by fifteen minutes after. I very seldom make it, so I'm getting beat anyway." I used to leave the kids at the door, go back out, party, dance, go to the movies, do whatever I needed to do. Then people would say, "You going home yet?" What's she going to do? Beat me? She beats me anyway. So I got that "beat me" attitude, you know what I mean? Then she realized she had to change her ways.

So my dad was the nicer guy. So one day he was telling me I had to do something I didn't want to. I said, "Dad, why"? He said, "Because I pay the rent." I see. I made more money than him. I said, "Ma, I want to pay the rent next month." My mom was a gopher. She was this country girl who you could bullshit. She said, "No, honey, you're saving because you said you wanted to move when you're eighteen." I said, "Ma, I want to help. I want to pay the rent. I made more money than dad. I want to surprise him. I don't want you to tell him. I want to pay the rent." I did. I paid the rent. I think it was two hundred dollars. We lived in the government projects. We lived in these nice projects because they made them to simulate the Jewish condos. Because we lived downtown so they didn't want us to feel poor so then they built this Henry Street Settlement. I'm sure you heard of it. And that's where I was raised. All my art and culture comes from the Henry Street Settlement. So the next time my dad told me to do something, I was like, "No, you do what *I* say." He said, "What?" I said, "Ask mom. I paid the rent." I really believed what he said. You said I have to do what you said because you pay the rent. Well, I paid the rent so you do what *I* say. [*Laughter.*] I taught them a lot about what you say. You've got to think about what you say to a child. And at the time, of course, you don't realize you're being so silly. I just was really wanting to be the boss. I said, "Shit, I got money, I'll pay the rent and I'll be in charge. Nobody has to beat me anymore." [*Laughter.*]

When did you come out to your parents?

When I was nine . . . or when I was eleven. My little sister was just born. She was learning how to talk, and I had a lover that was visiting me and we were kissing in the living room and my little sister told my mother that I was kissing this girl. And my mother said, "Well, they're friends." And my sister said, "No they were kissing and muah, muah, muah." So my sister outed me. A baby. And my mother was like, "Oh no, we can't have this." And I said, "Now wait a minute. I am what you made me. I was boy crazy, you sent me away. You could call me bisexual, but you can't disown me. I'm not your child only when I'm good. I'm telling everybody you're my mother." Because she really wanted to disown me because I was a bad influence on my brothers and sisters. I said, "Yeah, but before you knew, I was taking care of them, and my brothers and sisters know who I am. You're the only one who don't know who I am." Because my brothers knew. They knew they couldn't tell my mother. My dad was so hurt that for about two years he didn't even talk to me, and then he started loving the woman I was going with. When he died, he asked her please to take care of me. My mother respects me because I raised her children. I raised *her*. I told *her* what to do. And so she respects me and doesn't want me to think that she looks down on homosexuality, but she's a homophobe, but she hides it from me. But if you listen to her talking. Like when Ricky Martin came out she was like, "Why is he flaunting this?" and then she would look at me like, "Oh I forgot that you're a lesbian." [*Laughter.*]

It's so funny because my mother is my color. I'm the darkest in my family of my immediate siblings of my dad. My mother has African roots, and so we're the colors of the rainbow. But my mother will see a very dark-skinned person and not think they're pretty. She's a racist. And people go, "Aida, how can you say that?" I love her. She's my mother, but I've known her for seventy-four years. She's a racist. And when she thinks something, I get it from her, strong-willed. So if you don't know how to defend yourself in my household, you're in trouble. [*Laughter.*] But my mother would deny that she's a racist. She would deny that she's a homophobe. She's very much together. "Yeah, Ma, okay." But what do you do with your mother? You can't change her views. You learn to accept that. And a lot of older, definitely Puerto Ricans are homophobic, and that's in a lot of cultures, as we've been coming out. I remember when it was you could go to jail for being gay. Now you can ask for marriage rights. I've seen it evolve, which is wonderful. . . .

So, what is your favorite memory of the South?

Pride. . . . It was all of the bars and stuff were downtown. Outwrite [bookstore] had just gotten on the corner of Piedmont, which gave us a view. It was people who were coming from all over the world. It's Pride in Atlanta and you being part of that. It was so much fun, but we also raised money for so many causes and stuff, and it was the one time where the neighborhood really accepted gays. It was Gay Pride. Straight people would come in. I mean, I went to New York Pride, but New York is so big it was Pride and then it goes on. Atlanta was like after the Pride there were parties, before the Pride there were parties. It was the most beautiful time in the world is Pride in Atlanta because it's southern. People cook. People have events. People invite you to parties. People host people and they really mean it. For that one weekend, it's just a family that you so seldom sense that as a gay community, and I saw it evolve from an all-white thing. I was there when Black Pride opened and I was like, "Where y'all going?" And they was like, "Miss Aida, we need our own." And then every Black Pride opening with the Bayard Rustin breakfast. I didn't know who the hell Bayard Rustin was, so I looked it up, and then it was like, "Wow, Martin Luther King and Bayard." I'm one of those that reads and brings it to life and imagine what were they feeling, and so that Bayard Rustin breakfast in Atlanta to this day is an event that you shouldn't miss if you're in Atlanta and you're gay. So, Pride in Atlanta. The weather was beautiful, people were beautiful, you felt good because you did something. I was Grand Marshall one year, and you don't know how proud I was. It was like wow. And then they told me, "Miss Aida, you were unanimously picked." I was like, "Really?" That was a big thing for me because I'm not too impressed with status and all that, but that your community loves you and gives you the greatest honor. I think it's very important for my sense of being.

I started when I got to Atlanta with Latinos en Acción because that was the need. There was a lot of Latins coming into Atlanta and nowhere to go and nothing to do, and I formed Latinos en Acción and then we integrated with all the other organizations. I've learned that being multicultural, adopting it, and not being a racist. I tell my friends who say, "What's up with that white woman?" I said, "That's a racist remark." Because all of us have something to contribute. It don't matter if you're white, black, Hispanic, whatever. And we are so racist and don't even know it. "That white woman thinks . . ." Hello? Her name is Nan. You know? And she's trying to help you. She don't have to be here, you know. Because she's white, she does not have to be here. . . . I remember when they called me a spic. Now Latinos are *in*, but that was not always the case. Now there's all this hate because we're going to become a majority instead of a minority.

The other day a friend of mine was so good to me. She sent me like eight apology cards and I said, "You don't have to. I just wanted you to be aware." Because she didn't like the fact that whatever her name is [Zoe Saldana] is playing Nina Simone. I understand that, but she went and talked about spics and how they're taking over and how dare anybody think that this girl could play Nina Simone. And I said, "Hold it. Puerto Rican here. You've got to understand in spite of myself. Maybe I don't want to be Latina, let's say. I would love to be African American, but guess what? My mother and my father are Latinos, so I've adopted a culture because that was where I was raised. That was my heart. Spanish Harlem. I used to run into American Harlem, and my friends and I love it, and we all come from Africa. So I'm aware, but I'm also Latina, so what you're talking, you're beating up me. What the hell did I do to you?" She's like, "Oh Miss Aida, I'm so sorry, it's just that I forget you're Spanish." And I'm like, "You don't need to remember I'm Spanish, you could just be kind as a human being. I don't need to know what your background is or who your lover is. Just be kind. That's all that it takes. It covers all the bases."

Money in the gay community did not make that much of a difference as much as respect when I was growing up and you looked up to somebody that somehow commanded your respect. When I was growing up there was this woman named Gloria Tubby. She had a club and she was kind to everybody and so she was like our leader. "Tubby said . . . ," you know. I never really belonged to that rough lesbian crowd. There was something about me that I didn't want to be known as that. I thought, "Okay, I'm a lesbian, but I'm not a thug." But because I had a loud voice people would kind of treat me [that way] and sometimes and I would have to say, "Excuse me, I'm not the one." Yeah, it is important for you to know that I go to work and I am not dealing drugs or a drunk or that loud person that you don't want to be seen with because I respect myself. I want you to respect me. I never was part of that wild group. I aspired to be with artists. When *The Color Purple* came out, to be honest with you, I had to see it five times before I really understood it and remembered it all, but I wanted to. It was so beautiful. There's nothing in Puerto Rican culture like that because we don't do culture like that. We do music, and maybe now they're beginning to, but I don't remember my mom ever taking me to nothing equivalent to *The Color Purple*. I remember going to see Rainbow for Colored Girls [*for colored girls who considered suicide / when the rainbow is enuf*]. I had to see that about eight times. I needed an interpreter, but I loved it. It was like, "Wow."

Miss Aida stops abruptly, as if she has begun to feel self-conscious about not speaking in her birth language. I had been hanging on to every word and really perked up when she spoke about Ntozake Shange's *for colored girls*, given that it's one of my all-time favorite plays. I was introduced to it in college in a performance class where we had to perform monologues. I chose the lady in blue's monologue about spending time in a club in Spanish Harlem, the first line of which begins "my papa thot he waz Puerto Rican & wda been/cept we waz just reglar niggahs wit hints of Spanish."[1] Miss Aida's story clarifies for me the significance of what that monologue is trying to get at. Just as I am about to lean over to Miss B. and tell her my connection to Miss Aida's story, I realize that she has moved up to the porch and is sitting between Queen Mother Mary Anne's legs getting her head greased. Her eyes are closed and she looks so peaceful as the fragrant hair grease perfumes the air. For some reason, the sense of closeness I had imagined to Queen Mother Aida dissipates as I watch Miss B. wedged between this elder's legs getting her scalp greased. I am definitely not a part of this world but rather a guest of someone who has blood roots. And yet, despite being a stranger, this place feels familiar.

The woman next to Queen Mother Aida startles me out of my meditation when she rises and walks down to the end of the porch, bends down, and pulls up a loose plank in the porch. She sticks her hand down inside the porch and retrieves a knife, the blade of which is about four inches and slightly curved. She slides the plank back into place and walks back down toward me and down the stairs and out into the yard to the weeping willow tree, under which there is a white bucket. She grabs the bucket, carrying it with her arms wrapped around it like a bag of groceries. As she ascends the steps past me, the fish smell overwhelms the hair grease and my eyes begin to water.

This woman cannot be more than five feet, yet she carries herself like a giant. Her dark, rough hands know of work and weapons. As she plops back down in her chair and drops the bucket down in front of her, I notice her large, almond-shaped eyes. They seem to light up at the sight of the day's catch. She pulls the knife from her apron, wipes it on both sides on her thigh, and pulls a fish out of the bucket and begins to scrape the scales, the silvery translucent flakes popping off in every direction. After about three fish are scaled, she rears back in her chair and begins to speak.

Cherry Hussain

I was born in Daytona Beach, Florida, June 15, 1955, on a Wednesday. My childhood was good, I should say. I'm the last of seven survivors now. It was eight of us. My mom had a couple of miscarriages during that time, but I'm the last child. Two to six, two boys, six girls. I'm the last one. Everybody say you're the baby. I say no, I am not. I'm the last child because everybody know that the first child is always the baby. My mother worked in the school cafeteria across the railroad in a white school. I don't know anything about my mother's husband.

I grew up in South Street Projects. My address was 60, unit 60, and we moved from 60 to unit 1, number 1 in South Street. We lived across the river. White people lived closer to the river and closer to the ocean, and we lived on the other side of the river. We weren't allowed on the beach. The beach was eight miles away from my household, actually ten, and we couldn't go to the beach that was that close to us. Our parents or our friends or relatives would drive us to New Smyrna Beach. Actually, at New Smyrna black people actually owned the property and stuff around the beach, but you know eventually all that changed.

The number one subject [was] white folk. The Caucasians were always the subject. They were called blue-eyed. My grandmother called them ghosts. Yes, and the ghost thing resonates with me to this day because I was laying out at the unit 60, it was a summer day and I had my little quilt out on the front porch, because you get your little baths and you put your little underwear on and you go outside and relax until nap, and this car came by. I can't remember if it was a cop or a cab driver, but it was dusk dark, it was dark enough and it appeared out of the window and it scared me. It was a white man. That's why my grandmother called them ghosts. So that was really profound for me when she called them ghosts.

My grandmother was my best friend, and all of her friends were my friends, and so as I grew, older people were my friends because that's what I knew. I would rather be around the older women than the younger women, and then when I reached a certain age, then I started trying to hang out with my own kind, but then I found myself migrating back to the older [people] because they kept me settled. The wisdom and knowledge of those people were just amazing, and I must say I learned a whole lot from hanging around with older people. My skills as a mechanic or my skills at looking at something and figuring out how to fix it [are] because my grandmother lived in the rural areas of Thomasville, Georgia. We had a well. We had pigs. We had chickens. It was like a farm-type thing. My grandmother had a garden, so that's where the freshness comes from for fruits and vegetables and stuff. My grandmother was a root woman. I'm fifth-generation. I'm proud to say it. She was born in 1902, so that makes her parents ex-slaves, I guess you could say, and then it was just all girls in her siblings.

And they all practice?

You know everybody gets saddity. [*Laughter.*] But she did. She was our neighborhood healer. Used to get together and cut wood. During the wintertime, everybody got together and shared chores because people needed things when the wintertime come. There was an incident once where we were all harvesting, I would say wood cutting, and a man cut his leg with the ax, and my grandmother always wore a apron and in those apron pockets was goodies, a sewing needle, different things. Instead of a purse, it was the pockets on the apron. But she took care of that.

What did she put together?

She had something in her apron pocket. She said, "Jenny, run to the house and get my quilting basket," so that was my chore to always get stuff, water or whatever, and she took some orange powder out of her apron and by the time I was gone, she had it. And when I came back it looked like a patch of moss and mud from my point as being as young as I was, and the things that she took out of her quilting basket was a—I remember it very well—it was a piece of black thread and a hook needle, and she sewed him up, put another layer of something then patched him up, and he sat and he did what he could do, and then three or four days later he was up and walking and it didn't get infected or any of that, but she made sure that she always tended to the wound and then passed it on to his family to take care of.

When you on that farm, you throw on your boots, you throw on your dirty pants. You put a hat on or get a hat and you put them gloves on and you work that farm. You work. But then when you had to go to the city or the town or whatever it is, then you had to be, "Oh, let me get that for you." But when I'm on that farm, it's not that way, so why you want to act so uppity and so gently now when it's not the same when you're on the farm? And I tell Pat it was a difference between town and the city. Okay, in town, it's like the little general stores, little corner stores, and then the city, it's the fast-paced, sophistication, the uppity folks, the saddity people. We went to town and you hear things as a child and it pass you by, but then there was always the color code thing going on, and if you called somebody African, they wanted to cut you. If you called somebody black, they killed you. "You a African!" "I'm not an African!" That's a kill. And if you call somebody black, they want to beat you up because they talk about your nose, your lip size, your shape. That's what it was when we were growing up. And kids imitate what they see and hear, so it's passed on.

So, what did people prefer to be called? Colored, Negro?

I was born colored, raised Negro, I became black, I was an Afro-American, now I'm an African American, now I'm colored again. So, you know what? [*Laughter.*] I roll with the punches, but I'm still human. That's a dangerous thing, though. Being human is dangerous. The most dangerous animal on this planet is *human* because we take what we want, we kill for no reason, and if you got something I want, I'm going to take it from you. So being human, is that good? I don't know.

When did you first realize that you had same-sex attraction?

I was a late bloomer, but I tell you my first encounter with a female was in, I was in fourth grade. I'll tell you her first name. I won't tell you her last name. Her name was Deborah. She said, "We're going to play mommy and daddy, and I'm daddy," and she threw me down and laid on top of me, kissed all over the face and said, "Mmm, mmm, ah, ah." [*Laughter.*] That was my first encounter.

And that was it?

That was it. And in the . . . I want to say seventh grade, I had a crush on one of the cheerleaders. I will NOT say her name. I had her glove. She misplaced her glove and I had it. I didn't know what was going on, but I slept with that glove for three days until I saw her and gave it back to her. Poof, went on out. But my thing was by me being molested, by me being passed around from men to men, I thought it was something normal. It just had to be done. I'll tell you these bastards' names that took advantage of me. One was [man's name], which was the man that lived in our household. The next one was [man's name], which was a family member that all my, my brother and siblings knew and would work for and do things for, and that was the opening of me realizing what was going on was not right.

I was in the ninth grade. Yes. I called myself, "me, M-E," because every-thing that was happening was happening to Cherry but M-E was the strongest one that would say no, fight back, punch, kick, tell. [Man's name] was on the phone with his brother-in-law in Jacksonville, Florida, and I heard him telling his brother-in-law, "Oh that's no problem, I can bring her back up here and I'll let you have her when I get back up here." I heard that conversation. The light bulb went on. I'm being passed around. That's why all these men are having sex with me. I became a very mean person after that, brutal. Men didn't care. I was really angry, and by me being a lesbian it had nothing to do with that. I left my household for all the wrong reasons, but it was the right thing to do . . .

I left home at twenty-one. I left home in '77. I got married in '78. I left home in '77 and moved to Alabama because William [her husband] called and said come and I needed to go and I left. I got married and then we had our son. Yeah. I didn't want kids, but stuff happens. But I tell my kids to this day if I had known then what I knew now, I would not have had them. I love my children. I really do. And they were both mistakes, but they were good mis-takes. I love my babies. I do, and there was a reason for me having them, be-cause it kept their dad from getting killed. [Laughter.] That's another story. We were both young. I married him. He was a selfish boy. I called him one year after the divorce. I had so much stuff going on in my head. We were sleeping downstairs at that time in the room downstairs and I woke up one morning because I was hearing people saying in order to forgive somebody you have to forgive yourself first, and I'm trying to figure out what the hell you need to forgive yourself for things that happened to you, you had no control over? You know? And I was fighting with that. How in the hell do I forgive myself? I didn't do anything to me. Everything that was done to me was done to me, but then it manifest itself. And I called him, I think it was in January or New Year's, and told him, "You know what, William? I forgive you because I forgive myself. We can be friends if you like to and if you don't, that's okay, but I still forgive you. I'll be there if you need me." I said, "But we're still the parents of our children, and you can take this as any way you want it, but letting you know that I do forgive you."

And I did, because the things that happened to me in my life gave me a better understanding of human beings and I wouldn't be the person that I am today even though it was a lot of stuff on me, but it made me a lot kinder to people as I got older and it made me understand abused women. It made me understand that run-away from home. It made me understand that poor boy sitting on the corner over there who done robbed this woman but sobbing because he done that. That made me aware. That gave me a wisdom I didn't have—a forgiveness—because everything happened for a reason. Might not know what it is, things happen. Things happen for you, and I think that it gave me a lot of patience, 'cause I didn't have any.

I don't like nonsense. I don't like chaos. I like order and I demand it. It's like common courtesy. I tried to explain to a young man about common courtesy about the Negro race, colored folk, because it was a matter of life and death for us to know how to speak to Mr. Charlie and Miss Ann when they walk down the street. It was a matter of getting what you need if you were polite enough to the white folks to get what you wanted. It was a matter of survival to say "Please" and "Thank you," "Good morning," "Excuse me" and not look those white folks in the eye when you were doing it. It was a matter of survival for us. What's wrong with common courtesy? It's just being a human being and saying, "Excuse me," "Please," and "Thank you," "Good morning," "Good evening," "Good afternoon." What's wrong with that? It gets you what you need. Because I'll do more for you with your common courtesy than I will with your cussing and demanding what I need for you to do for me. Because if you demand anything from me, I give you what I'm supposed to give and let somebody else deal with you. But if you giving me common courtesy, I'm going to do everything I can for you and sometimes do things I'm not supposed to do to make sure that you get what you need. That's the difference between me. No nonsense. I need order, not chaos. I'm sorry. I get kind of crazy, don't I?

No, no, no. So, when you and your husband separated, did you keep the kids?

No.

They stayed with their father?

Yes. William, by us being young, by him being an educated man, he knew that I wasn't [at] his intelligent [[intelligence]] level when we got involved. I think William liked me because of my caring of him, making sure that he had everything he needed. I think that's what he got because he didn't get that. He was a educated man, a very selfish man. I'll tell him that to his face today. In his role of thinking that he was trying to motivate or help me, he would call me dumb. He would tell me that I wasn't going to amount to anything, but the light bulb came on when this fool told me, "When I finish my degree, I'm going to take my children and I'm 'a leave you."

He told you that?

Yes. Now, why would a dumb person like me stay with a smart man, stay with him and he's telling me he's going to leave me? How dumb would I have been? He said, "You too dumb to even teach your children how to read or write." But every gift that I got my children were educated stuff and I would make them read the instructions. I bought this thing called SMath. It was a thing of spelling and math together thing. I said, "William I bought this for the children. If you read the instructions, we can play this game with them." He said, "See how dumb you are? You can't even read these instructions to teach the children." But you hear this all the time. When I was growing up I heard enough of it, but then when I married this man on an educated level that was supposed to been able to help me and bring me up, he wasn't smart enough to know how to do that. His intelligence wasn't at that level of intelligence to do that. But if a man telling you he's going to leave you, how dumb would it have been for me to sit there and wait? So I left him.

When I decided to leave my children's father, I would've taken a job in Tahiti as long as I had a job and somewhere to stay. If someone had offered me a job in Timbuktu, Egypt, I would've gone. But when I left my children's father, I went bound on the word of someone I didn't know. "Come live with me. I'll get you a place to stay and a job. Come and stay." When I left my children's father, I left my children with their father. They had room and board and clothes. They were in school. He had a job. He could feed them. He could clothe them. He could get them back and forth to where they were going. When I left, I had no place to stay. I had no job. I had no car. I had no school to put my children in, so where was the better place for my children? If I was going to be homeless, I wasn't dragging my children with that. If I was going to be homeless because of something else that had happened, yes I would've had my children, but I was leaving their father. I wasn't leaving my children. I was leaving *him*. He was abusive to *me*, not to them. To the *mommy*, not the children. So when I left, I left them in very good hands. He got me on abandonment.

Do you think your kids felt resentful?

I don't know. My daughter says she felt abandoned.

How old was she?

She was eight. And [*long pause*] I did things in my mind that I thought were better for them because, you know, as we look along the way we could've did things, if I had of, ought of, should of, and other things, but my children, talking to them as life got on within they time of aging, my children were saying, "We heard a lot mommy, we knew a lot," and I was trying not to cry out because I didn't want them to hear but then after they had told me their dad had started in on them. My son showed up at my door with the clothes on his back. He said he didn't want to live with him. He loved his dad. He said he was standing at the top of the steps wanting to push him off the steps. Something happened, but whatever happened, my children are adult enough and mature enough to forgive him and still have him as a part of their life. My daughter stayed too long with him because he was saying if you leave me, you'll never get to see me. You know how they play on your emotions, and being a girl, and her ways are like his, too. But that's my child. I don't like my child, but I love her. I don't like my children, but I love them. And I fault myself for their behavior because I left them too long with their father and allowed them to manipulate that guilt part of motherhood, and then after a while, it's like that rubber band. That rubber band is giving for a long time, and when it get tired of you stretching what it does is it pops your ass on it. It does.

When was your first lesbian sexual experience?

Huntsville, Alabama, with a married woman with two children. [*Laughter.*]

And how did that happen?

My friend, Jessie, we hit it like this [*puts her index and middle fingers together*] when I met her in Huntsville. She worked at the cafeteria at A&M campus; Alabama A&M in Huntsville was in Norman, but everybody say it's Huntsville. But anyway, I met her through one of my children's father's friends, one of his fraternity brothers, because he was over in the cafeteria. This loudmouth girl. We both loud. We hit it off just like that [*claps*]. We were sisters from another mother, and we are like that to this day. All of the little knickknacks and the signs were there, because she had girlfriends and they all lived together, and I didn't think about anybody sleeping in a bed together. Hell, I still sleep with my sister. I didn't think anything about it, and they had a one-bedroom apartment. So what? That's normal for me. Ten children? Come on. [*Laughter.*] I won't call the other girlfriend by name because she went through some stuff, but her other girlfriend, and then the light bulb came on. BING! She's a dyke but she's my best friend and that was okay. This other young lady that I met because we used to go out to the post, well the arsenal in Huntsville, and play basketball because Jessie drove a bus for them and we would get on and I drove a cab. That's another story. But I met this woman through Jessie and come to find out that she was also a dyke with two kids, two beautiful girls, and wow, bells and whistles and lightning. That orgasm was just phenomenal. But I said that out loud. But yeah, her, and then I met another young lady.

And at this time were you married?

Mm hmm, still married.

What was the BING!, the click, the "Ah-ha!" or whatever, because you had had traumatic sexual experiences with men but then you had children with your husband but something was missing? What was it that happened with this woman? Was it just the sex, the difference in the sex, or . . . ?

It probably was. I think it was the touching, the embrace, the gentleness, the emotional experience that you got with somebody just holding you, understanding you. I think that's what it was because that's the only thing that I'm like, "Oh my, is this the way it feels to be touched and caressed and not forced?" Now don't get me wrong, now William, I taught him everything he knew. He was a good sex partner. I mean, look at all the lessons I had. You got to get it right. You gonna be with me, get it right, but sex was wonderful. I had orgasms with him, but there was something missing, and it was that emotional, that feeling, was the thing that was missing. I loved him, I did. I cared for him, but I wasn't in love with him. He was my ticket away from home. That's what he was. I was grateful. I was grateful for the escape from home because I would've been in trouble.

So, you met this woman, bells and whistles, and you had other experiences. Did you at that moment decide, okay I'm definitely a lesbian?

Yes, because William and I got in a battle. I told him, "You know what? I don't even like you. I like girls." And we fought. But I told him that was the last ass whooping I was ever going to take from him, and we fought, and he was one of the kind like Pat's mother, he wasn't happy unless he was screaming at the top of his voice at you. It had gotten so mental with me that at three o'clock no one had to tell me it was three o'clock, because I already knew it was three o'clock because I knew the beast was coming. I found myself sitting in the closet one day, and when he came home, just those few seconds of not having to see him was so wonderful. Just sitting in the closet and he hollered, calling my name, and then it dawned on me: What's your stupid ass sitting in the closet for? Get out of this damned closet! Don't make that man make you fear him like that. Get your ass out of the closet! So I sat on the edge of the bed and he came in and said, "I've been calling you" and I said, "I've been sitting right here." "I didn't see you." And I said, "because you were too damned angry calling; you didn't see me sitting here." [I was] playing his cards.

William told me, "Here. You call your sisters and brothers. You call them." I said, "I'll call them when I want to." "You tell them you like girls." Dialed my mother's number. I hung up the phone. I said, "You can't make me do anything anymore. I'll call when I want to." And so he went through all that. He wants to call my sisters and brothers. I said, "You're an adult. You can do whatever you want. Pick up the phone and call them if you like." So I called. The only person that really, really crushed my heart out of my siblings was my sister Gunh, my sister Gwen. My nieces and nephews couldn't say "Gwen"; they called her Gunh, and my brother, Lucius. But everybody else, I would've got over it even with my mother, but those two . . . and Linda. Linda said, "Okay." And I told my mamma. I said, "Mamma, I need to tell you something." She said, "Okay." I said, "Are you sitting down?" And she said, "Are *you* sitting down?" I said, "No, ma'am." She said, "You're walking and rubbing your head, aren't you?" And I'm not aware that I do this, and when I find myself doing it, I stop because my mother brought it to my attention and Pat did, too. And I said, "Yes." She said, "Well, what is it you need to tell me, you should sit down?" I sat down and I said, "Mamma, I like girls." She said, "You like girls?" I said, "Yeah." She said, "Are you happy?" I said, "No." She said, "Well, you need to find somebody that make you happy." I said, "But I wanted you to know that." She said, "Okay. Are you okay?" I said, "No." She said, "Pull it together." My mother told me that. I said, "Yes, ma'am." I called all my siblings. I have a brother that's a Church of God in Christ pastor. He said, "You're my sister." He said, "I might not approve of what you do, but you're my sister and I still love you. Hate the sin, love the sinner." I said, "I'm not a sinner [*snaps*]. I just happen to be a human being that loves women." He said, "You're my sister. I might not approve of what you do, but you're my sister and I love you." And Gwen, she said, "Damn. I thought you had pneumonia or something." And I told them all. And my sister Patricia. If you look up the word to be Christ-like in the dictionary, you would see my sister Patricia because she lives it. She doesn't preach at you, but if you asked her a question, she'd talk to you. You know? But my siblings were okay with that, and that was good, and my nieces and nephews are just fine: "Oh, my auntie is a dyke. My auntie's a dyke!"

[*Laughter.*] You know how nieces and nephews are, but my family's okay with me and that's all that matters.

When I took Pat home to meet my family, my mother had a list of things that she wanted to get for Pat. She said, "Jenny let's go. We need to go to the store and get Pat's stuff." Pat's allergic to the sun, so we couldn't survive in Florida, so my mother loved this ice cream parlor called Dippity Dan. It's not around anymore. They used to make homemade ice cream and stuff, and she wanted to introduce Pat, so we had to go out, and she was getting a list of stuff. I said, "Hell, Pat's not special." She said, "Cherry." I said, "Yes, ma'am." She said, "That woman loves you. You're going to make me a promise that you're going to do everything you can to make her happy and keep her happy because no one else is going to love you like her." My mother told me that. And I do everything I can to keep that promise to my mother because she deserve everything I can give her and all the things I wish I can give her. Because I work very hard to make sure that she gets everything that she needs, and that's the promise I made to my mother.

That's really a beautiful story and not one that I would have expected given everything else you said. Why do you think your mother was so accepting?

I'm her child. What mother wouldn't want their child to be happy? What parent wouldn't want their child to be happy? And I am very honored and thankful that my ancestors gave me my mother that allowed me to be in the family that I have. I'm thankful for my ancestors for putting me with the people who love me, and I'm very thankful for that because I've heard horror stories and I've lived some horror stories, but I'm thankful for my family as jacked up as they are, they're mine and I love and honor them all.

What are your current feelings about being a black lesbian?

My current feelings? [*Smacks her lips.*] I am a proud black dyke. My feelings about being a dyke, I have no feelings. I have feelings of being human, and when I told you before it's a dangerous thing, right? I am happy with me. I am happy with my wife. My feelings about being a dyke, being a black dyke [*giggles*], I love me. I love Miss Cherry, you know. I can't say I have any feelings. I can say what I can feel about Miss Cherry, and that's a happy Cherry. That's how I feel about being me but not the other me.

I am emotionally spent by Queen Mother Cherry's story. I tried not to go into the ugly cry a few times while she was narrating her abuse, but I couldn't help it. I was also moved by her capacity to forgive all of the men who had abused her or taken her for granted. I write down her line "The most dangerous animal on this planet is human." I find it both an obvious and yet profound observation. And given what she has been through, I totally understand why she believes that to be true.

Miss B. and Queen Mother Ida Mae have gone out by the weeping willow to have a cigarette, but I can faintly hear their voices through the rustling leaves. As I begin jotting down a few more notes about Queen Mother Cherry, Queen Mother Lori comes over and sits down beside me on the steps. She stares at my writing pad and then slips it out of my hands and begins to flip through it. She gives it back to me after a while and then smiles before sharing a story about her life that seems to start in the middle of its telling.

Lori Wilson

My mom just stayed pregnant most of the time, so she didn't work a whole lot, and then when she did she worked as a maid, and my dad was a construction worker, and so it was just kind of in and out. What always stands out the most for me and my childhood is that we were just very poor. We lived in the same house for a few years and then we moved a couple of times. We moved throughout Houston, and I think at one point we moved when I was like in the fifth grade to live in a better neighborhood and a better house or something, so I'm guessing my dad must've gotten a better job. I had a brother right under me, he went to live with my mom's mom, and then I had a sister, a younger sister, and she lived with her godmother, and then my youngest sister lived with my aunt and uncle. They had ten kids, but some were there and some were not. I just remember, like, "Damn, every time she go to the store she come back with a baby." [*Laughter.*] The last baby was born at home, and so it was like, "Oh, mama done found a baby on the porch." It was all very crazy. She was very sick with that baby, and every time she had these kids, it's like it was so obvious in my life because every time she left I got sick. It felt like she left me, and so I would get like physically sick, and so people for many years thought, like, oh Lord, she ain't gonna never leave home, she just ain't gonna never leave home. Like when I went to school, I think I went to school when I was six, and so I just cried like the first week. I just didn't want to be there. I just hated school and wanted to be at home with my mother, but I was actually the first one to leave home basically. My dad was an alcoholic, very abusive physically. He fought my mother a lot, terrorized the house most weekends, unpredictable. You didn't really know if he was going to buy everybody on the block ice cream or if he was going to come home and try to kill everybody.

At some point, my mother started dating the guy that is my stepfather now, and one day we left home on the weekend and we never went back. I was fourteen at the time. It's, like, okay, and that wasn't really out of order. We would sneak around and leave and go be with him on the weekends sometimes, but we would always go back, but this particular weekend we left and we didn't go back. It wasn't a discussion they had with us. I guess my mom just decided she had had enough.

And how many of you kids were around at that time?

It was probably four of us at the time, and then I met this guy, this boy is what he was, boy because I was a girl, and I was fourteen. At the time that I met him my mother had people [who] had some kind of concern that I wasn't liking boys. It's like it was cool. We played basketball, shoot marbles, steal bikes, fix bikes, go carts, da da da da; that was cool, but not really. When I met this boy, they just kind of got excited [*laughter*] that I was even interested and just kind of pushed that issue. He lived in Angleton, and so he would hitchhike and everything. I was fourteen. He was sixteen. He would hitchhike to Houston to come see me and just all of that, and so when I was fifteen, I turned fifteen in October. In November, I got pregnant, and then that was in '77. In February of '78, I left home, went to Angleton and never came back. My mother was like, "Can't have no babies in my house, can't stay in my house having no babies" kind of stuff. She never really said that to me, but I could hear her—and never talked to me about it, never said, "Are you pregnant, what are we going to do?" any of that. But the message was just very clear. And so I was going to have to have an abortion or whatever. The guy wanted his baby and his mother was not up for that whole thing happening and so she was like, "You can come live with us," and I did.

When I went to live in Angleton, he was actually in jail at the time for burglary of a building. I went there, and for me, it was like being grown because I couldn't wait to be grown. I wasn't fast. I just wanted to smoke cigarettes and cuss. [*Laughter.*] And then, of course, that's kind of like your rite of passage in this society. When you have a kid, that kind of like defines you as an adult. You grown and you got a baby kind of stuff, but what people don't realize is that the responsibility of having a baby don't really make you grown. If I think about it, it should have been like, what are you thinking? You need to take your ass back home, but that never happened, and the relationship was basically the carbon copy of my parents' relationship—he was abusive, he cheated, he did all of that, so we just fought like we didn't have nothing else to do most of the time. We stayed together with his mother, had the first baby in August of '78, so at the age of fifteen, I started having sex, I got pregnant, I left home, and had the baby that year. It was a girl, Tanisha. And then nine months later, I was pregnant again, another little girl. It was just like [things] had gotten progressively worse, so by now I'm just feeling stuck in this situation, and my mother, they never say that you can come home. My mother actually was at the hospital when I gave birth to my daughter. They were going to do the little epidural or whatever, and so she told people that no, that it was in my best interest because I wasn't going to sit still long enough and I was going to be paralyzed, but what I later realized was that she was trying to punish me.

She wanted you to feel all that pain.

Yeah, and I did. And I did. But it wasn't enough to deter me apparently from getting pregnant again. And so, you know, got pregnant again and just already realizing that it's not a good situation with this man.

Had you dropped out of school?

Yeah, I dropped out of school when I was in the ninth grade, which meant I had an eighth-grade education. Then, you know, just kind of had the baby. She was born December of '79. I was working, started working at a nursing home, and this lady next door was supposed to watch the kids and she couldn't and so my mother-in-law watched them. And I got home from work and the baby was dead. Actually, I came home from work, the oldest one like [*mimics a baby crying*] "Eh, eh," you know. I got two kids, neither one of them talked, both of them sucking bottles, both of them in Pampers, and she was like wanting these crackers, and I was like, "Shhh." So I was asking my mother-in-law where's the baby at and she was like, "The baby's in there and she's still asleep." And I go in there and sit on the side of the bed and she's not waking up, she's not doing anything. I was just like, What's going on over here? I shook the bed, she shook with the bed, shook the bed and she shook with the bed, and she was dead and that was just really crazy. The dad was already [saying], That ain't my baby, that ain't my baby, that ain't my baby" kind of shit.

Were y'all married?

We got married. We eventually got married right when I turned eighteen and he was in jail.

Again?

Again, and on his way to prison, so the rule basically was that he couldn't have any contact visits unless we were married, so we got married, so it wasn't like because we was in love. [*Laughter.*] It was convenience, that kind of thing. Because he was like really stressing the hell out of me with this baby, and then when she died, he was just devastated, and so I was just angry at him for being so devastated.

He said it wasn't even his.

Yeah, as recently as the night before.

Did they find out what happened? Was it sudden infant death syndrome, SIDS?

Yeah that's what they ended up, because that was back in '80, so that's what they called it. So they investigated and all that, and I just remember going to the hospital and riding in the ambulance with her and that was like the longest ride of my life and it probably was like five minutes, ten at the most, but it just seemed like a long ride. No panicking, no real emotion at this point because I'm probably by now so emotionally detached from life that I don't know what the fuck to feel. [*Laughter.*] Happiness wasn't a good deal in my house. Sadness, you too poor for that, and so really the only acceptable emotion was anger and everybody understood that, and so, of course, needless to say, I fought a lot growing up. You couldn't say stuff like, "My feelings are hurt," "That made me sad," you know? Those were not my household words and nothing like that, so that's how you dealt with whatever it was, whether it was sadness, whether it was disappointment, whatever. You just got mad and everybody understood mad. So, you know, she died, and probably a few months after that we ended up moving away from his mom's house and getting our own place.

You and your daughter?

And him.

Oh, I thought he went to jail.

He went to jail. He went to jail and got out of jail, went to jail, got out of jail. The story of his life.

Why did you stay with him?

One, I was still very young, and he was crazy, too. At that point the thought, considering leaving, that wasn't an idea at that point. What would I do? My mother had already put me away from her house and had never said you can come back. But to this day, I've always been pretty committed to whatever it is I'm going to do, so I've always lived by my own rules—good, bad, indifferent— and yes, took some bumps along the way. So when my daughter was born, I just remember making that commitment to her, like thinking it doesn't really matter. I'm going to take care of you no matter what. I decided this, and this is what this is going to be.

So we moved, and he now is trying to gather his thoughts and he gets a job working for the railroad and that's a pretty good job. We living in this little one-bedroom shack house kind of deal, but it's our house. We are very young and doing better than grown people, and I'm working, he's working and trying to raise this kid. Plus, I think when my daughter died, I got pretty detached emotionally, and so he was still pretty attached to her and that was his baby. He didn't know as much about being a father as I knew about, but him probably even less. Like I had some idea, because girls do, because it's real alright for us to play with dolls so we learn that whole thing, nurturing my baby, get the bottle, change the Pampers, baby don't cry kind of dolls and shit. So that was all about preparation, where with boys, it's like if boys get caught playing with dolls, it's like a whole meltdown in the house [*laughter*], so then they have these kids and society expects them to be fathers and they never learned how to nurture anything, so they don't know what to do with that. But you know, that was her daddy, and that was his baby. And we got high. We got high. We got high. We got high all the time. We got high. That was the thing that we probably had in common. We smoked weed, drinking, you know. Before I got pregnant with my oldest, I was drinking. I was like a blackout drinker. So, yeah, we got high and I drank and then I got pregnant and I stopped drinking but I still smoked weed. I smoked weed throughout my pregnancies. And thank God, they didn't do what they do now, which is test the babies. That little baby would've been over there in CPS custody. So, smoke weed and it was probably a couple years before I started drinking again. Well, actually, the day that the baby died I remember, like, making a conscious decision about getting drunk and don't really remember getting drunk but drank but I don't remember getting drunk and so I think at that period is when I started drinking again. Not a whole lot, didn't really drink, but it got progressively worse. And then at some point, I had a bright idea—I'm always a sucker for a good idea, so I thought I would start selling weed. It was like sell weed, keep some weed to smoke, sell weed, just kind of keep that going. Did that, and then the whole intent was to just not have to buy weed, you know, have enough to smoke and sell it and just have enough. Well the demand got great and so, you know, it was like, and then, so it went from a quarter pound of weed to a half pound of weed and from a half pound of weed to a pound of weed, and so it just kind of got bigger, and then, but I'm still working. He's still working. At this point I'm working at a nursing home, at a different nursing home, and so I was thinking earlier that day, how am I going to get home? A couple hours later, the police was coming to pick me up to take me home. They raided the house and came and got me and took me back to the house and it was just a mess in there. And it was crazy because in my high, in my craziness, and this man that I'm living with, and we crazy, and we basically growing up together, right? So, we have this Polaroid camera, and so I'm high, he high, we just decided we just going to take naked pictures. [*Laughter.*] Naked pictures, lingerie, so we got like a couple of photo albums of pictures and so the police come and they take the photo albums. I was like, why you got to take that? "Well, there's pictures in here." You know I'm posing and smoking weed and they like you smoking weed. I'm like, "I ain't never said I didn't smoke weed but there ain't nothing in there showing me selling weed or anything." So, you know, they take me on to jail and a little while later he shows up at the jail. Somebody told him that they took me to jail. I was actually the one that was doing the dealings with the guy selling the weed, so he came and got me. He paid my bond to get out and all of that.

Where was your daughter?

With my mother-in-law, because I was at work so she had been at Head Start so she was there, which was good, which was a good thing. So, we go to jail, get out of jail, and go on with life, and of course now I'm thinking, okay now I've got to pay this attorney. So I got to sell some more weed [*laughter*], and actually the weed that was in the house wasn't as much weed as I had because the majority of it was down the street at a friend's house. But what I don't know is, is that this guy [her husband] is using cocaine. We used it together, but he had by now started shooting dope. And I didn't know. It was just kind of like a decline in life because there was something real attractive about that. Like, he had this guy that lived around the corner that shot dope, too. He didn't know how to hit himself so he would always get this guy to do it. And so this guy wasn't at home [and] so he don't give a shit at this point [and] he comes to the house and he's trying to fix it and fix it and fix it and so he's trying to hit himself and he keep missing, keep missing, and I'm just like, "What are you doing?" Like what the hell? And so I say, "Okay stop that, let me see that," and so I hit him and the guy comes and he does it again. The guy does a shot of dope [and] it's like he just breaks out in a sweat. I don't know why, it was something appealing about that to me, and so now I want to try it, not today, but the next time he gonna do it I'm going to try it. So, I was like, "Oh yeah, I'm going to try the cocaine." The first time I tried it, the needle got clogged up, so that was a sign from God I'm sure. Stop that. Stop, don't do that. Don't do that. So, a couple weeks later it does [work], and so we started shooting dope, and so now we got a whole habit. The drug using got bad pretty quick and then we pretty much at a point where we're not homeless but we're living in a house where it's no running water and something happens and he goes back to jail and so he's on his way to prison. This friend of mine, the one that I've been working with, the one who's my best friend, she came to Houston and she was like, "You need to come home." So I went back and I lived with her. I go to Houston, stay for about five or six months, she comes up there, I'm just out of control. This is my every day all day thing. I'm criminal like hell, on probation for eight years, been put on probation for eight years and not doing nothing right, getting high as hell, drinking, drinking, drinking excessively and just was like real hopeless at this point. Like, life as I knew it was no longer so I was just like couldn't gather my thoughts. And so she came and I started losing weight again. She's watching this madness.

So, I go back to Angleton and I live with her and I go back to work and stay there, but I was smoking crack. We smoking crack. She's smoking too, but she's a different kind of crack smoker. [*Laughter.*] I really appreciate her because it didn't matter what the hell was going on, we was going to work the next day. We'd stay up all night and watch the sun come up and we still went to work and that was her check. And for me it was like as long as you got a job you can always get dope on credit because now, crack is out so that's just coming through like a fucking tornado and you just watching women just get butt naked for nothing for men who they never would've thought about having sex with two years ago. So, it was just like mm-mm, can't suck no dicks, nope, nope, can't do it, can't do it. [*Laughter.*] But I'm just working and smoking. I'm working and smoking. My daughter's still over there with my mother-in-law. So, it's just bad. It's bad. It's a bad situation. So, my commitment to my daughter, I was not living in that commitment and so that made life worse for me and I didn't know how I was going to come out of that. Like what the hell am I going to do? Because there would be times that I would say I wasn't going to smoke and shit, I'd be smoking. So I could never get a footing to like get back right. Like, I could not stop smoking.

I met this woman and there was just something that was really inspiring about her. She was a black woman and she was standing up there and she was so eloquent and she was pretty. She was down from Houston and she was driving back and forth doing this presentation for the, it was like this OJT [on-the-job training] that you had to deal with if you was getting food stamps or welfare. So, I was like, "Okay." So I met her and we just stayed in contact and so while I was in hiding one of the times and she said she was going to Angleton and I said, "Well, I need to go and report." She said, "Okay." I said, "My cousin's going to take me. She said, "Well, I'll bring you back home." Okay. So I meet her and so we on the way home and she said, "You know, if you stop getting high, if you stop using drugs, your life would be so much better." I said, "You know, if you started getting high, your life wouldn't be so boring." [*Laughter.*] "Mm, why would I want to do that?" That just didn't seem appealing to me. That just didn't seem like anything I want to do. So they make this thing mandatory for us to go to at the courthouse. These two guys are there from prison and they're doing this presentation and the one guy who was like twenty years old, he was talking and he's in prison for like ninety-nine years or something like that, and he was a football player and all this stuff and he was doing really good and he got on probation; he'd go over and give his probation officer [football] tickets, "Come see me [play]," you know, so he thought he was bullshitting the system and still doing shit. I think his dad was some kind of prominent attorney in Houston. Black kid. Mom was a schoolteacher, so he just thought he could get away with shit and this time it wasn't going to happen for him, so he's in front of the judge. And so he told the judge, "I'm using drugs, I'm a drug addict," and so the judge told him, "You should've told your probation officer." I don't know why but that stayed with me. And so I had decided, because I would never report like I was supposed to, so people would always come to my job, "Okay, I haven't seen you in two, three months." They used to be at my office at eight o'clock. So, I didn't do shit right in the first two years I was on probation and so I had decided that the next time I go, I'm going to tell this woman I'm a drug addict; I need some help. And so I go in and I said, "I'm a drug addict and I need some help." So, she like, "Let me see your arms." When I got put on probation, I had these tracks on my arms so that was like distinguishing marks on my body and I was like, "No, I started smoking because I knew you'd be looking for that." She was like, "You don't look like it." Yep, because I understood the game this time. It was rules like eat before you start getting high so you don't lose weight so you don't have those telltale signs so I had all these rules in place. And so she was my second probation officer. The first lady she just couldn't send me to prison so that's why she got rid of my ass because she knew my situation. I was going with this crazy boy, I had this kid, I was young, and so she just couldn't do her job with me. So the new PO goes and tells her, "She says she's a drug addict," and so she found me somewhere to go, which is here over at the Austin State Hospital, they got a unit over there. And I'm thinking, "Well okay, wait a minute, that's for crazy people" and then I thought, I guess I'm crazy just smoking shit, losing my mind, over here doing all kinds of shit because I'm criminal, you know what I'm saying?

So I come to Austin and I go to treatment. My brother goes to treatment the year before and he still smoke weed but he didn't drink no more. That's good. They gave him these pills, Antabuse. And so, my idea of treatment was that I was going to get me some crack pills or cocaine pills or whatever and then I could still smoke weed and drink. So when I got to treatment it was like, "No, that's not how this goes. You can't do anything." I said, "Really? I don't think this was the place I was supposed to come to." It was, but by now I'm just so hardened, my heart is just hard and everything about me is just like crazy and so I'm just very angry and pretty volatile and just really want to be left the fuck alone. Okay. And so I go to treatment for twenty-eight days and probably the second week I realize, because they say okay you can do whatever you want to do. You can go back home and smoke you some weed but I'm telling you you're going to be smoking crack. I said, "I don't want to do that," and so I made a decision that I wasn't going to go back, and so I left there and went to a halfway house for like four months and then got an apartment and stayed in Austin.

You weren't going through any withdrawal or anything?

Not anything physical as far as . . . people who did heroin, alcohol, they have really bad withdrawal. Alcohol will kill you if you try to detox if you physically addicted to alcohol. Like, you cannot detox on your own. You could go into DTs and die. Heroin just makes you feel like you gonna die. Cocaine was more like psychological. For the first couple of days that I'm there, I'm just hungry and tired and so it's like, you know, and so the second day I'm just thinking. The withdrawal wasn't so much, it was just like my body was rested a little bit and so it was like, "Okay what are we doing here? Let's go." So, it's like that feeling of wanting to use, needing to use, but in this locked facility and it's not coming out and I'm in a city where I don't know nothing. I'm just over here on these grounds and I don't know where to go if I left. You had to be committed because it was the state hospital grounds.

So this other friend of mine, she took me there and the judge had to sign off on it, like I was being committed. They could take me to jail and shit, too. So, I was like, "Okay." And it was probation, but I didn't give a shit about that. Like I couldn't think like that. I didn't have that kind of concern. Shit, I was on probation, I didn't give a shit about probation. That was not a deterrent for me. Because by now I done went to jail myself four or five times in between that time. We go to jail one time and we somewhere sitting on the side of the road shooting dope. They come, police take us to jail. Just different times and stuff had happened so I don't give a shit about that, and so I stayed and this friend tells me if I stop getting high my life would be better. When I decided to go to treatment, I called her and said, "Hey, I'm fixing to go to treatment." She just was excited; she was excited about it. And she was like, "Well, when you get there and you get situated and everything call me and let me know and I'm going to come visit you." I was like, "Okay." "I'll be your first visitor" and everything. I called her and she came. She is still my friend today. And I've been clean for twenty-five years.

Given everything you've been through, how do you feel about the life choices that you made in relationship to being a black lesbian?

[*Long pause.*] I know that for me the first thing that I am is just a woman. And how people or why people define me as a lesbian is mostly because of who I sleep with, but who I am throughout the course of my day is that I'm just a black woman in America. I have to acknowledge the black because that's what people see when they see me. That's the first thing they see is my color, and for people to say, "I don't see color when I'm talking to you," you must think that I'm clear. So now you've denied that, too, in your efforts to be politically correct if your best friend is black or whatever. I understand that about myself and before I really understood me as a gay, as a lesbian woman, I understood myself as a person, a female, girl, woman, just trying to live through the chaos and the confusion of the life choices that other people had made for themselves that included me. And as a child you're just really powerless. You don't have the power to leave. It's not like, "Fuck you all, I'm fixing to leave and go somewhere" when you eight years old. "I don't like what y'all doing and I can go live somewhere else." You just don't have that power and so you have to live and for me living in the choices that my parents continued to make for themselves and then having a child at such an early age and going from one [set of] parents to somebody else's parents and then having a child, becoming a parent, my life still was not my life. So I went from being my parents' child to my daughter's mother, this boy's live-in girlfriend to his wife and all that, and then, and so things happen, like, in just functioning in life and so you just wake up, you go to work, you come home, you cook, you clean. You make sure the kids alright, you make sure he's alright, and you do it all the same way the next day. For me, that worked because it's consistency and so I knew what to expect. People call it control issues. I like to know what's happening in my life.

So the choices that I made for myself, I shot dope, I smoked crack, I got clean, I stayed clean and managed to get some kind of license where I can have a career, and then I made a choice to open my own business and people didn't necessarily support that. People just haven't supported a whole lot of my decisions, but that doesn't matter to me. So, it's like I understand that I don't expect you to have my best interest at heart; I have to have my own best interest at heart, and so I live in that. And so I'm very thoughtful about the choices that I make because I do know that they affect other people. Some days I would like to smoke a joint and drink a beer, but I don't know what the end result of that would be. I don't know that I would just smoke the joint and drink the beer. Or I don't know if I would smoke crack. So, since I don't know, I just don't even start it, and then I don't have to stop because the rule is, if I start smoking, y'all better get the hell away from me because I'm telling you, you better take everything you got because it's going down.

Queen Mother Lori pats me on the knee and gets up and walks into the house. I'm paralyzed by the story she just told and not sure I can handle hearing any more like it. I long for the love stories I heard in the field of wildflowers, but they seem a lifetime ago. How could one person survive so much heartache and strife and still be so resilient? Queen Mother Lori comes back outside with a glass of mead on ice and hands it to me. She knows I have been shaken by the stories I've heard so far. I down the glass quickly and give it back to her. I feel more settled already. She goes back to her chair and up walks Miss B. and Queen Mother Ida Mae.

"I hope you didn't think these were going to all be uplifting stories just because they told by elders," Miss B. says, pursing her lips. "Yes, we have stories of love and sex, art and politics, and what have you, but we also have stories about what a fucked up—oh, excuse my language, Queen Mothers—what a messed up place the world is—and especially for women. And when you add black and sweet on women to that list, you can best believe it's going to be on and popping."

I am about to come up with another excuse for why I can't hear more stories and I remember the club. *There is no absolution here.* I feel stuck in this place I don't want to be, hearing stories I don't want to hear, because despite my disavowal, I have lived them, too.

Growing up, my family and I lived in a one-bedroom apartment where my mother and I slept on a pullout sofa in the living room and my six siblings slept spoon-fashion in bunk beds and a single bed in the bedroom. There was a dirt driveway that separated our apartment from two rows of white, cinderblock two-bedroom apartments. There were a total of eight of them, but there were probably close to forty or more people living among those eight apartments, if you counted all of the parents, grandparents, children, and grandchildren.

In the first apartment at the end of the row lived Mr. and Mrs. Lukes and their two children. I always knew when it was payday because that's when both of the Lukes parents got drunk and started fighting. First came the cussing and carrying on, following by the physical violence that often spilled out of the apartment onto the dirt driveway or even into the street. No one ever broke up their fights. It was a ritual spectacle by which the folks in the community set their suppertime or for which they substituted their Friday evening entertainment.

Next to the Lukes was the Hughes family. The parents and their children (I can't remember the exact number, but there were at least five) lived there. The Hughes parents were often drunk, too, though they were quiet drunks and, as far I can remember, didn't fight—at least in public. They just slept around on each other. I learned after I was an adult that I shared the same father as two of the Hughes children.

Next to them was my Uncle JT, who worked hard and drank hard. He died of a heart attack at the age of forty-six. And in the final apartment lived Mrs. Sims and her three daughters. Mrs. Sims didn't drink. She was a holy and sanctified woman. Trouble for her came by way of her youngest daughter, who served time for stabbing a man to death, and her grandson, the child of the daughter serving time, who was my age and was also prone to violence. He ended up serving time for armed robbery. That was just the first row.

Queen Mother Lori's story was across the dirt driveway of my childhood—a memory I wanted to leave in the dusty corners of my forgotten past. I have moved on. I am not poor anymore. I don't live next to or across from my kin anymore. But no matter how much running I might try to do, the ghosts of my past keep kicking up dust in the driveway that bridged the gap between my childhood neighbors' and my own family's poverty and dysfunction. And so I sit faced with a choice to get up and run down the dirt road before me, away from these familiar familial stories of black pain. Or I sit and listen to my life through these women's words, transported back to that dirt driveway of my past to reckon with my own survivor's guilt. I am paralyzed by the choice.

Queen Mother Ida Mae, who is still standing next to Miss B., cuts her eyes over to Miss B. as if to ask, "Are you going to handle this or do you want me to?" Miss B. puts her hands on her hips and I brace myself.

"Look, Dr. EPJ. I can click my heels three times and buzz your behind back home faster than a roach flees light, but that's too easy. You must run toward that thing that frightens you the most. I know it's hard listening to these stories, but what do you think it felt like to live them? You were chosen for a reason. According to your publications—and I have read a few of them—you claim to be invested in ethics this, and ethics that, and wanting to be a 'coperformative witness' to others. But it ain't ethical to run at the first sign of trouble, little brother. You can't be a coperformative witness only to the 'uplifting' stories. Life don't work that way. And it *certainly* don't work that way for those of us in this hive—and these queen mothers are a living testimony to that. You have to take the good, the bad, *and* the ugly. This ain't a hit-it-and-quit-it kind of adventure you're on, you understand? Don't be like some of your colleagues who cozy up to folks just to get the 4-1-1 to write a book and then when you really need them for something—say, a little help with the light bill—they ain't nowhere to be found. Now, I know you have better home training than that—I know your mother, Miss Sarah, well—but that also goes for sticking with it when things get uncomfortable. How are you going to call yourself a professor who is training students if you can't even make it through an interview because the material makes you uncomfortable? What kind of 'teaching' is that?"

I realize that Miss B. is performing for the queen mothers, but her soapbox lecture cuts me to the white meat, as my grandmother used to say.

"Yes, you're right. I need to walk the walk. I want to hear more stories," I say finally, trying to reconcile my hypocrisy and guilt with my empathy.

All of the queen mothers high-five Miss B. with their eyes, except for Miss Ida Mae, who shoos Miss B. to the side, as if dismissing a child, and walks up to the step where I'm sitting. She's even taller from this angle than I discerned from afar. She's a handsome woman whose masculinity fits her like a tailored suit. She smiles down at me, revealing her gold-plated front tooth cap. It looks like the one my Aunt Nevatrice has. I have no idea what's about to happen next, when she pulls a toothpick from her pocket, pops it in her mouth, and plops down beside me on the step. Miss B. slowly squeezes past Ida Mae up the stairs, still beaming from her read of me, and sits next to Queen Mother Mary Anne, who seems to be her protector. Ida Mae leans forward and spins a tale.

Ida Mae

My childhood was an easy childhood in my eyes because my parents worked really hard to keep me in the dark about what actually was going on because this was a civil rights thing and my father and my mother were very protective of us and not letting us experience it. So it was an easy childhood, and it was fun and everything; I had a really good time because you don't understand what's going on around you. So if it's not right, you don't know it as long as the Kool-Aid's there and Santa's there, everything you need to be comfortable is there. So that's the way it was, and I tell you, it must've been until I was about maybe in high school before I started to really realize that there was a lot of fear. There was a lot of fear in the community. And what was actually going on, you know, because you know how grown folks were in the South, "Y'all go on the porch." We didn't talk about it, so when it got to the point where I could understand the dialogue and I'm like, "Oh, they're scared" or "Oh, they're going over here," I started to get an understanding of what actually was going on.

My mother went to Odenville because her mother lived there, and I was born in a house, okay? So I was born at home. My mother was a resident of Birmingham, Alabama, so as soon as I got up on my feet, being premature and all, I was relocated to Birmingham, where I went to school. I went to a little school. My first year of school was at an old schoolhouse that was right not far from our house. My father was very disappointed with the level of education so he pulled us out of that school and put me and my sisters in [name of school], which was a parochial school. I stayed there until I was an eleventh grader. And at that time, he felt that it was safe enough and the educational boundaries had balanced enough so that I could go to a public school, so I graduated from [name of school]. During that time during my childhood, it was so much going on as far as civil rights was concerned. I think I was about maybe a sophomore in high school or freshman in high school when my father decided he was going to be a Baptist minister. That changed every damned thing because he just got involved in trying to help out the civil rights movement and everything. He was a minister of the church and pretty much it was the civil rights thing most of my childhood. I remember we used to get the *Jet* when *Jet* was black-and-white. I remember seeing Medgar Evers hanging up from a meat hanger and his flesh was completely turned inside out.[2] That's the kind of stuff that *Jet* was showing. This is what I started to understand what we're dealing with. They would find kids hung. They would find people, pull them people out of, what was the name of that river that was close by? Choctaw River or something like that. They used to find bodies in there all the time. It was really a thing. And then we had the civil rights movement and Martin Luther King came in and we had the boycott of the busses. I will never forget that because when my father got off work—he worked at US Steel—he would drive his car around to pick people up from work and help move people around. There was a lot of that going on in the community, in my community. There was a lot of "Help us because we walking, we can't get on the bus." And it turned out pretty successful in that they got what they wanted. They brought that bus system to a screeching halt. I had no idea that minorities actually carried the transportation system. When they got them off the bus, it shut it down, so they won that battle. Then I remember the sadness of Dr. King dying and both the Kennedy boys dying. I remember how everything in our world just kind of stopped for a minute. It was a focusing moment. It was like, "Oh my God." People continually show you how awesome they can be, how terrible they can be, not awesome in that way, how terrible they can be and the way that, and it just kind of like shut things down. It kind of suck the life out of you. You know what I'm saying? But everybody was determined to keep on because this is life how we know it. This is life how we know.

I left Birmingham in the eighties and came to Texas because there were no economic opportunities. There was no work. I graduated Miles College and I was trained to be a teacher. I didn't want to teach because I didn't want to conform. The whole thing was killing me and I talk about this a lot. This whole being a girl thing, you know? My mom used to make me wear a longline bra.

What's that?

A longline bra? It's this bra you put on that come way down here [*points to her waist*] back in the day.

> *Down to your waist?*

This was before Spanx, okay? Then they had the metal stays in it so you be like this. [*Laughter.*] Then you had the damned girdle on. It came down to here [*points to her midthigh*] from your waist down to here. It had metal stays in it, had a zipper on the side so you'd be like, suck it in. It was crazy; you know what I'm saying? But that was the way women dressed, and there was no pantyhose, so we had stockings. We had to put them up and then you had to hook that to some shit. So all of it was like [*gasping*]. I hated it. I just couldn't conform. I remember when I first went to Miles College. We used to always wear dresses. I was a big girl all my life, I mean really. I maxed out at 400 [pounds] to tell you the truth, and so when I went to Miles I was about 350, 400, close to it. Shit, I was a big girl. And I had these shifts. My mom would always buy shifts for me, so I remember I was standing out there and I had these little spoon heels and I was so fat that they were sticking out on the side because they had that gap in 'em on the side and there was a squishing going on every time you take a step [*laughter*], you know that nylon going shoop, shoop, shoop. I was the most miserable person in my freshman year in college. And I had no pants. My father did not allow us to wear pants, so I had no pants, so it was the shift every day with the long line girdle and the bra. It was killing me. It was killing me. The kids in school were starting to call me "church girl" and I didn't know that they referred to me as that behind my back, and then, one day I was sitting in front of the student union. I was sitting up there. I was so uncomfortable. I was trying to read a book, just trying to fit in any goddamned way I could, excuse my language. And I'm sitting and this guy came and sat beside me. I still say he saved me. His name was Frederick. Everybody laughed or looked at or paid attention to Frederick because he had his hair permed and he had this big head of hair; it was just permed like a woman, and he had his shirt tied up under here [*points to her chest*] and he had on these cutoff blue jeans and they were so short you could see the pockets and he had on these little sandals and shit and he come up there, "How you doing church, girl?" I'm like, "What the fuck?" You know? I mean nobody ever bothered to speak to me. I was just some strange motherfucker walking around that people were talking about. I'm so timid I was totally out of my zone because my father came home one day and told me. I was laying on the couch after graduation and I thought I was doing real good. I was sitting at home watching TV and he walked in and he said, "Look baby, every day I come home you laying on this sofa. Let me tell you what, let me tell you how this going to go now. You got three choices here: you need to find you a job, go to school, get in college, or you need to move." I'm serious. I sat straight up. Because I had never thought about not being out of my father's house and I never thought about work. For what? You said I had to finish high school. I finished high school. I'm done. Shit. I got up, went to Miles College, and enrolled in there. So, anyway, I met Frederick, and Frederick sat down and he said, "Church girl, what you up to?" And I didn't say that much to him. Every day we would meet there and we just developed a friendship. So, I got a job with work-study and it was working with kids outside, so when I showed up at four o'clock to start my new job I had on the shift and the same little teaspoon shoes. He said, "Where you going?" I said, "I'm here." He said, "Oh no, honey. We out here hitting balls and bats and shit. You can't be out here." I said, "I don't have any pants." He said, "C'mon," and he took me to K-Mart and bought me my first pair of jeans. He bought me a pair of Bucks. Remember them old Bucks and things? And a shirt and a denim jacket. Yes, he did. I went back to the school and I felt so free. When I was taking off that stuff he was like "Oooh, oooh!" He just cut up, you know? [*Laughter.*] "What the fuck? Why you got all this on?" He was just cuttin' up. He turned out to be my best friend. I swear to God. He died two years ago, and we talked every week. He had to have dialysis.

Frederick took me to my first gay bar. I was so freaked out because I was sitting on the thing and he said, "You like her, don't you?" Because there was this girl and I really like this girl and I would just watch her walk across the campus but I would never say anything. I didn't know people were watching me watch the girl. [*Laughter.*] He say, "I see how you be looking at her. You like her, don't you?" And I looked at him because I don't know nothing about what you're talking about, you understand?

I had never had a relationship, so Frederick took me to this bar. I wish I could remember the name. It was a beautiful name for a bar but I can't think of it right now. But when I walked in there and we walked up some steps and there was this big old carpet and everything and they had lights and the floor would go around. Lights were up under the floor. They had this big ball so everything was moving. It was like, "Wow." But it was dark, so we walked in and he sat me down at the bar and said, "Wait a minute, I'll be right back." I'm sitting at the bar and I don't drink, I don't do nothing.

This was in the sixties. This was in '69, about my second year of college. And I was sitting there. It was the Out of Focus—that was the name of that damned bar, the Out of Focus. And I was sitting at that bar and I was just so glad to be around people and hear that music, Marvin Gaye and them in the background, because my daddy didn't allow us to listen to secular music, so all this was new to me. I had never been to a game. I had never been anywhere unsupervised. I had never been to the movies, so every damned thing I experienced in college was totally new to me and I was too enamored and I sat there in that club. I sat there about ten minutes and I said I wonder where he at because I started to feel nervous because I'm out of my element now. I don't have a car. My mamma 'nem don't know I'm here. I'm like, I'm out of my element. Finally, I started to notice. I started to pay attention to the folks, and it was men dancing with men and women dancing with women and I was like [*gasping*]. So, I ran to tell Frederick. [*Whispering*] "Frederick, did you see this motherfucker?" He said, "What you think we come here for? Go on over there and sit down some damn where." He got some man. "Go on and sit down somewhere, make yourself comfortable." He sent a girl over there to talk to me. He told her, "This bitch gonna run out of here; go over there and calm her down." And it kind of calmed me down; and that woman was so nice to me and I thought she was going to be my first girlfriend, but looking back it wasn't going to happen, but they were very nice to me and I got to where I would come there a lot. I would always be at that club and I started looking around trying to learn about the community, because I see I had no idea that there were other people, I knew nothing about gays. I was just a woman that was different. And then after that, I moved out of my mama's house and started dressing, like cross-dressing. I became the sharpest man that I thought my daddy was, so it was white shirts, Stacy Adams, canes and hats and shit. I was on my own. My folks forbid me to come to their house.

Really?

"Do not come here."

Did you cut your hair, too?

I did. I sure did. I had a nice little butch cut. Cut my hair, had my little shiny shoes on. The minute that boy [Frederick] pulled me out that garter belt and that girdle, it was on. For years, I didn't own another dress. I didn't buy them. I didn't fool with them. The discomfort of the whole thing, the whole hair straightening thing, that used to drive me nuts. Top of my ears be burning. Cut this shit off. Cut the hair off. Give me some boots. Give me a pair of jeans.

Let me chill on Friday night. I'd get sharp, go out to the club, have me a few drinks, hang out at the overnight joint. Everything changed.

I got into the drug business, became pretty much of a drug pin. It was me and Dr. Drake, and he was a doctor on the corner and he would give me the strawberries, was the drug of choice back then. It was speed. It was speed, you know? It used to be strawberries or blackberries, or whatever them black ones. Different color pills, so we sold those. I was alienated from my family. I picked up. I met a girl. I had surgery on my knee in the hospital. I had to have a transfusion. That's how I got Hepatitis. That was in '72. Then after I graduated from college, I met this woman. She was five years my junior. She was an RN, so when I was having the surgery she would come in and out my room and she put shit in the closet. I didn't know what was going on. So one day I asked her, "What you doing? Why you keep sneaking in here?" She said, "Girl, I got my medicine in here." She was stealing drugs from the hospital.

And she was putting them in my room, so she was jonesing. See, that's why I say you should expose your kids to most everything, because if somebody else show it to them, they won't give it to them like you're going to give it to them. So I didn't know about drugs, so I didn't know about addictions. I didn't know none of that shit. When I got out of the hospital back in the seventies, they wouldn't give you no pain medication. You get your ass some Excedrin or something. They wasn't writing no prescriptions for no pain medicine. You can forget that. So when I got home I was in so much pain because they had removed my kneecap, so I was in pain a lot and I would just whine and cry. One day that girl came over to my house. She said, "I know you in pain." She was not wrong, and she had the fix. She hit it. She come by and hit me every day. Pretty soon, we was into this thing, so okay, I got me a girlfriend. She was a nurse, had her own car and everything, but she was a junkie, and she took me right down that junk ass road with her. Then, they caught her at the hospital, fired her ass, and then we were in downtown Birmingham looking for the drug man. You know? She turned me on to heroin. She turned me on to coke and all kinds of shit. So that went on for about four years. Then finally, because I always said that you need a base. I resented my folks and shit for the way things went down, but you know what? You know [how] you used to hang your foot on the floor to keep the bed from moving? Even when I would be that fucked up I would still be trying to say my Lord's Prayer. [Laughter.] Because I was raised you don't go to sleep without saying your prayers. "Our Father." People used to laugh at me [slurring the words], "Who art in Heaven, hallowed it be thy name." They'd be going, "Girl, be quiet." I'd say [slurring], "I gotta finish my prayers." But I swear I do believe that that saved

me because the shit that I went through and put myself through, I was supposed to be dead. Do you know what I'm saying?

Did you graduate from college?

I did. I graduated from college, got all of that taken care of and everything,
and then after I got off the drugs my friend Marilyn, who I still talk to every
week, who was my roommate in college, she had a nervous breakdown and
don't remember none of this. I tell her all the time, "Girl, you saved me." She'd
say, "How'd I save you?" Because she came to the apartment where I was and
I was so fucked up, she went into the hardware store and got a lock and put it
on the outside. I couldn't get out of there. I was on the second floor. That bitch
had me up there for three days, but when she come back I was sober and I was
thinking. I was like, "Oh my God." I could look at my body. I could tell by the
smell in the damned place. I could look at the puke in the corner and know
that I had been somewhere. I never touched drugs again, man. She saved me.
I never touched drugs, even today, I don't even want to give blood. Like when
they come at me to give blood, I'm nervous because I still, I got a really bad
experience in my head about that.

So I came to Texas, and I came with a friend. We left Birmingham running. She was in trouble with the law. She had wrote bad checks for groceries.
I mean, it really wasn't nothing. We was in a bad place in Alabama. When you
see white boys on the garbage trucks, you know it's bad because they didn't
do work like that. It was all black folks, all black folks in the service area, and
everything but that was gone. So I left, and she left and we both still are here
in Texas. She's with another partner. She's a lab analyst. She does lab work
and she makes very good money. There was no need for us to be unemployed.
We were both highly educated; we just couldn't find work. She's doing quite
well. I went over my life, several women, one, two, three women later. I run
into this one woman who has vision. You know what I'm saying? But she, too,
was an addict, but I recognize them when I see it now, but I didn't recognize
it because she was a different kind of addict. She was a prescription drug user.
Now, I didn't know nothing about them girls, but they all over the place. Them
Vicodin heads, that's what I call them, Vicodin Heads. To me, Vicodin is just
about as bad as heroin. Anything you can't get rid of. But I didn't know that.
I spent two years with her, loving her, and she was the first person to tell me,
"You know you write good poetry," because she had me motivated. This chick
had me writing. I was writing her love letters and shit, poems and stuff.

And so one day she was reading this shit I had wrote for her and she said, "You know, you're really good with this poetry thing." I was like, "Eh, that's just something I do." She would always look forward to those poems. Then one day she took me to an open mic and I read one of my poems and it felt good to read it, and it felt good for people to understand what I was saying, so I just started writing. I just started writing. Man. I had wrote a lot. I started doing open mics and then I started to doing schools, published one book. I never published another one. I still got stuff stacked up to be published that is not published. I like performing my work.

> *You said your father became a minister. So I assume that you had to go to church quite a bit.*

Oh, Lord. I mean, that's all we did was go to church with BTU, choir rehearsal, prayer meeting, revivals. That's all there was. We sang in everybody's choir. If you need a choir, that's five of us. Choir done. [*Laughter.*] You know what I'm saying? No problem. And . . . I always wanted to do what other kids do. I wanted to, Miss [last name] lived behind us, they were having little parties for the kids and shit. My mamma never had no parties. No secular music. No games. No football. None of that stuff the other kids do. When the streetlight came on you were at home, and if you wasn't at home, then you got beat. It was a lot of corporal punishment going on around then. Looking back, if it was to happen today, their ass would be in court. [*Laughter.*] There was quite a bit of that kick ass going on.

> *So you didn't enjoy church?*

I did, because I like to sing and I was doing fine in church until I found out that, after I found out I was gay and what that was about, and then I would sit up in church and listen to them talk about homosexuals and try to make people feel bad and "You're going to hell." I got so tired of hearing that until really I had to work on myself because I really thought that I was at odds with God. And I was mean to myself. When I was doing drugs, I was mean to myself because I really felt like, you're damned anyway. You're not going to heaven. Your daddy told you so, which was not the truth. So once I got the truth and could see the light. First of all, I don't even agree with organized religion. I'm not *down*. I have removed myself from organized religion pretty much. I need to step back and reassess some things because I'm not going to be a part of any institution that's going to make me feel indifferent about Ida Mae, so I stepped away from the church. Right now, I have church here. I had to have a long talk with God about this. We did. We had to have a long discussion in my mind and my heart about church and I told God, I said, "Listen. I won't abandon you if you won't abandon me. He let me feel in my heart that yes, there's something wrong there. You're right. You got that feeling. It's right." It's something that has been tampered. It's not what it was set out to be. And my father was so damned—they were so judgmental. OMG. Like they would be like, love the, what's that thing? Love the sin, hate the sin, love the sinner but then they still treat people crazy. You know, this one was welcome, that one wasn't. Even after I was gay and had girlfriends, they were not welcome. They wasn't feeling no love. [Laughter.] Nobody feeling no love here, you know what I'm saying?

And then my father sent so many mixed messages because him and my mamma used to fight. It was a violent relationship. So, how you going to stand up in church and hug on these gals over here and make peace with these over here and then you come home and kick my mamma's ass? I ain't feeling you. It was definitely some things going on about religion early on. You know? And my father, I can tell that he was a product of his raising. I had to lighten up on him because his light was dull because it had been dulled in his youth. He only was acting in good faith on what he thought was the truth. I just don't agree with his truth. We have a right to disagree. So he was firm about his belief until I put him in the ground. He felt like he was on the right track. He was remorseful about some things concerning my mom, but he did tell me one day, he said, "You know, I don't know about this gay thing, Ida Mae." He was pretty old when he said that to me. I know he sat on that porch and thought about all the shit that we went through and how he could've been different being the head of the household to actually have more peace in the house, more togetherness. Him being the head of the house, he dropped the ball, and he knew it in the end and he was very apologetic about it. I had to forgive him on them notes. And so, my father being a minister, it didn't make it no better for me. The shit heated up because you have to look a certain way to be a minister and your kids have to look a certain way. There can't be no abhorrent behavior because you Reverend John's daughter. So it didn't work for me.

What are your thoughts about homosexuality in terms of do you think people are born gay, do you think people choose to be gay, do you think it's a little of both?

I think it's a little of both, because I myself, I noticed my difference early on. I just enjoyed cutting grass. I enjoyed being under Papa. I never really had that "give me a boyfriend" kind of thing. I always just admired pretty girls. Always.

Even when I was little, I just admired girls. I loved pretty girls. So I do believe people are born in their mix. I believe I was born in the mix. I ain't never entertained that whole regular shit. I've always run like a rabbit. No! I'm not conforming. I ain't going there. Now, maybe it was because my mom and dad done fought so bad, maybe I didn't want a man because of that. I don't know. All I know is I never felt the urge to do that. I look at gays now, and I look at my friends, how they have kids they have adopted and did [things] like that. Things have changed so radically since I was young, I wish I was young now. I would do it probably a little differently, but I'm not. But I am so glad to see, because my niece, seventeen, she's gay. I've got a nephew that's gay. So, just the fact that she can hold her girlfriend's hand and her dad ain't tripping. That's major shit, because when I was coming up it was, "Get the whip."

I remember going in Out of Focus one night and I got out [of] the car and I walked across the street. They had the lines and there was police sitting around, but I wasn't paying no attention because there's always the police, but when a guy was crossing the street, if you broke that line, before your feet touched that sidewalk they was taking folks to jail in front of the gay bar. There were so many people, when they drug my ass off the street, "C'mon, you're under arrest," and they took me on the side of the building and they had people lined up down the block. I hadn't noticed that. Then when the paddy wagon come, they used to have the paddy wagon come and take you to jail, me and my girlfriend, they wouldn't let me in with the girls. They put me in with the boys. I had to ride down in the paddy wagon with the men. It wasn't a bad ride because they all had on makeup and shit. It was so fun. We had such a good time. Then we got to jail. They let my girlfriend go and told her that I was gone and they had done isolated me and stuck me in a room in the back somewhere and they wouldn't let me be with the boys nor the girls and held me there for damned near twelve hours before she found out where I was and had to come back. Now this cost us, between the two of us, we paid out over $500 to get us off us for jaywalking. That's the kind of harassment that you used to have to go through when you were gay. It was harassment. It was just straight-up harassment. And they used to get away with that stuff. You had to be very careful. They would put you in jail for sneezing. I hear the women before me used to go to jail for wearing pants. You know? You couldn't wear jeans and shit. It used to be against the law to dress like me, and now I'm like, "I'm glad I wasn't living in that moment." That was a bad moment for me. I'm like, are you serious? Yeah, you couldn't wear pants.

Was Out of Focus a black gay bar?

Umm hmm. Sure was. I was tripped out. And then another one used to be the 21 Club, and I tell you the truth, we was a dry county, so it was a lot of afterhours going on. We used to have a lot of afterhours joints and that used to be everything. You leave the club. They'd shut it down twelve or one o'clock. Go to afterhours joint and you'd play cards and you'd eat pork chops until you fell out the door and the sun was up. I used to love them afterhours joints. They would be the death of me. There wasn't nothing in there but pretty women, liquor. You could smell the food frying because there was plenty of fried food, and they'd be there until the morning time and then there'd be a card game in the back. You could lose all your money or win all of somebody else's. That's how they was rolling, honey. I tell you, when I moved out of my father's house, I got completely turned out because I didn't know what was going on, so I had all the crazies giving me instructions. I'm just glad to be here.

Tell me about how you came out to your father.

There wasn't no coming out. I didn't have to come out. I'm telling you we dealt with that tomboy thing and then when I got to college, I flipped the switch on that cross-dressing. It was like [*gasps*] I ain't telling nothing. They saw me coming. I heard my mamma talking to my daddy one day about it. He said, "Look, what you want me to do?" She was trying to get him to take a hard line or something, do something. He was like, "What you want me to do? Ida been doing the same ever since we known her. You know she was different when she was two years old. We done talked about this." I heard him say that to her. They knew I was different that early on. You'd think somebody would of sat down and try to explain it to me. You know what I'm saying? Let me know what was going on. Miss Shuford had to show me around the ropes.[3] Why Miss Shuford had to be the one? Y'all could've told me something. "You're a little different" and "Don't you feel bad about yourself," "You're still a good person." I didn't get no shit like that. I didn't get that. So when I came after I changed my drag and everything, I went to my mom's house and that's when my dad told me, "You're not welcome here. Don't come here." That's cool. So I used to have to sneak around to see my little brother. Sneak around and shit. I'd wait until my daddy go to work and I'd come and sit on the porch and talk to my mamma because she was so hurt about the whole thing. She didn't know what side to take but she was not turning her back on me.

I remember sitting there one day. This was a turning point for me. I was sitting on the porch. I came there one day and had a bottle of wine in a brown bag because she knew I drank and I sat there with that wine. I didn't open it. I just sat it on the porch. I said, "I just wanted to see how you were doing, Mama." She said, "I'm fine, how you doing? You dragging that wine around." I said, "Well, it's my wine." I said, "You want some?" She said, "No, your dad will be home in two hours." In other words, if he hadn't come home, would she have taken that drink? So I started to realizing that she was in a predicament, too. You know what I'm saying? She told me one day, "I didn't know I had options." I told her I was going with a girl, she said to me that day I was sitting on the porch with the wine, she said daddy's so upset about me. And she said, "At least you figured out you had options. I never knew." You know? Shit. Then I started realizing that you somewhere you really don't want to be. You're doing something because that's what they said you supposed to be and you're surprised about options? It blew me away. She was in a prison herself and she had no tools because she was uneducated. She had raised all of us and my daddy took advantage of her because she had no tools. She had no education. She didn't want to be there, but she didn't know the first thing about getting out of there. She was scared. He towered over her. I feel sorry for her. I feel sorry for my lack of understanding because, hell, I was fifty years old before I could figure out okay, they were operating on what they had to work with. That narrowness is attributed to the fact that they were uneducated and they hadn't seen a thing.

My daddy just totally wrote me off. He was like, "You're lost, you're lost." That's the way it was, and after I finished college, I did. My daddy let me live in a house that he owned. That shocked me but he let me live there. He let me and my girlfriend live there. But my daddy, as hard as he was, I think he was more understanding of me than my mom was. I think my mom put a lot of pressure on him to do things concerning me that he would had not have done if she wasn't putting pressure on him. She told me one day, she was putting a damned chicken in the pot and pulling out a rooster. She said, "Tough as hell." [Laughter.] So, stuff like that. That's the kind of shit we used to get into it about. I remember her cornering me in the room one day, "I want to know what you're doing with the women. What are you doing? They're calling all night long. What you doing?" No answer. I have no answer for that. It was a miss. It was a miss. I have no answer for that. Then they would call me Don instead of "Ida Mae," and that just burned her nerves, honey. "Ain't no Don living here! Who you talking about?" She'd get on their nerves more. "I tried to call, but your mamma wouldn't even call you to the phone." I know she won't. [Laughter.] This the kind of stuff that I went through.

Is your mother still alive?

No, my mother and my father are passed. My mother passed about ten years ago, and my father passed about five, maybe four.

Did you and your mother reconcile before she passed away?

Not really. We were not enemies. I was there when she died, but she still wasn't having this gay lifestyle, honey. That was one of the things she said before she had the last stroke, "You know you're going to hell if you keep fooling with these women," and I say, "Yeah, Mama," because I have no more argument for her. She believes that. Let her take it to the grave. If that's what she believes, that's what she believes. I'm alright with that, so I just pat her on the back and say, "Yeah mom, I know."

I believe in God because I can't do it by myself, and it has worked for me. I'm sixty-two years old and they say, "Well, you ain't rich and you ain't nothing, and your God ain't done nothing to you." Yes, it is, because my God kept me peaceful while all this shit was going on. Do you know how much that's worth, just the peace? So, yeah, I'm fine. I got peace and I know that if anything go down, my first human reaction is to go [*gasps*]. Just be still for a minute, just be still and believe in your heart that you got angels all around you and God is working on your behalf. Sometimes I see change that don't look right to me but I just be still because some of the worst shit has made me a better person. You know what I'm saying? Something I perceive as totally horrible, like losing this three inches on my leg, but I have slowed down and done my writing. My life has not been terribly bad, but when I was there up in that hospital, I let my mind go places that it did not need to go. So that's what the love of God has done for me. That's what having God in my life has done for me. It calms me down. I feel like I got a husband or a wife or whatever I need, whatever support I need. They say, "Well your God . . ."; don't tell me nothing about my God. I give my God a lot of heavy stuff, and it's all taken care of. God has done well by me. You know what I'm saying? I don't work nowhere. . . . I get my little check every month and I make it. But God be looking out for me and then my needs will be met. All I have to do is be still and believe. That's what I do. But all that shit I went through, all that shit I put myself through was a process, and I was never alone. I can name you some times when I knew it was straight-up miracles. I was never alone and I never felt alone, even when I was at my worst.

Queen Mother Ida Mae stands and lights a cigarette and walks back out to the weeping willow tree. Her walk has a sadness to it, like a ritual processional of mourning that one has to make in order to heal. It strikes me that melancholy clouds the air after a story that is mostly filled with humor and resilience.

Still nestled against Queen Mother Mary Anne's leg, Miss B. raises up a song:

> Ain't gonna let nobody turn me 'round
> turn me 'round
> turn me 'round

The queen mothers join in on the "turn me 'round," Queen Mother Aida and Queen Mother Cherry on soprano, Queen Mother Lori and Queen Mother Mary Anne on alto, and Queen Mother Ida Mae booming a baritone from the yard. I add my tenor.

> Ain't gonna let nobody turn me 'round
> I'm gonna keep on walkin'
> Keep on talkin'
> Marching into Hymen land

The queen mothers continue to hum the song as Queen Mother Ida Mae makes her way back to the porch and takes a seat in her rocker. Miss B. is weeping, her head buried deeply in Queen Mother Mary Anne's thigh. The women's humming continues until Miss B.'s weeping subsides. She wipes her eyes with the hem of Queen Mother Mary Anne's skirt, stands, and works her way down the steps past me and heads out toward the tree. I get up and run after her to make sure that she's okay and she stops, turns to me and says, "I'm okay, baby. I just need a minute. You go on back to the porch. I'm sure Queen Mother Mary Anne will share something once the spirit moves." I head back to the porch as Miss B. walks down the road into the heat of the day.

The queen mothers are back at work scaling fish, peeling papayas, and snapping beans. The only sound in the air is that of their hands in motion and the trace of their singing still ringing in my ear. After a little time passes, Queen Mother Mary Anne starts talking.

Mary Anne Adams

I was born in Oxford, Mississippi, in 1954. [*Long pause.*] As I grow, evolve, and learn more about the location of my childhood, I find myself describing it various ways at different times. But, you know, I'm certainly not going to give you these tired clichés like my childhood was really happy, because it wasn't. I would say it was challenging, at best. Oftentimes, I felt very disconnected, very disjointed from my family. I felt as though I was in the wrong family much of the time. And wanted to be someplace else actually. Never got the opportunity, unfortunately. I just felt so different. I was left-handed. I was almost a breech birth. I was born with a caul over my face. And if you know anything about that, you know that you are told from an early age that you can see things—that you're special. And later I realized it's a membrane that's just extra. But nonetheless, I kind of grew up with that kind of hanging over me and being really afraid of it. Being actually pushed to explore it and to embrace it. But based on a lot of other things that happened in my childhood, I was afraid of that. I had a childhood very much marked by suspicion and a lot of myth. And a childhood very much marked by death at an early age. A lot of loss, a lot of grief, a lot of poverty. And I think my saving grace was the fact that I was a bookworm. I grew up in kind of a two-generational family. There are ten of us—five girls and five boys. I'm the second oldest . . . my brother is the oldest. He insists, though, I'm the oldest because there's a lot of responsibility that my brother certainly shrunk from. And I had a different sensibility about the world, so I always felt things very deeply. I would find myself . . . literally crouching under the table in the house.

There were three of us for a long time, my brother and sister. I'm the middle child. So, people would come to the house and they would look at my brother and say, "Oh, he's so strong," because he was very rambunctious. He was just all into everything. And my sister was really cute. Then they'd look at me and say, "Oh, okay." I mean, probably not in those words, but that was the sense that I got. And so my claim to fame became the fact that I was really smart. I was really respected for that in my community and I can remember that I was encouraged to be smart. I got away with not doing a lot of chores because I was reading. My mother would often say all I had was book sense and no common sense, and I believed that for years. And finally, one day, I had this epiphany because I had just done something that required common sense. And I was like, "Oh, I do have some common sense." I mean, really, because I heard it so much that I internalized it. And so, after that day, it was like,

"Wow, I do have some common sense." I can actually screw in a light bulb or [*laughter*] connect something. I don't have to go read and try to figure out step one, step two, step three, step four. So it was that kind of childhood. Various paths along the way. It was different. It was wonderful. It was horrible. There was nothing static in my childhood.

I was very much introverted. I was alone. Not lonely but alone, oftentimes by my own design. So, I couldn't jump rope. I couldn't play ball. I couldn't play marbles. I couldn't bat the ball. And so I don't think I ever tried to develop those skills because it was just I couldn't do them. I was in the house reading a book, sitting near my mother and her friends as they discussed who did what and how. I was that kind of kid who [they would tell] you need to stop listening to grown folks' business. So much so to the point where [they] became oblivious after a while. It was like, "Oh, it's Mary Anne," and they would continue to talk, because they just came to expect me as a fixture under the table, reading a book. After a while, that's just who I was, that was just my role in the family. Whereas my brother and my sister were out and about. But I generally was home, on the back porch, reading, under the house, in the house, that kind of thing. I was considered the good kid, a quiet kid, a kid who read. They liked that because this is in the sixties where education was very important to folk in my community. The community I grew up in was called Freeman's Town. And after Reconstruction, there were black folks who lived out on the farms and stuff and they migrated into town, into a certain area in Oxford. And they developed their own businesses. The schoolteacher lived next door to the domestic worker, to the minister. I mean, we all lived in Freedmen's Town. And Freedmen's Town had about maybe less than ten streets, really. It was a black section. There were maybe three black sections, but Freeman's Town was the first and the one that was most widely known. And so education was just highly valued. So the fact that I'm the little kid walking around with the book. Because we could walk to school, we could walk to downtown. We were a stone's throw away from Ole Miss, that's how close we were. So everywhere I went, I would walk with this book in front of me.

What were you reading?

Anything. Anything I could get my hands on, [Dr. EPJ]. That's what I read. I would read soup cans, literally. My mother would read these *True Romance* magazines. I would read those. I would read the *Farmer's Almanac*, because that was popular, because folks were growing stuff. And I remember the first time I read it, I realized my mother and I had the same horoscope, I cried. [*Laughter.*] I will never forget that because I did not want to have the same horoscope as my mother. [*Laughter.*] I'm Libra, she's Libra, you know, September 25th, she's October 7th. But I read everything. Books saved my life. It allowed me to imagine a world outside of where I saw myself kind of being stuck. And I realized there's a whole world out there.

> *Freedmen's Town, was there a physical barrier that separated it from the white side of Oxford? Was there a railroad track, a river?*

Actually, there was an invisible barrier. If you drove through Freedmen's Town and right at the edge, it's where the white streets began. So it wasn't anything physically, I mean, we did have a track. There is a railroad track. But on the other side of that were black folk. But you didn't venture down there too much. So it was just literally at the end of this street, that's where the white housing began. There was no river. And actually, as you walked to town from Freeman's Town, there were some white families. So, yeah, you just knew not to venture onto those yards or into those houses. [*Laughter.*]

My mother worked off and on. Mostly, she didn't. When she did work, she would do domestic work or she would do babysitting. She would take in ironing and do that from home, seamstress, that kind of work. Out of the ten kids, I'm the only one who ever knew her father. And there's a whole story behind that, which I'm not averse to sharing. So I had a stepfather, who actually adopted me, and who actually went to prison when I was maybe six years old.

I remember my sister being born. My earliest memory is my sister being born; I was three. And shortly thereafter, he and my mother got married. His name was Bubba. He had just come back from the war. I was born in '54, my sister was born in '57. . . . Bubba was actually reared in Chicago, but he never really knew his father. When he came out of the military, he migrated to Oxford so that he could really spend some time with Mr. Clarence and get to know him, and he met my mother. And then they got married. My mother's maiden name is Adams, and so of course we're going by my mother's name. And my mother had two kids at this point. And this is the first time that she was married, when she married him, because she had my brother at fifteen. And then she had me at seventeen. And I remember him coming to my school, after he got out of prison, and asking for me. Because he was a carpenter, so he would come and get us out of school.

> *Did you know why he had been in prison?*

Oh, absolutely. It was funny, because when he married my mother, my mother had these two kids already, then she had a third, so they had three kids. And I remember there was a time when we didn't have a lot to eat. And then all of a sudden, one day we just had all this food. [*Laughter.*] And it was like a feast, feast or famine—hot dogs, we were just eating hot dogs. I later found out that there was a black minister in town, Reverend Davidson, Hamp Davidson. And he had dropped his check. And so Bubba found the check on the sidewalk and he forged his name, because he was trying to buy food for us. Because he's a carpenter at work. And so his father [Mr. Clarence] had a prominent place, and I guess some of the people in the community [had said] "Please don't press charges because, he's trying to do the best he can." And he refused. He said, "No," he was going to press charges, because he needed to teach him a lesson. And I remember my mother taking us up to the jail before they shipped him off to Parchman Prison. And I actually have a picture I'll show you of us being at Parchman with him. At that time they used to wear the stripes, black-and-white stripes. And so my mother had me in a black-and-white striped dress. My sister [*laughter*] in a striped dress. And my brother in a striped shirt.

So that you could take the picture?

So that we could feel some kind of affinity with him [*laughter*] is my guess.

So she stayed loyal to him while he was in prison?

Oh, absolutely. My mother was an interesting woman. My mother had a difficult childhood herself, as did my grandmother, so a lot of that woundedness was passed down, as is wont to do, unless you get some resolution. My mother was not wanted by her mother. And so my grandmother would not allow touch to enter into my mother's life. And my Aunt Sarah, who was like fourteen when my mother was born, would take my mother and hold her and hide under the bed, so my grandmother, who was her sister, would not see her holding my mother. My grandmother didn't want anybody to touch my mother. And so my grandmother had five kids and my mother was the second child. But she treated her very differently. My grandmother made my mother leave school to go take care of her in tenth grade. And my mother often told that story. And it was just a lot of pain around that. She was just treated like a stepchild. She's the child that my grandmother never wanted. And my mother was always, forever, trying to get my grandmother's approval.

I remember my grandmother would come to our house when I was eight or nine, and just completely change the whole house around. It was almost as though my mother was rendered a little girl again with my grandmother. My grandmother never respected her. She didn't really have any kind of tangible relationship with my mother. Now, her children, she loved us, because the three of us—for six years, there were just the three of us. So we would go every summer, on the weekends. And my grandmother, for us, was a place of stability. It was a place where we knew we could get three hot meals. We knew the place was going to be warm. We knew that there were some institutions that were introduced to us that were church, for one, family reunions, for another. And it's just really interesting to me, this disconnect between my mother and my mother's children. My grandmother would take me . . . around to the neighborhood and brag about how well I could read. Now, I'm about eight or nine or ten. And these women were probably, I don't know, in their sixties or seventies. And she would say, "Give her a book, she can read it." Now, these big, old, huge, dusty books. I didn't know half these damn words, but they didn't either. So a lot of them were illiterate. They had low literacy skills. And so I would get these books and I would like, fake the funk until I could. And they were, "Oh, baby, oh, that's so wonderful." [*Laughter.*]

So, this is my grandmother's way of showing love to me, because my grandmother was not affectionate. She was very much the matriarch of the community. I'm named after my grandmother. So everybody called my grandmother "Miss Mary"—everybody. She was very prominent in the church, could bake and cook like nobody's business. Somebody was always coming to the house for her to bake them a cake or she was also a quilt maker. I have quilts to this day. So she had that kind of prominence for those skills in the community. And was considered to be a woman of high integrity, which is important. And so that is the picture that was painted for me, from other people, about my grandmother, early on. My aunt lived with my grandmother. And my aunt was considered at the time an old maid, that's what they called her. She taught French at the high school and she was a librarian.

So there was three of you for six years, and then seven more came?

Yes. One more came. And then the other six came. So Bubba was in prison for about no more than two years. Bubba came out of prison. Because this was our house and the school was right there [*points across the room*], literally we could walk across to the school. I remember coming home for lunch, I was probably in second grade. And I remember just not really wanting to have anything to do with him, you know? I don't know if I felt abandoned. I don't know if it was because he was in prison. Because I was a kid who—I was just kind of strange. But I didn't want to have anything to do with him. But once he got home, I loved him. I mean, he would pick us up from school. My sister was in kindergarten. Come to the school, get my brother and I, because my mother would be at work. He was a carpenter, he was self-employed. Take us home, build these big fires, we'd roast hot dogs and marshmallows. And he was a fun-loving guy. He was an alcoholic, but he was a fun-loving guy. He was a very loving guy. So when he came to the school and asked for Mary Anne Shaw, because that was his last name, and they said, "There's no Mary Anne Shaw here," he pitched a fit: "I've adopted her, her name shouldn't be Adams," and I'm sinking in my chair. [*Laughter.*] Because I felt things very deeply, everything embarrassed me, I was that kind of kid, you know. And so, I'm like, "Oh, my God." So for the rest of that year, I had to go by "Mary Anne Adams-Shaw. I had the first hyphenated name, because they were like, well, they had my Adams on everything and they just put Shaw, you know. And I hated that, because I was always the first person they'd call with Adams. Now, all of a sudden, I'm almost here at the back, you know what I mean? [*Laughter.*]

So he must have come back in the summer, because I remember we were just really just happy. I remember when James Meredith, that whole weekend, I remember that whole weekend, because we were very close, and I remember hearing the shots. And I tell the story about my stepfather, I'm hearing these shots. And I'm like, "What's going on?" He said, "Oh, those peckerwoods don't want this colored man to get into the university." But that didn't really mean a whole lot to me. And the next day was Monday. I was going to school. And my brother, we would walk to school. So one day we were walking to school and my brother decided he wasn't going to go to school. So he would walk me to school and he was going to shoot [play] hooky. So, he'd walk me, he'd say, "You can walk that," it was probably maybe a block or so, so I was walking, and I saw all these soldiers. I mean, for me, eight years old, it was like just a million soldiers, white soldiers with these guns, right? And I walked up and one of them said, "Little girl, there's not going to be any school today." [*Laughter.*] I'll never forget that, as long as I live. And I turned around, I run back as fast as I could. Well, my brother had stopped to throw rocks into the squirrels or whatever, so I was able to catch up with him. And we walked back out of the town. Freeman's Town was actually shut down, all the black sections, for like a week, that week. We didn't go to school. We couldn't really go into town to shop, because people were afraid. We had had threats on the community, the black community. And so I remember that, that time really, really well. Not knowing that eight years later I would be entering Ole Miss myself.

So, I think it was September. And then October 7th is my mother's birthday. And that morning, my mother said to my stepfather, she said—we had an elderly friend who was in the hospital. He said, "I'm going to go visit him." And my mother said, "You should not go, because I had a dream last night." And he was like, "Oh, you don't know what you're talking about." So he walked across the track, because it was a railroad track where we were. Now, we were on one side of the track, and the black folks were on the other side of the track. [Laughter.] So he didn't have a car, so he was going to walk to see him. And my mother told him she dreamed that something bad happened to him. Now, when he was in Parchman, he was a really smart guy, outspoken, take no prisoners. I would read the letters that he would write to my mother, because I'd read them, and just very, very, very bright, just a smart guy. But he told my mother that there was some white guys he had gotten into it with when he was at Parchman, and they told him that if they ever got out, they were going to kill him. Well, he had come home that week and told my mother he had seen those white guys in town that day, so I don't know if this was weighing on her when she dreamt about it or what, but she said he shouldn't go. He was like, "Uh." So that night, I'll never forget, it was a Sunday night. My brother and my sister had gone to bed and I was up with my mother. And Mr. Clarence, his [Bubba's] father, came to tell us that he had been killed and his body was found on the tracks. So there was some speculation: was he drinking and did he fall asleep on the tracks? My mother always believed that those white guys killed him and put him on the tracks, because he had seen them in town that day.

Had he been shot?

Well, the train had just kind of cut him; it just pulverized him.

So he got hit by a train?

Yes. Yes, he got hit by the train. And we left the house that night and went to my grandfather's house, to their basement, because he had a house with a basement. And so we literally went to live in the basement. My mother just became, just comatose with grief. And I remember the next day, that Monday, my brother just did not go to school, but I went to school, because I guess I craved some sense of normalcy, I had to go to school. I didn't have any books with me but I went to school. And after school—when I think back on it, it's just so insane—but his father and my mother and some other folks had all the kids together. We had a bunch of cousins and things. And we went and walked up and down the track because we were looking for his brains. Because suspicion was that if your brains are outside your body and the birds peck on them or eat them, whatever, that the spirit will not rest.

Did you find them?

Probably not. I think we were all just kind of numb with grief, didn't know what to do. We did as we were told. The adults, I don't know what they were thinking. They weren't. I guess they believed that. I mean, they believed it. So that's what we did. We went to look for them. And I'm sure we did not find them. I can't imagine that we would have or could have, you know what I mean?

Did they not find his head?

I don't know. There was a lot that they exposed us to but also a lot that they kept from us. I'm not really sure. But that was my first experience with death, at eight years old.

So I would say by the time I was sixteen we had lived in probably eighteen different places. Moving oftentimes in the middle of the night. And we were probably moving just on the heels of eviction. But we moved a lot. And oftentimes, we would move up the street. So we would carry stuff. Or down the street or around the corner. It was not really too far away. So that's why today stable housing is very, very important to me. I'll pay the mortgage before I pay anything, because nobody's going to ever tell me to leave anywhere, unless I decide that I'm going to leave. That's why I would never move in with any partner that I had. We had to move into something together, 'cause nobody was ever going to say to me, "Get out," for any reason. That's a lasting legacy from my childhood, in terms of that whole piece, you know.

My mother . . . died of ovarian cancer. And I had become guardian of my three brothers and sister. So, I was like twenty-four or twenty-five and they were like nine, eleven, and thirteen. And the boy was eleven. And Linda was nine and Rita was nineteen. And my sister who was nine developed a rare form of rheumatic fever, where she all of a sudden couldn't walk, she couldn't talk, she couldn't do anything. At the time that my mother was in the hospital in Jackson, Linda was at the hospital in Memphis. And my grandmother and my brother would not help out. My grandmother said that my mother had cancer because she was a sinner and this was God's way—oh, yeah. And

I remember being in Memphis with my sister, Linda, and the social worker calling me, saying that, "Your grandmother cannot stay in the hospital with your mother, because this is what she's saying to her. And she's upsetting her." And my sister, who is three years younger, didn't want to go to the hospital at all, no how, she just couldn't deal with it, and my brother wouldn't go. So it was just . . . craziness. And my mother, she probably was in the hospital for about a year, yeah, for about a year. Yeah. So, essentially, it was my sister and I would take care of seven kids.

And so I had just moved to Jackson and I was on my own and then this happened. And so my sister and I just said, "Okay, this is what we're going to do. I'm going to stay in Jackson and work, to get money for us. You're going to take care of the kids. And on the weekends, I will come home to give you a break." And so that's what we did. Sometimes, I would come on Friday and my sister had a boyfriend, she had a baby. She was already gone to start, [and the] little kids are at home by themselves. They were being literally like readied for me. My sister was not the type who was nurturing in that sense, you know what I mean? She would provide a place. But in terms of doing homework and all that kind of stuff. So, literally, I would get home and help them and do all this. And my mother's in the hospital. So I don't know how we made it, we just made it. And when my mother died, we decided I would take the girls, because my aunt and my grandmother, they said they wouldn't take anybody, that we should put the kids to foster care. . . . And it never crossed my mind to put these kids in foster care.

So my sister and I decided that I would take the girls. So there were three girls. And she would take the four boys, because she already had two kids. And we were going to do that, that was our plan. Except my middle brother, one day I was going to the laundromat, he said, "I heard you going to take the girls." And he was eleven. I said, "Yeah." He said, "But I want to live with you." And I thought, my God, this kid is asking to live with me. And when I would come home to take care of them, he would always go with me. He would always be with me. So I'm thinking, this kid is asking to live with me. So I decided at that moment that I would take the older kids, the four older kids, she would take the three younger kids. That way, he would be included, because I had an older brother who was sixteen. So, nine, eleven, thirteen, and sixteen. Two girls and two boys. Well, he came to Jackson with me. And I didn't have any relatives in Jackson. I hadn't been in Jackson but like a few months, you know. And I didn't have any relatives. And I had a job working for the Federation of Southern Cooperatives.

And actually, after I got the kids—now, I think this is a really important part of my story—I subscribed to the *Gay Community News*. And it would come every week. And it had fifty million staples in it. And I would just look for it. And I learned a lot about gay culture through the *Gay Community News*. I learned who the writers were. I learned who the activists were. I learned what was going on. And, I mean, it was just a huge education for me. It was out of New York. It was huge for me. And then I had a friend, my best friend who had gone to Ole Miss with me, who I was working with at Legal Services in Jackson at the time, had went away to some conference. And I was like, "Well, can you bring me back some books?" And I asked her to bring me back Audre Lorde's books because we didn't have them in Jackson. So this is how I was able to kind of get literature and to get stuff to read and that kind of thing. But yeah, the *Gay Community News* was like, that was my Bible, you know. I mean, those rags were so vitally important, and people just don't know what tremendous impact they have. Particularly with somebody like me, who just didn't have a lifeline. I didn't have a lifeline.

And how did you find life in Atlanta, once you got here?

I think initially, it was somewhat challenging for me. I didn't really know anybody. Jackie was in Athens. And she'd kind of come back and forth because it wasn't that far. And then I knew Donna. But I didn't really know anybody. And it was difficult in the sense that I was really grappling with a lot of things, with being in that relationship, because based on my background, for me to be with a white woman [*laughter*] is totally not ever anything I would ever fathom, you know. I'm "black power!" I'm reading *Lookout Whitey Black Power Gon' Get Your Mama*, just totally, totally out of my reality zone. . . . I had gone to Ole Miss and I had white friends, but by and large my world was really black. And I didn't know what the politics were of the black lesbians here in Atlanta. I didn't really know how to meet them. I was trying to find a job. I was just trying to find myself and situate myself someplace early on. I met the women of ZAMI because there was this white lesbian that I met who introduced me to them, actually.[4] She had a gathering at her house and she was the only white woman there and everybody else was black. This is a true story. And that's how I met some of the women of ZAMI. And then after I met them, I was kind of on the periphery because I just kind of saw myself as being a little bit more political than they were at the time. Lisa Moore, and there was a sister named Angel, and I did the newsletter for ZAMI. So the three of us did that. And that kind of was my initial involvement. And so I started to feel a little bit more settled in that regard. I started to work at Emory. And started to meet people. I would say probably my second year here, yeah, second, third year here, I started to kind of get my feet under me. And started to kind of embrace the city and what it had to offer. And the relationships that I was cultivating.

Why did it [ZAMI] stop?

Because I was tired, for one thing. We kind of looked around and realized that we were aging in place, the women of ZAMI. And thought that it would be really good for us to try to focus on that. And so, we kind of morphed into ZAMI NOBLA, you know that NOBLA is National Organization of Black Lesbians on Aging. And we wanted to kind of shift the paradigm a little bit. And have us start the conversations about aging. Because our community, our culture is so youth-oriented. And people don't even want to talk about aging. So we want to start the conversations and shift this whole paradigm from seeing aging as this whole death and dying model, but to folk who are empowering, affirmed, and who are living their lives and doing that community. And so that's really why we stopped. We're going to do the scholarship again, but we're going to make sure—we're going to really focus this time just on black lesbians forty and older, because there are a lot of women who haven't had an opportunity to get their training or education, who really want to do that and just don't have the funds to get it done. So, that's something we know we can do, we can do that with our eyes closed.

I believe in coalition politics. When I moved here, I joined the ethics board for East Point, well, I was appointed to the ethics board for three years. Because it's where I live [*laughter*], you know. And I think if things are better for everybody then things, of course, are better for me. But at the same time, of course, I do queer organizing, because that's important to me. But I think we need to bring all of ourselves to the table. I need to go to the ethics board meeting as Mary Anne, the black lesbian, social worker, who works at Georgia State in research. That's important. Who works in HIV. I need to bring all of my selves to the table. And so I think it's important that we do that, and that's kind of what I try to do. And actually, I've been pretty well received. Yeah. I'm the secretary for the Home Loan Association. They all know I'm a dyke. These folks, I mean, "Can she keep the minutes?" [*Laughter.*] But I've grown up here. I've really grown up here—in so many ways. Most days it's just so much work to do, because there's Atlanta and there's Georgia. There's just so much work to do. Because there's a pull here, I think people really appreciate community. And it's one thing I said about the black folk, queer folk. We fight, but when we need to come together, we come together. That's a fact. I mean, the men will tell you that. If there's something that we need to come together, we're going to come together. I appreciate that about this community. There's no doubt about that. If there's something, we would call each other, we're there. We're like brother and sister. [*Laughter.*] We all know each other.

You hear all the time that turning forty, turning fifty, turning sixty, are the best times. At fifty-seven-years old, I can literally say that when I entered my fifties, I am at the best place in my life than I've ever been—personally, emotionally, spiritually, professionally. I know who I am. I know what I know. I know what I don't know. I appreciate the fact that until the day I leave my body, I'm going to be learning something. And most importantly, I have a willingness to learn. And that's important to me. I don't really spend a lot of time worrying about what people say about me, I really don't. I believe that the only reason we're put on this earth was to help each other, I really believe that. And that's really kind of how I try to live my life. And people who know me, if I can help you, I'm going to help you. I think my life's work is to just continue to try to build community and try to bring us together.

And right now, with ZAMI NOBLA, I really want us to try to develop a new paradigm for aging. I don't think that we have to live by this whole medical model of death and dying as we age. I want us to start to begin to even have the conversation. So, many of us don't want to have the conversation, because we even look at the whole framework of aging, the next thing that we associate that with is dying. And for all the black folk who preach about God and Jesus and the pie in the sky, they're afraid of dying. They don't want to go there. That's another story for another day. But we have seasons, we're going to leave at some point, and we need to prepare ourselves for that. We need to understand that aging does not mean that you have no more dreams, you have no more goals, that you can't continue to grow. There's so many folk I see who are so—who have so much agency now. Who empower me and affirm me. We have these models for what it's like to age successfully and to have a quality of life. And if we can't do it individually, we can do it collectively. I understand that. But I know together, we can build something. We can have collective housing. We can help each other. So that's what I'm trying to do. I'm just trying to build this different paradigm. And to do it in a multigenerational way, you know? I think we owe that to each other. I think we need to comentor. I've been trying to get this whole concept of comentoring out there. It's not doing very well. Because I think that in order for us to really be in conversation with each other, it's not about the fact that I'm older and I know more than you. No, it's not the fact that because you're young, you think you got—no. We need to continue to grow and learn and teach each other. And so, we're working toward that, you know.

For all the angst that I experienced and that I put on myself oftentimes, at the end of the day, there were people who believed in me, who encouraged me for what I was, as opposed to what I wasn't. And I'm very clear that I became a woman in Atlanta. But in Mississippi, I do believe that the skills that I learned, the way of being in the world has been the cement and the glue for me. The moral values I learned. That community at Ole Miss, for example. The community at the Black House. The community among my siblings. Invaluable. Priceless. I wouldn't give anything for that.

Queen Mother Mary Anne gathers her hair grease, combs, and brushes in her lap, unties her apron from the back and methodically folds it around her tools. The other women begin to do the same with their things and, one by one, leave the porch and return inside the house. The porch still bears the mark of their scents and voices. I begin to write copious notes to follow up on many of the things they told me, and especially about the civil rights movement. I happen to look up from my notes and see Miss B. approaching, her heels leaving a dust trail in the wake of her gait. When she reaches the porch, she looks spent, sweat dripping from her brow and her hair even more out of place than usual. She doesn't say anything to me but sits down on the step below me.

"I was worried about you. Are you okay?" I say, gently.

"I watched my daddy be dragged out of Hymen," she says, skipping over my question. "He was one of the few drones to be allowed to stay in Hymen after his prime as long as he lived on the outskirts of the hive. One day while he was walking into town, he decided to take a shortcut and walk through a part of the hive where most of the ashies live. Well, some little ashy drones thought it would be fun to harass him. When they saw the path he was taking, they set a booby trap under some leaves, such that once he stepped on it, his feet would be stuck. It's like what you all would call a bear trap. Sure enough, Pops stepped in the trap and those ashies strung him up by his feet from a tree. While he hung there, upside down, they poked at him with sticks and threw rocks at him. Once they grew tired of playing with him, they just left him hanging there. After a few days, some old women who were out gathering roots, including Queen Mother Mary Anne, found him swinging from the tree, but it was too late. He had already passed. They cut him down and dragged him to the opening of the hive and pushed him out into the Osun River. So when Queen Mother Ida Mae started talking about all of that stuff about how folks were being found hung and drowned, it just took me to a place." She reaches in her purse for a cigarette.

"I'm so sorry, Miss B."

We sit in solemn silence for what seems an eternity. "Me, too," she says after a while, and takes the last drag of her cigarette and smashes the butt into the top step. She then opens up her yellow purse and drops the butt in while she contemplates pulling out another cigarette. After a minute or two of reflection, she looks at me.

"I know you don't like cigarettes. My parting gift to you will be to stop cold turkey. Right here and now," she says, with a very serious look on her face.

"Really, Miss B.? You're just going to give up cigarettes just like that?"

"Just like that," she says, snapping her purse shut and throwing it down the stairs.

"Wow. That's amazing. But you know, you should not do it for me. You should do it for yourself. Smoking causes cancer and all kinds of health problems. And, according to the CDC, black women have a higher incidence of cancers related to smoking . . ."

She gives me the side eye.

"You really do know how to fuck up a tender moment, don't you? Hand me my pocketbook so I can get me another cigarette."

I walk down the steps, pick up her pocketbook, and hand it to her, shaking my head. I should have known it was too good to be true. She lights up another one and I sit down beside her, looking out over the vast landscape of the hive. What a beautiful place, I think to myself as we watch the sun head toward its westward resting place. We sit for a while more in silence, the vibration of all the activity around us paralyzing.

"Come with me," Miss B. says, standing up, putting out her cigarette, and extending a hand to me. I grab her hand, thinking we're going to be magically transported to another place as before, but we're not. We walk hand in hand through the town square and up the road, past the places we visited when I first entered the hive. After a while, I realize that we are headed back to the field of wildflowers where I listened to the women tell their love stories. And, as we come to the clearing, Miss B. turns to me.

"Remember when we were standing at the entrance of the hive and you said that you couldn't hear anyone talking and I told you that you would once you tuned in to the frequency?"

I nod.

"Well, I bet you don't remember that the first time you heard talking in the hive was actually when we passed by the drones, sitting under the tree."

"You're right. What does that mean?"

"Now, before you go into your academic analysis, all it means is that the drones' frequency is also part of you and that you first had to acknowledge that before you could tap into the women's frequency. I told you, the drones are a necessary evil, but that's not quite right, because they aren't evil. They were not born into this world to do harm. In fact, this activist group I used to belong to that met down at the Combahee River on the other side of Hymen drafted a statement about drones that in part states that 'we do not believe that it is their [droneness], per se—i.e., their biological maleness—that makes them what they are.'5 It's just that sometimes the world teaches them to do harm because it seems like the easy way to deal with hurt. Or the world punishes them the way it did my father. So we keep holding out hope for our brothers."

"Well, thanks for holding out hope for *this* brother in particular," I respond, only half joking. I pause for a bit, my head bowed, and moving rocks about with the tip of my right foot. Then the confession: "Miss B., I need to tell you something. At first, I was resistant to coming with you on this journey because, well, I didn't know you and I think it's rude to be taking people from their homes against their will to go on unplanned trips. I think they call that kidnapping." We both chuckle. "But, seriously, after you started introducing me to your sisters and I started listening to their stories, I was resistant because I felt guilty—about a lot of things. And sometimes I just felt . . . a lot less smart than everybody thinks I am, when I'm used to being the smartest person in the room. Listening to these stories forced me to come to terms with a lot of my own stuff and humbled me in the process. And, in the meantime, I got to meet some incredibly courageous women. And for that, I'll always be grateful."

Miss B. digs into her purse and pulls out a small vial.

"Here," she says, placing the vial in my hand. "This is a little vial of propolis. We use it for many things here in the hive—sealant, protectant, caulk, chalk, healer, peeler, antifungal, antibacterial—you name it!" she screams, channeling her inner Shirley Caesar. "Use it sparingly," she continues. "A little goes a long way. Just put a little dab on your lips to speak truth to power or on your hands to write authentically. And as you become more in tune with the frequency of your truth, the other uses will be revealed to you. You have the gift of gab. That was your birthright as a southerner. Now you have been given the gift of others' stories. Your burden is to hold them."

I take the vial, open it, and dab some of the propolis on my finger and smear it on my lips. Miss B. holds out cupped hands, as if offering me a sip of water from them. Not knowing what to do, I mimic her and cup my hands as well and extend them toward hers. When our hands meet, a ray of light bursts through the clouds and a symphony of sound erupts. I look up and a black zigzag mass hovers hundreds of feet in the air, alternately hiding the sunlight. As it gets closer, the ground begins to vibrate and the words of the sonorous buzzing become audible:

We speak our truth to you today, tomorrow, and always. You have listened with an open heart. You have listened with an open mind. You have listened. Remember that these are not your stories. Remember that these are your stories. Both/and. Neither/nor. Remember.

Dedra. Kate. Nancy. Malu. Alpha. Emilie.

Remember

Julia. Darlene. Lynn. Spirit. Shannon.

Remember

Joy. Lisa. Monika. Bluhe. Wynee. Lenore.

Remember

Almah. Diane. Felicia. Nora. Michelle.

Remember

Laurinda. Shetikka. Rose. Tommye. Pat. Sharita.

Remember

Shonda. Q. Iris. Joan. Priscilla.

Remember

Aida. Cherry. Ida Mae. Lori. Mary Anne.

Remember

Miss B.'s head begins to elongate, her mouth and nose disappearing into her face. Her eyes stretch downward to resemble black diamonds. What were once tendrils of twisted hair harden and move about robotically. Brown and golden fuzz sprouts all over her body and her ass balloons toward the ground. Her arms and legs seem to grow attachments that extend to the ground, while out of what once were her hips burst another set of legs. Her purse is stuck to her left hind leg. Another purse appears on the right hind leg.

The swarm soars out of sight. The sky darkens.

Miss B. is now facing me. My heart is beating out of my chest. She rotates slightly to the left, then to the right, and then hobbles toward me, her mandibles caressing my face. "Remember," she says.

The swarm surges back above and the sun slivers through the darkened sky. Out of each of Miss B.'s shoulders emerge two translucent sheaths. They pop and whistle as they extend the length of her buttocks. I study the weblike veins running through these enormous sheaths, mesmerized by their intricacy and how their translucence should not be mistaken for fragility. Miss B. steps back from me, gently moving her new additions. Flap. Flap. Flap. Flapflapflapflap-flapflapflapflapflapflapflapflflapflapflapflap. The wind from the flapping wings knocks me backward onto the ground. Miss B. is in flight.

"Miss B.! Miss B.!" I shout into the windstorm as the sky envelops her trace. I look down at the vial, clinch it with my fist, and pull it close to my chest. I savor the sweetness smeared across my lips, and listen for a sign to remember.

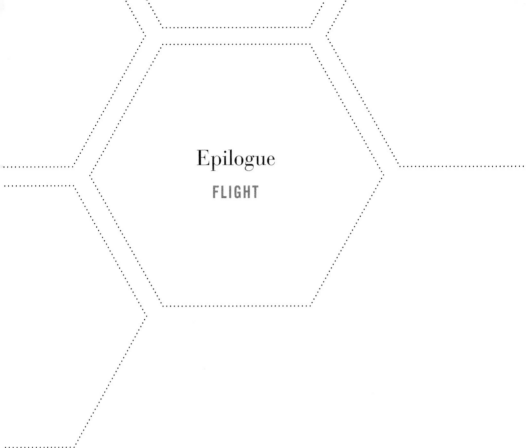

Epilogue

FLIGHT

Summer solstice in the South marks the longest sundown of the year as dusk winks into nightfall. Amid these hot, humid days is a smorgasbord of sensory overload: the shrills of children on the playground, swinging toward the sun with each and every push from their big brother or sister, saddled with their care; grandmothers sitting gap-legged, their aprons creating a basket to hold the green beans they're snapping for Sunday's supper, while gossiping grown folks gossip; old men down by the stump, drinking brown liquor and telling lies while slyly ogling fast-tailed girls who ought not to be wearing those short skirts; the smell of Bergamot, Royal Crown, and a burning kitchen, accompanying a little girl's teeth sucking and head jerking when the hot comb gets too close to her ear; the calming sound of the river's stream rushing over rocks while neighbors dip their fishing lines for a quick catch of the day; or the smell of crappies floating in a black cauldron of grease, waiting to be scooped up and lovingly placed between two pieces of light bread slathered with mustard and coleslaw on a cheap paper plate.

The backdrop for this carnivalesque theater is the kaleidoscopic brilliance of flowers in bloom—a splash of pink azaleas here; a cascade of honeysuckle there; a bouquet of Stokes' aster and phlox huddled near a burning bush; a spray of golden forsythia reaching toward the sky; a cluster of irises, Indian pink, and false indigo, beaming with pride; a gathering of stargazer, swan lily, and lily of the valley, kneeling in prayer; a smattering of bee balm and hibiscus, arrogantly throwing shade at the pestering flies; a blanket of summer snow, blinding with its virgin whiteness the buzzards circling above. And in the lull of light and lush and scent is the ethereal sound of twelve thousand beats of wings—the buzzing of the honeybee. Up and over, down and around, she tickles the noses of the children playing in the sun; rests for a while on one of the grandmother's apron strings while taking in some of the "tea"; stings one of the old men on the eye and runs off with his whisky; dodges the curling iron to deliver a droplet of honey salve for the seared ear; plunges toward the river's fury and skims the surface to quench her thirst; and, feasts on the fish sandwich long enough to make sure it has enough Old Bay seasoning, the big bones picked out, and fresh grease—all of this before following the beeline to the anther to receive the flower's offering of pollen in exchange for fertility.

She gorges on history's nectar, her proboscis primed at the ready for each sugary sip of sustenance; her legs arched back in time, she brushes her hair on pollen reveries. Full and thick with history, her pollen baskets bursting at the seams, she journeys home to unload her story to her sisters, who will follow her back to the river of Osun's flowering. The elders swarm and tremble, tremble and swarm, dancing on daisies, dandelions, and daffodils, this succulent place of memory feast: three hundred trips for slavery, one hundred trips for Jim Crow, fifty trips for civil rights, and countless trips for the burdens of black women who love women. Their loads are heavy, for they are aging. Their buzzing is labored, for they are tired, but they must make the journey to feed the royal jelly to those yet unborn. They must be told from where they have come. Twilight is near. Dancing is done. The hive is still. There is only the tender touching of wings gathered around the queen. She is pleased with their work. Stories are being spun here. There will be food for the winter. The drones will die. And the children will come in spring.

I know only from what their wings have whispered in my ear. This book is where the dreams of bees are kept. I am a beekeeper, patiently listening to my sisters' stories as I continue to harvest honey for the honeypot.

Appendix

LIST OF HONEYBEES

AIDA RENTAS Born in Santurce, Puerto Rico, 1938. The interview took place on November 18, 2012, in San Juan, Puerto Rico.

ALMAH Born in Louisville, Kentucky, 1976. The interview took place on August 21, 2013, in Rockville, Maryland.

ALPHA Born in Dallas, Texas, 1957. The interview took place on September 15, 2012, in Dallas, Texas.

BLUHE Born in Anderson, South Carolina, 1968. The interview took place on August 22, 2012, in Winston-Salem, North Carolina. Bluhe was assigned female at birth and given the name "Bonita," the name they used during the original interview. A few years later, they transitioned to male and began going by "Bluhe Elijah."

CHERRY HUSSAIN Born in Dayton Beach, Florida, 1955. The interview took place on August 9, 2012, in Decatur, Georgia.

DARLENE Born in Las Vegas, Nevada, in 1961 and reared in Fordyce, AR. The interview took place on August 9, 2012, in Atlanta, Georgia.

DEDRA Born in Prentiss, Mississippi, 1966. The interview took place on August 22, 2013, in Prentiss, Mississippi.

DIANE Born in Spartanburg, South Carolina, 1977. The interview took place on July 31, 2013, in Winston-Salem, North Carolina.

EMILIE Born in Durham, North Carolina, 1955. The interview took place on September 30, 2014, in Nashville, Tennessee.

FELICIA Born in Mobile, Alabama, 1970. The interview took place on October 14, 2013, in Lithonia, Georgia.

IDA MAE Born in Odenville, Alabama, 1951. Pseudonym. The interview took place on September 11, 2012, at her home in Houston, Texas.

IRIS Born in Miami Beach, Florida, 1955. The interviews took place on August 27 and October 14, 2013, in Atlanta, Georgia.

JOAN Born in Washington, DC, 1951. The interview took place on August 28, 2013, in Atlanta, Georgia. Joan passed away in 2017.

JOY Born in Houston, Texas, 1966. The interview took place on September 9, 2013, in Dallas, Texas.

JULIA (SANGODARE) Born in Gastonia, North Carolina, 1979. The interview took place on August 26, 2012, in Durham, North Carolina.

KATE Born in Winston-Salem, North Carolina, 1981. The interview took place on August 29, 2012, in Durham, North Carolina.

LAURINDA Born in Memphis, Tennessee, 1959. The interview took place on August 22, 2013, in Prentiss, Mississippi.

LENORE Born in Wampee, South Carolina, 1962. The interview took place on March 31, 2014, in Columbia, South Carolina. Lenore passed away three months after the interview.

LINDSAY Born in Jacksonville, Florida, 1993. The interview took place on March 23, 2013, in Tallahassee, Florida.

LISA Born in Detroit, Michigan, 1972; reared in Grambling, Louisiana. Pseudonym. The interview took place on August 6, 2012, in Atlanta, Georgia.

LORI WILSON Born in Seguin, Texas, 1962. The interview took place on September 10, 2012, at her home in Austin, Texas.

LYNN Born in Jackson, Mississippi, 1968. The interview took place on August 13, 2013, in Jackson, Mississippi.

MALU Born in Cincinnati, Ohio, 1980 and reared in Davidson, North Carolina. The interview took place on July 30, 2013, in Davidson, North Carolina.

MARY ANNE ADAMS Born in Oxford, Mississippi, 1954. The first interview took place on August 9, 2012, and the second one took place on August 27, 2013, in Atlanta, Georgia.

MICHELLE Born in Winston-Salem, North Carolina, 1965. The interview took place on August 22, 2012, in Winston-Salem, North Carolina.

MONIKA Born in Birmingham, Alabama, 1979. The interview took place on October 13, 2013, in Birmingham, Alabama.

NANCY Born in Maxton, North Carolina, 1950. The interview took place on July 30, 2013, in Davidson, North Carolina.

NORA Born in Houston, Texas, 1983. The interview took place on September 12, 2012, in Dallas, Texas.

PAT HUSSAIN Born in Atlanta, Georgia, 1950. The interview took place on August 9, 2012, in Atlanta, Georgia.

PRISCILLA Born in San Antonia, Texas, 1967. The interview took place on September 9, 2012, in Austin, Texas.

Q Born in Dallas, Texas, 1980. The interview took place on September 13, 2013, in Dallas, Texas.

SHANNON S Born in Baton Rouge, Louisiana, 1972. The interview took place on April 19, 2013, in Baton Rouge, Louisiana.

SHARITA Born in Washington, DC, 1979. The interview took place on October 5, 2013, in Little Rock, Arkansas.

SHETIKKA Born in Atlanta, Georgia, 1975. The interview took place on August 25, 2013, in Lithonia, Georgia.

SHONDA Born in Columbus, Georgia, 1959. Pseudonym. The interview took place on September 12, 2013, outside of Dallas, Texas.

SPIRIT Born in Washington, DC, 1977. The interview took place on April 18, 2013, in New Orleans, Louisiana.

TOMMYE Born in Orange, Texas, 1958. The interview took place on April 20, 2013, in New Orleans, Louisiana.

WYNEE Born in Jackson, Mississippi, 1962. The interview took place on October 4, 2013, in Little Rock, Arkansas.

Notes

PREFACE

1. The female hip-hop artist Nicki Minaj has also made the word famous by referring to young singers as "honeychild."

2. This derivative of the word "honey" comes from drag culture and has been made popular by the black drag star RuPaul and his show *RuPaul's Drag Race*. The term also has derogatory connotations, since it riffs off of the misogynist word "cunt."

3. See Kid's novel *The Secret Life of Bees* (New York: Penguin, 2003).

4. Zora Neale Hurston, *Their Eyes Were Watching God* (New York: Harper & Row), 14.

5. See "Out of Africa: Scientists Uncover History of Honey Bee," Science-Daily, October 27, 2006, http://www.sciencedaily.com/releases/2006/10/061025181534.htm.

6. I should note that while the violence the women experience at the hands of men is a feature of the majority of the stories I collected, these stories should not be taken as representative of all black queer women in the South, but rather as a reflection of the specific sample of women I interviewed. Further, sexual trauma caused by men should not be read as an explanation for why these

women express same-sex desire. Indeed, many of these women had positive romantic relationships with men after their experiences, and many of them state explicitly that their sexual abuse did not turn them toward women.

7. For readers who are interested in a more traditional rendering of oral histories, replete with descriptions of actual towns, interview settings, and the women themselves, see *Black. Queer. Southern. Women—An Oral History,* which is meant as a companion text to *Honeypot.*

8. I should also note that beekeepers use smoke to calm bees.

9. Jacqueline Freeman, *The Song of Increase: Returning to Our Sacred Partnership with Honeybees* (Battle Ground, WA: Friendly Haven Rise Press, 2014), 39.

10. The narratives included in this book are only excerpts from the longer interviews. They have been heavily edited for clarity and brevity. I have also taken creative license with the context under which the interviews were conducted to reflect the fictional world of Hymen.

CHAPTER ONE **THE HIVE**

1. The waggle dance is a behavior used to describe the movement of a honeybee in the hive through which it shares the direction and distance to food sources, such as flowers with pollen and nectar, and water sources, such as streams and rivers.

2. Mason, carpenter, miner, and ashy miner are all types of bees.

3. The ashy mining bee is a European species, widespread throughout the United Kingdom and Ireland.

4. Paul Lawrence Dunbar, "In the Morning" (New York: CreateSpace Independent Publishing, 2017), 226–27.

5. Dunbar, "In the Morning."

CHAPTER SIX **ALL HAIL THE QUEEN (BEE)**

1. Ntozake Shange, *for colored girls who have considered suicide/when the rainbow is enuf* (New York: Scribner Poetry, 1975), 11.

2. I have not been able to locate this image of Evers in *Jet Magazine* or find any other references to it.

3. Pseudonym.

4. ZAMI was a multiracial lesbian activist group founded in Atlanta in 1995.

5. The Combahee River Collective, "A Black Feminist Statement," in *Words of Fire: An Anthology of Black Feminist Thought,* ed. Beverly Guy-Sheftall (New York: The New Press, 1995), 235–36.

Index

CPSIA information can be obtained
at www.ICGtesting.com
Printed in the USA
LVHW010042280620
659157LV00031B/741